Ten years ago it was an ordinary department store.

Today it's a glittering, glamorous, elegant show-place, known as *the* most exciting fashion center in the world.

# BLOOMINGDALE'S

The store, the event, the phenomenon—A place that dreams dreams and dares to make fantasies come true!

How did a few innovative business people create the most smashing succes story of the decade?

- **By discovering the hottest young designers and letting their imaginations run wild**
- **By turning the marketing of clothing, food and home furnishings into an art**
- **By searching the globe to uncover—and invent—new trends**
- **By creating sophisticated boutiques to rival the finest galleries**

Bloomingdale's is the prestigious leader of the fashion industry and much, much more—a place to dress up and be seen, a meeting place for swinging affluent singles and a center of the classiest trend-setters. Here is the first and only book that tells all about the hottest spot in town—the store and the sensation that put 59th Street on the map!

"Like No Other Store in the World"

The Inside Story of

BLOOMINGDALE'S

## Mark Stevens

BALLANTINE BOOKS • NEW YORK

To Carol, who has nurtured me with love and friendship and has enabled me to lean back and have a damn good time with my life

# Contents

Acknowledgments      ix

1. A Disneyland for Adults      1
2. Social Climbing      24
3. Fifty-ninth Street and Third:
   The Flagship Store      47
4. The Bloomingdale's Blitz:
   Strike, Conquer, Retreat      69
5. The Top Two: Apparel and Furniture      93
6. The Propaganda Machine      114
7. As Bloomie's Goes, So Goes the Nation      141
8. Transplanting the Magic      155
9. Where the Real Power Lies: Cincinnati?      174
10. The Trade      196
11. Clouds over Fifty-ninth Street      215
    Index      233

# Acknowledgments

The author thanks the following people for sharing their intelligence and experience: Halston, who is as interesting and dynamic as his reputation holds him to be; Ralph Lauren, a design genius; Cathy Cash Spellman, a charming and talented woman; Warren Hirsh; Gloria Vanderbilt; Edwin Bobrow; Gordon Cooke; Harold Krensky, a first-class gentleman and a first-rate executive; Stanley Marcus, the dean of American retailing, whose observations are worth their weight in gold; Barbara D'Arcy, one of Bloomingdale's greats who still loves her work and loves to share her memories; Lawrence Lachman, a strong and gutsy executive, who is starting a new career at a time when others would be polishing off the golf clubs; Bob Gumport; Mary Merris; Vincent Draddi; Steve Fass; David Bell; Doris Shaw; Richard Zolt; Steven Forrest; Nancy Stern; Cheryl Forshner; Roslyn Bloom; Jay Bloom; Lee Stone; Judy Zolt; the lower-ranking Bloomingdale's employees who had the courage to talk about their employer; editorial staffers at the *Washington Post* and the *Boston Herald American;* Barbara Walz; Lawrence Greenburg, for his great camera work; my agents, Rus Galen and Scott Meredith, for having full faith in this idea from the start; my editor, Arnold Dolin, for demanding the best from the author and for the book; and my family, which lost me, for the better part of a year, to a lover called Bloomie's.

# A Disneyland for Adults

*Diane Keaton and Woody Allen in a scene from the film* Annie Hall:

*Keaton: "Sometimes I wonder how I would stand up to torture."*

*Allen: "You? The Gestapo would take away your Bloomingdale's charge card and you'd tell them everything."*

The business we know as Bloomingdale's occupies a special place in the world. It is one of a kind: the richest, most influential and most successful major department store on earth.

Forget Harrods, Tiffany's and the bustling markets of Marrakech—nothing is comparable to Bloomingdale's. Located in the affluent, pretentious, free-wheeling and free-spending Gold Coast of Manhattan's upper East Side, Bloomingdale's attracts an extraordinary multitude of shoppers and browsers. On any given day, the sales floors are crammed with the likes of Canada's Prime Minister Pierre Trudeau rubbing elbows with struggling actresses from Indiana, Sutton Place matrons sampling Givenchy perfumes beside gay waiters from SoHo, breathless tourists sharing elevators with Turkish pashas, and the spoiled charge-card-carrying twelve-year-olds of New York's rich, pushing past famed psychologist Dr. Lee Salk.

Greta Garbo, Robert Redford, Margaux Hemingway,

Woody Allen—they all come to Bloomingdale's. The rich, the talented, the legal secretary, the busboy, the, transvestite—all want to experience the store and to be associated with it.

This powerful appeal can be traced to something called the "Bloomingdale's mystique": a partly contrived and partly spontaneous image of the store as the authoritative source of information on fashion, taste and style. Bloomingdale's is a business success story, but it is more than that. Its very position as a cultural force makes Bloomingdale's an economic, social and psychological phenomenon. In fact, it reflects an increasingly significant aspect of the contemporary American psyche: the need among the upper middle class as well as young white-collar workers for easily recognizable status symbols and instant sophistication, which translates into the search for a trendy, fashionable look.

Bloomingdale's success is also based on its realization that adults like to have fun too. Ever since management started transforming the store in the late 1940s from a tacky bargain outlet to a top-of-the-line emporium, careful attention has been paid to making Bloomingdale's a place where people could really enjoy shopping. To cater to an adult's version of fun, Bloomingdale's has designed its stores as fantasy-like worlds of exotic gifts, international fashions and lavish displays. The result is what *Time* magazine has called the "adult Disneyland."

In the process of building this quasi amusement park, Bloomingdale's has revolutionized the way goods and services are sold throughout the world. The store's contribution to retail science is the movement away from the age-old product-by-product sales system to an "umbrella" scheme utilizing broad themes, promotions and merchandise categories. According to traditional merchandising methods, which went virtually unchallenged for more than a century, each item in a store had to stand on its own. Attempts to tie merchandise together were limited to dividing stores into departments.

In changing this unwritten law, Bloomingdale's managers picked up on innovations that were already taking place in the small shops of London, Paris and New

York. Throughout the late 1950s and '60s the influence of the emerging pop culture produced new and interesting kinds of boutiques in bohemian sections like the Left Bank of Paris, London's Chelsea, and Greenwich Village in New York. For the first time, stores installed jukeboxes, offered unisex apparel and combined unrelated merchandise lines like health foods and casual clothes under a single roof. As happens in many industries, the small and more flexible retailers were the innovators.

What Bloomingdale's did was to incorporate these new merchandising techniques at the department store level. It was the first major retailer to recognize that department stores could be collections of small stores within a store, that the excitement of the boutiques could be reproduced on a larger scale. Thus, with its great financial resources, Bloomingdale's was able to lead the way in imaginative merchandising.

The store became a hotbed of exciting developments in American retailing. This was most evident in the discovery of new fashions and their presentation in such fresh and original settings as in-store boutiques. In a move that was crucial to the store's transformation, management also decided to work with European designers, manufacturers and vendors to obtain merchandise that would be unique for the U.S. market. Buyers for everything from food to fashions to furnishings were dispatched to the Continent (primarily France, Spain, Switzerland, Italy and Great Britain) to purchase exclusive goods for Bloomingdale's. A search was also conducted in the U.S. for domestically produced goods with a European flair.

To pave the way for the new imports, Bloomingdale's had to help its customers cultivate a taste and appreciation for European merchandise. And to do this, it started hyping an image: the image of a savvy, sophisticated and Continental American, the image of a chic, worldly and affluent lifestyle. The significance here is that an established store suddenly turned away from the classic solidly American merchandise its customers were used to (for example, the Ivy League look for men), and said, "This is what you should want. This is how you should look—and how you should live." Thus, in men's wear, Bloomingdale's buyers sought to provide clothes comparable to Brooks Brothers' quality and fabrics but interpreted with a European accent. The aim was to appeal both to those existing customers who were open to change and to a new breed of consumers moving into the area.

"Store executives don't even know this now, but my first contact with Bloomingdale's goes back to the 1950s, when I was a sales clerk selling sweaters in the men's wear department," says Ralph Lauren, the award-winning designer and owner of Polo fashions. "It was an exciting time to be on Manhattan's upper East Side because the neighborhood was changing from a dingy, blue-collar area to a place of flashy new office buildings, apartment towers and interesting shops. The change was attracting affluent and fashionable people in the vicinity and Bloomingdale's was starting to upgrade its merchandise lines in order to position itself for this new market.

"As it happened, this turned out to be a great blessing for me. After leaving Bloomingdale's, I got a job as a salesman for Beau Brummell Ties. At the time, everyone was wearing very narrow ties; there wasn't much imagination in the tie business at all. I convinced Beau Brummell to let me do some original designs and I came up with the very wide tie—about three and a half inches wide compared to the then standard two inches. Bloomingdale's, which was then one of my accounts, liked the new style and decided to promote it heavily. Frank Simon, the men's clothing vice president at the time, bought a full showcase full of the ties, gave them window space and heavy advertising support. Soon the ties were the hottest things in the store, I made a name for myself and left Beau Brummell to start Polo.

"The wide tie is a perfect example of what Bloomingdale's was looking for at the time: an original style with a European flair that would help to build the store's reputation as a fashion leader. They wanted to move customers away from the prevailing tastes for Ivy League clothing and toward a more Continental look. Simon encouraged me to move from wide ties to wide lapels to fitted suits, and the store backed me up all the way, promoting my designs as the fashion ideal."

Bloomingdale's developed its own version of the "ideal" lifestyle and held it out to New Yorkers as the ultimate objective of hard work and success. In line with this, the merchandise carried in the Bloomingdale's stores had to meet a greater test than simple profitability: each and every item, from Mic Mac coats to country French sofas, had to mesh with the theme of "high fashion." Retail goods were no longer just isolated numbers on inventory sheets; all were tied together to achieve just the right look for the Bloomingdale's customer.

This attention to image is integral to the Bloomingdale's story and contributes heavily to the store's success. "Above all else, we sell image," says Bloomingdale's chairman of the board, Marvin Traub. "We sell the sizzle rather than the steak," is the way former senior vice president Joseph Schnee liked to put it. "For years, we refused to locate any of our branches near another department store," says retired board chairman Lawrence Lachman, one of the prime movers in the Bloomingdale's transformation. "We were afraid their drab image would somehow rub off on us and spoil our magic. We never wanted the public to associate us with the likes of Sears. There's no excitement there."

True to its image, Bloomingdale's has for years been an exciting place to shop, and this quality has helped make it the most successful major retailer in the U.S. Judging success by the retail industry's favorite yardstick, sales per square foot, Bloomingdale's New York store weighs in with more than $400—almost four times the national average. And this is only the tip of the iceberg. Bloomingdale's is well ahead of the industry norm in such other recognized performance indicators as:

- Stock-Turn Rate—Simply put, this is the number of times a store sells out its inventory in the course of a year. Among the factors involved are the price of the goods, the proportion of the merchandise mix that is devoted to breaking fashions, and the store's location. In general, high-priced merchandise turns more slowly, but such things as a high-fashion image and a good location can speed up the rate. Every store's stock-turn rate must be viewed in the context of its market niche: K-Mart, a discounter, has a much higher rate than Bloomingdale's. Compared to its department store competitors, however, Bloomingdale's is known to exceed the average by at least one stock turn per year—a major accomplishment. A high stock-turn rate is usually an indication that management is doing a good job of buying, pricing and displaying merchandise for its market.

- Average Gross Sale—This is the dollar amount of gross sales divided by the number of sales transactions. Obviously, the higher the average gross sale, the better the store's ability to move more expensive merchandise. And most importantly, bigger gross sales can yield bigger gross profits. Bloomingdale's average gross sale is believed to exceed that of its closest competitors by a significant margin.
- Pretax Earnings—This most vital indicator, expressed as a percentage of total sales, tells the story of a store's profitability. Here, too, Bloomingdale's is believed to surpass all other stores in its category, turning in an estimated 13 percent compared to the industry average of less than 10 percent. Annual pretax profits for all Bloomingdale's stores combined exceeded $58 million in 1977\* (and could be estimated at about $70 million for 1979.)

No one factor can be singled out to explain this success. Bloomingdale's has been blessed with outstanding management, great financial resources and one of the best pieces of commercial real estate in the world. Add this all up, however, and you find that Bloomingdale's

---

\* This figure, which has never before been made public, emerged in the course of a probing interview the author had with a Federated Department Stores executive.

as a whole is greater than the sum of its parts. Other New York stores have enjoyed similar blessings but have never achieved such extraordinary success. Like the Model-T and McDonald's, Bloomingdale's appears to be one of those businesses that transcend their obvious virtues and for some reason simply "catch on" with the public. This is evident in Bloomingdale's enviable store-customer relationship: many Bloomingdale's customers are devoted followers who call it by the familiar nickname "Bloomie's" and who think of the store as their personal pleasureland. Fanatics, Bloomie's "freaks," they are willing to shell out exorbitant sums just to have the big "B" printed on their umbrellas, T-shirts, and even toilet paper; sales of the store's "Bloomie's"-inscribed panties generate more than $1 million annually.

Bloomie's fans are so eager to gobble up practically any fad the store promotes that they routinely part with eight dollars for a small bag of ordinary peanuts simply because the magic name is on the wrapping. And when the store's alert buyers decided to cash in on the women's movement, they sold thirty thousand neckties imprinted with the words "Male Chauvinist Pig"—just the kind of tongue-in-cheek, "hip" item Bloomie's people adore (and proof positive that even at Bloomingdale's, poor taste can be profitable). Similarly, Bloomingdale's was the first major store to advertise the now infamous Pet Rock (an ordinary rock in a cardboard box for four dollars) and is widely credited with making that insult the success it was. Bloomingdale's hold over its customers has helped the store develop—through word of mouth and major press coverage—a national reputation. "People the world over like to talk about Bloomingdale's, write about Bloomingdales, share Bloomingdale's stories—I see it wherever I travel," says top designer and former Bloomingdale's protégé Halston. "It's a strange and awesome attraction to a business."

This "attraction" is what caused official Washington to greet the opening of Bloomie's suburban Virginia branch with all the excitement of a presidential inauguration and made 67,000 Washingtonians sign up for credit cards even before the store opened. Bloomingdale's reputation precedes its branch expansion, preselling new markets before the foundation is poured. For this reason, all Bloomingdale's branches opened in recent years have achieved profitability in their first year—a rarity in the retail industry, where major new stores commonly operate in the red for several years.

Certainly a major ingredient in the Bloomingdale's success formula is its identity as an "adult Disneyland." The New York store is a glittering showcase of sumptuous merchandise, beautiful faces, blatant sex appeal and total self-indulgence. Displays at Bloomingdale's break through the old-fashioned reliance on mannequins, racks and static settings and put new emphasis on sound, color and movement.

"The in-store environment builds a crescendo of excitement in a store, gets the shopper turned on and cultivates a powerful image. That's why we prefer to put more of our promotional dollars into displays and such than into standard media advertising," says senior vice president Gordon Cooke, the young Madison Avenue-bred advertising executive hired away from Macy's in late 1977 to run Bloomie's big promotion department. Ambitious, aggressive and self-confident, Cooke represents a rare example of the reverse brain drain, where Bloomingdale's raids a major competitor for top talent. It is also evidence of Macy's position as the toughest competitor in many of Bloomingdale's markets.

Feeling no loyalty to standard parameters of time or space, Bloomingdale's brazenly opts for the unorthodox without an iota of self-consciousness. Like Disney's characters, Bloomie's promotions are larger than life. They are designed to thrill and capture observers—to make them surrender to the fun of it. When the store's jewelry buyers launched a promotion for French-made watches, the familiar display booths were cast aside in favor of a white-faced professional mime (brought in from Paris by the distributor) wearing dozens of watches up and down his arms. To cultivate tastes for primitive artifacts as home decorating accessories, Bloomingdale's displayed stunning reproductions, including shields from New Guinea and sculpture from Africa, in a makeshift museum that was carved out of existing floor space.

One of the originators of the rage for handmade area rugs, Bloomie's started the ball rolling by setting up an in-store international rug bazaar featuring works from India, Afghanistan, Haiti and native Navajo tribes. The scene—with rugs hanging from the ceiling and walls and strewn on the floors with baskets, palms and brass decanters—created the effect of a crowded market street in Calcutta. The lifelike environment is delicate, as is the manufactured elegance of the apparel floors, where bold brass and chrome signs herald the location of boutiques. It's like a private club for the clothes-conscious. Most of the big-name designers are members— Saint Laurent, Calvin Klein, Halston, the Missonis, Ralph Lauren—and all have an appropriate setting in which to exhibit their collections.

Bloomingdale's central merchandising strategy is based on what chairman Traub likes to call being "true to the merchandise." This reflects back to the Bloomingdale's notion that merchandise should be tied together in unified themes, rather than being forced to sink or swim on its own. The retailer's function is not simply to stock and sell products, but also to package and promote them with great style and appeal. So when Traub says "be true to the merchandise," he demands that a display of English bone china be presented in a replica of a London town house or a country cottage in Surrey. And when Cuisinart food processors are promoted, play French ballads, hire a Parisian chef and demonstrate the preparation and cooking of ratatouille.

A strategist supreme, Marvin Traub is that rare breed of executive who can concentrate on the big picture as well as on the smallest of details. Appointed Bloomie's chairman in 1978 after rising through the ranks for thirty years, Traub is a master of theme merchandising. All the store's promotions in recent years, from the successful China Passage to the disappointing India Fantasy, were Traub inspirations and he supervised their implementation with the energy and persistence of a driven man. More than any other Bloomingdale's executive since the founders, Traub views the store as an extension of himself. Although he denies it when asked, many say that Traub gives himself most of the credit for making the store the great success it is. He is proud and extremely sensitive to criticism. A negative word about Bloomingdale's is enough to make the man defensive.

Traub's critics claim that he is publicity hungry and that he has played only a small role in the store's transformation. It is just in the past decade, they say, that his influence has been felt, and the reviews on his performance are mixed. One of his greatest goals, to make Bloomingdale's a successful marketer of top-of-the-line women's clothing, has still not been achieved. Industry observers all agree that although Bloomingdale's does a big business in quality ready-to-wear (the trade name for mass-produced clothing), it has never been able to sell respectable quantities of the really high-priced lines, like Oscar de la Renta and Givenchy. The price gap between quality (like Ralph Lauren's clothing) and top-of-the-line (like Oscar de la Renta) can be as much as double, and it is at this steep end of the market (the $300 blouse, as opposed to the $150 one) that Bloomingdale's has never been successful.

But there are a great many Traub admirers as well. Many say he is a master merchant whose most visible accomplishment is the union of retailing and showmanship. As Las Vegas nightclubs fill the casinos, Traub's promotions build the traffic, stir the excitement and put the masses in the mood to spend.

Just what will happen next is never quite predictable, and the limits to which the store will go to shock and amuse are being extended all the time. For example, when Bloomie's lingerie buyers decided to feature the avant-garde collection of Zandra Rhodes, a designer associated with the punk rock movement, they knew something "tastefully kinky" would be needed to set the scene. The solution, as described by Gordon Cooke and former vice president Arthur Cohen, was to dress shapely models in panties only and have them parade around the sales floor in a topless fashion show. The

Bloomingdale's executives considered the show a smashing success: an original presentation of innovative fashion.

The truth is that extraordinary promotions are part of the Bloomingdale's razzle-dazzle—the kind of unusual goings-on that maintain the store's powerful mystique. Selling Rhodes's designs was not the sole objective—her collection is too radical for most of Bloomie's customers. The real point was to keep the Bloomie's name at the forefront in lingerie fashion.

Bloomingdale's has a lot at stake here. The store set the intimate-apparel industry on its ear in the mid seventies with the introduction of the now famous "Sighs and Whispers" catalogue. Produced by Bloomie's former marketing vice president Arthur Cohen (hired from General Foods specifically to give Bloomingdale's strength in mail order marketing, Cohen later left the store after being passed over for the top promotion spot by Gordon Cooke's appointment), "Sighs and Whispers" positioned intimate apparel for the first time as sexy fashion accessories. Before this, women had basically two choices: the traditional lackluster bras and panties or the tawdry mail order numbers popularized by Frederick's of Hollywood. Bloomies' catalogue changed this by offering a middle ground of sex appeal with style and elegance. "Sighs and Whispers" use of erotic photos taken by photographer Guy Bourdin did set off a minor controversy with those who objected to receiving "porno" material in the mail, but it also increased the store's bra, pantie and nightie business. In one masterstroke, Bloomie's established itself as a pacesetter in intimate apparel, and events like the Zandra Rhodes show are designed to keep that image alive.

The parallel of Bloomingdale's and show business holds true when it comes to fitting out the store with most of its products and displays. Here, as in a Broadway musical, floor space becomes a set and the accent is on staging. A tour of Bloomingdale's New York store reveals that the retail choreographers know their job and do it well.

"The closest you can ever come to being in a pinball

machine," is the way one customer describes the dazzle
of the Manhattan store at Christmas. Bright fantasy
worlds come to life to fill children and adults alike with
the feeling of make-believe. A replica of New York's
Chinatown pulses with silk kites, paper dragons, coolie
hats and bamboo umbrellas. A floor above, grotesque
faces and huge Lucky Strike packages greet the buyers
in the form of bold-colored satin pillows, price-tagged
at $150 and up. From top to bottom, the store erupts
with the jangling noises and clashing bodies of a futur-
istic carnival.

But is Bloomingdale's all show? Is there too much
"sizzle" and not enough "steak"? Are the store's promotions first-rate but its merchandise only grade B?
The answer depends on whom you ask. Store critics at
the powerful trade newspaper *Women's Wear Daily* as
well as such designers as Halston and Ralph Lauren
contend that Bloomingdale's merchandise is not as
imaginative as its displays and promotions. Behind all
the fancy footwork, they say, is a store selling mostly
fashionable "but not really ground-shaking merchandise."

"I can't sell the better Halston line at Bloomingdale's," says the designer about his own collection.
"Shoppers there just won't put up $1,000 for a dress
that is very new and very expensive. They just don't go
to Bloomingdale's for that. They go, instead, to Bergdorf's, Bendel's or small specialty stores."

But the truth is that the snobby attitude of some top
designers distorts their perception of the store. Halston,
a charming and elegant man who likes to be called
"opulent" and who fancies himself "an American hero,"
looks down on $75 blouses as near-trash. (Halston's
top line is considered a bridge between mass-produced
ready-to-wear and couture clothing and sports price
tags of up to $300 per blouse.) This is plainly out of
step with the views of all but a few wealthy consumers
and is not an attitude that Bloomingdale's or any other
major store can adopt. Although Bloomingdale's would
like to sell more expensive apparel, broader market
groups must also be serviced in order to keep up the

kind of large yearly volume Bloomingdale's generates in all its stores—roughly $550 million.

The only meaningful way to analyze Bloomingdale's merchandise mix is to compare it to other stores of similar size and personality. Here Bloomingdale's scores well in the effort to sell interesting goods. More than at any other major department store, Bloomingdale's buyers work closely with manufacturers to develop unique and exclusive products. In the production of sofas, for example, buyers huddle with furniture makers at the initial design stage, sketching in special features like rattan armrests or Indian gauze fabrics. This painstaking effort is unusual: most major stores simply accept the manufacturers' finished products as a *fait accompli,* just as consumers are forced to.

Bloomingdale's bothers to be different because this is the only way to assure availability of merchandise specially tailored to what it considers to be the needs of its own customers. Philip Hawley, president of Carter Hawley Hale Stores (owners of Bergdorf Goodman), contends that 80 percent of the merchandise in comparable department stores is virtually identical—and much of the industry would agree with this estimate. The inventories of Bloomingdale's, Saks Fifth Avenue, B. Altman and the like are top-heavy with the same brand names, such as Gant, Capezio, Izod and Blass. It is the 20 percent "fringe" or unique merchandise that really makes or breaks a store. How well does it reflect its customers' tastes? How much publicity, excitement and fashion appeal does it build for the store? Bloomie's scores very well on both counts, and it does so by devoting the lion's share of its fringe goods to trendy, flash-in-the-pan fashions.

To focus attention on this type of merchandise, Bloomie's invented the now widely imitated "swing boutique," a display designed solely for ultra-hot fashions with a brief life expectancy. As one fad rises to a peak and then dies just as quickly, the latest item replaces it in the swing boutique. This is precisely where Bloomie's really earns its stripes: the career girl in search of a great outfit for Saturday's party often finds that Bloomingdale's has that one dynamite number no one else has. The store stocks more late-breaking fashions than any of its competitors.

At Bloomingdale's, virtually all its fringe or exclusive merchandise is invested in high-fashion goods with temporary appeal. This is unusual; most stores will not gamble more than 5 or 10 percent of their inventories in such goods. The risk is simply too great: unless the merchandise is sold off quickly, it goes out of style and prices must be drastically reduced.

Bloomie's accepts the risks because it has developed the image and the clientele to sell these kinds of goods and, most importantly, because there is big money in it. It is a well-known law of retailing that the greater proportion of fashion versus commodity merchandise a store sells, the more profitable the store will be. According to a major report on the retail industry prepared by analysts* with the prestigious Goldman Sachs investment bankers: "Well-presented fashion—which appeals to impulse as well as to the predetermined need of the shopper—makes a considerably higher gross profit margin for the seller, representing the higher merchandising value added by the selling store."

Bloomingdale's does boast an appealing variety of fashionable merchandise. The following is but a small sampling:

- One of the world's great delicacy shops, featuring among its more than 150 kinds of bread, 300 cheeses, and other specialties: Swedish limpa bread, White Mountain Loaf, Swiss whole-grain pumpernickel, Jamaican Blue Mountain Carib coffee, English orange marmalade with cognac, currants in sugar syrup from France, Dorset's lemon curd, smoked goose breast, spa water from Belgium, Lebanon bologna, quail eggs, and julienne of celery root
- Stone Siamese pussy cats from England
- The Cartier pen from Paris
- Gold lamé backgammon sets from Taiwan

---

* Joseph Ellis and Ellen Harris.

- White Spanish-influenced patio sets for the ultimate New York terrace
- Italian silk ties
- Twelve-foot flexible Glow-Worm lights, resembling snakes
- Madras shirts from India
- Temple paintings from India
- Flor de Blason soaps from Spain
- Calvin Klein women's cotton sweaters made in Hong Kong
- Giant two-foot satin pencils from Brooklyn
- Plastic hot dog puzzles from Japan

The products span a wide price range and this is no accident. Savvy retailers view price consistency as a mark of inexperience. "I would make a plea for price inconsistency," says Stanley Marcus, chairman emeritus of the famous Neiman-Marcus stores. "A buyer should never be so wedded to a price-line concept that she becomes musclebound and incapable of recognizing a worthy article of merchandise at a price far below her regular range. If she is buying gifts which retail from twenty to fifty dollars, there is nothing wrong with buying a gift of good quality and taste which retails for five dollars. She will attract new customers and delight established ones by offering something new and exciting at a price lower than usual."*

The collection of exclusive, trendy and variably priced merchandise offered at Bloomingdale's is irresistible to its young-thinking, cosmopolitan customers and is integral to the concept of Bloomie's egocentric slogan: "It's Like No Other Store in the World."

"Our exclusive goods serve as a showcase for the vast bulk of merchandise," says Gordon Cooke. "It's our way of making everything else look great, by means of association. Put a Picasso in an ordinary house and suddenly everything looks better, more elegant."

In an age of increasing plasticity, sameness and mass production, the opportunity to buy exclusive mer-

---

* Stanley Marcus, *Minding the Store*. (Boston: Little Brown, 1974).

chandise is attractive to Bloomie's customers. The chance to do, to be or to wear something "different" has extraordinary appeal for the millions of Americans intent on distinguishing themselves from the workaday, blue-collar, silent majority—the "double-knit rubes" in Columbus, Moline and heart of Searsland. Add to this the cachet of "shopping where the greats shop"—of rubbing elbows with celebrities—and you have another ingredient in the Bloomingdale's success formula.

Bloomingdale's policies concerning celebrity customers are ingenious and two-faced. While at the same time shielding its superstar patrons from "the great unwashed" on the sales floors, and thus pretending to protect their privacy, Bloomie's all but goes to the front door and screams as loudly as possible, "Guess who's shopping here!"

"We bring Jackie Onassis down to the Missonis' fashion show and she is immediately crushed by the hundreds who want to get near her," says Gordon Cooke. "So we have ways of letting Jackie and the other famous people who shop here do so with their privacy intact."

The "ways" Cooke refers to is a little-known Bloomingdale's department called At Your Service. Ostensibly available to any customer who phones ahead and makes an appointment, this VIP feature is designed primarily for the who's who of the Bloomie's crowd: the big spenders and the glamorous faces right off the covers of *New York* and *People* magazines. It is a high-service, one-on-one shopping courtesy. The VIP calls Bloomingdale's, asks for the "personal shopper," reserves a time and date, comes to the store, is ushered into a private salon, tells of her wants and needs, and the appropriate goods from around the store are brought to her for her personal inspection. Better yet, the regulars at this game hardly need say anything at all: the "personal shopper" makes it a point to memorize individual tastes, sizes and preferences. So when a well-known Park Avenue media heiress takes a seat on the couch, attendants are programmed to bring out the latest Sonia Rykiel collection before the woman even opens her mouth. At Your Service is Bloomingdale's attempt to act as a "specialty store," rather than a "department store," for select groups of customers. The distinction between these two kinds of retail operations is best described by Stanley Marcus: "A visiting manufacturer once remarked that the difference between a department store and a specialty store is the telephone. By that he meant that the specialty store sales staff had both the time and the training to communicate with customers over the phone, to tell them about new arrivals of merchandise which would meet their particular needs. Our sales people are provided with what we call a 'clientele book' in which they are required to record the purchases for each customer's birthday, anniversary, and any other information that might be useful in making contact by phone or letter. By the proper utilization of the customer's purchasing history, it is easy to relate new mechandise to that already in the customer's wardrobe."*

Neiman-Marcus, Bendel's and Saks Fifth Avenue are specialty stores; Bloomingdale's is not. At Your Service is intended to provide the availability of specialty store service in a department store setting. Although the service is free of charge and is technically available to all customers, Traub and company want to protect themselves from undesirables. "We have some weirdos who come in this store every day, get lost in the crowds and buy nothing at all," a top store official reveals. "The last thing we want is for them to learn about this service, claim their rights to it and then destroy the privilege for the celebrities who deserve the privacy and protection they need to shop here without annoyance."

This aura of privacy is, however, an illusion carefully cultivated by the Bloomingdale's staff. Recognizing that the urge to imitate big-name jocks, film idols and society queens is strong among its customers, Bloomie's wants every ounce of publicity it can get for the biggies who buy its goods and fill its coffers. This is accomplished through a steady stream of press leaks planted to ensure that media coverage of Bloom-

---

* Stanley Marcus, *Minding the Store.*

ingdale's will associate the store with its famous customers. Bloomie's publicity flacks know full well that the media love celebrity anecdotes to color otherwise drab stories, so they drop well-known names like a proud mother bragging about her prodigious children. Press people find it difficult to be with Bloomingdale's promotion executives for ten minutes without talk of Liza or Jackie O. or Garbo.

The atmosphere in the store's public relations quarters is rather haughty. With the notable exception of Gordon Cooke, the staff members there tend to be a snooty bunch, convinced that their contact with glamorous people makes them important too. Some act like near-royalty—too busy and exalted to deal with anyone whose name is not in the Social Register. In fact, they are simply small cogs in the Bloomingdale's wheel: stepchildren executives in a company of merchants.

Sometimes the staff's zeal for name dropping gets the store in deep trouble. Upon learning of false rumors that she would pose nude for a Bloomie's shopping bag design, Princess Yasmin Ali Khan (the daughter of Rita Hayworth and Ali Kahn) sued the store. Bloomie's settled out of court and issued a public apology to the princess, who had never agreed to the project. Whether Bloomingdale's started the rumor was never established.

Bloomingdale's equivocal stance concerning celebrities was made most evident by its handling of one of the greatest retail publicity coups of all time: the tour of Bloomingdale's by Queen Elizabeth. When Her Majesty visited New York in 1977, she announced that Bloomingdale's was on her itinerary. Management greeted the announcement with feigned surprise and made a big to-do about the queen's coming. The impression conveyed to the press was that the queen had long been straining at the bit to visit Bloomingdale's— that she, too, recognized it as the greatest store in the world. The truth is that Bloomingdale's begged, pleaded and twisted some powerful arms to arrange Her Majesty's visit to the store. For months, top executives leaned on contacts in and out of government to get Bloomingdale's name on the itinerary. Only through this influence did the effort succeed. The queen toured the store, and although she never dipped into the royal purse to make a purchase, the visit was enough to boost Bloomie's reputation even higher than its already stratospheric level.

Royalty aside, visits by the rich, powerful and famous are an everyday occurrence at Bloomingdale's. Bloomie's is the fashionable place for celebrities to be seen and admired while the sun is up. Many seem to enjoy the experience. "It's the obvious place to go for everything," says Lee Radziwill, Jackie Onassis's sister. "Oh, gosh, it's the most fantastic and exhausting store in the world."

For some Bloomie's lovers, the chance to see and rub shoulders with the stars is the key element in their addiction to the store. "I'll admit it straight out," says six-days-a-week Bloomie's nut Lee Stone. "I go to Bloomie's to see stars and there's hardly anything I know that's more exciting. I've been in an elevator with Barbra Streisand, drunk coffee next to Johnny Carson in the store's 40 Carrots restaurant and got Dustin Hoffman to give me his autograph. I buy things here sometimes, but most often I come to see who I can spot. This place is concentrated celebrity."

Among the store's superstar customers, baby doctor and political activist Benjamin Spock lingers in the men's furnishings department, carefully matching up Ivy League shirts and ties. Walter Matthau likes the suit department, and basketball star Earl "The Pearl" Monroe says he stops in for cologne and to "see how people with money act." Jackie O. does a good part of her Christmas shopping at the store (using At Your Service) and has gifts sent to friends around the world. Catherine Deneuve and Marcello Mastroianni have shopped together for sheets and pillowcases in the linen department, where socialite and businesswoman Gloria Vanderbilt makes personal appearances to sell her own line of designer linen.

"We see so many famous faces here that we are numb to it all," sighed Arthur Cohen. "The truth is we are very blasé about it." But this does not stop the PR people from grinding out endless celebrity gossip for the media mills. What's more, the store uses a device to give its John Doe customers the impression of celebrity status. Knowing that many of its most loyal (some say "insecure") customers want to be known as insiders or "Bloomie's People," management set up the Gold Card system. Based on illusion rather than substance, Gold Cards make ordinary customers feel like VIPs without actually giving them any special privileges. Here's how it works: Established charge card customers who spend a substantial amount of money at the store, and pay their bills on time are identified by the credit department for Gold Card status. After approval by management, the "fortunate few" are notified of their selection and are sent gold-colored credit cards (in contrast to the standard yellows and silvers). Presentation of the Gold Card is intended to bestow the recipient with the impression of instant status, recognition and insider privileges.

In reality, the Gold Cards are not even worth the plastic they are made of. Except for the color, they are exactly the same as all other Bloomingdale's charge plates. The vast majority of employees do not even know that the Gold Cards are intended to signify customer status. (No mention of the cards is made in Bloomingdale's training programs.) The only benefit bestowed by the Gold Cards is in the recipients' mind —in the appeal to personal vanity and in the fact that they can show their friends that they have something "special." Still, thousands clamor and beg for the cards as if they were pure gold and the token of admission to a private club. One delighted housewife was so moved on receiving her Gold Card that she composed a love poem to Bloomingdale's expressing her heartfelt pride on being one of a chosen few.

Store executives refuse to say just how much has to be spent to qualify one for a Gold Card, but outsiders put the figure at $10,000 per year. As with so much of the store's operations, this very secrecy is part of the mystique, the image, the illusion, the magic. People want Gold Cards. They pray for them. They try to spend more to get them. That is all that matters.

\*    \*    \*

This seeking after a piece of meaningless plastic is a dramatic illustration of Bloomingdale's powerful influence over many of its customers. Bloomie's people are obsessed with the store—they try to make love to the store, rather than the store trying to please or make love to them. In fact, the store's attitude toward its customers is evident by the way it services them. Switchboards at the New York store are manned by surly and abrasive operators who seem to be trained to keep callers with legitimate gripes from getting to top management. The switchboards are also understaffed. It is not unusual to have to wait for up to thirty rings to get an answer.

The same is true on the sales floors. In an effort to control costs, Bloomie's keeps its sales force down to the bare minimum. It is typical to have to wait ten or fifteen minutes for help in any of the store's major departments, and longer during the crowded lunch hours. Even more damaging than the shortage of employees is their lack of experience. "Management recognizes this as a real weakness in the Bloomingdale's operation," says Doris Shaw, a former Bloomingdale's vice president of advertising, who later served as editor of *House Beautiful*. "There tends to be a real crush of people in the New York store and most of the sales help there really can't handle it." Bloomingdale's routinely hires novice clerks, speeds them through a two-week training course aimed mostly at proper cash register operation, and then puts them out on the floor to deal with customers. Most do a poor job, and there is a good reason for this. Bloomingdale's pays its starting help about $3.50 an hour, adding a dime or so per hour for limited experience. Comparable stores like Saks, on the other hand, make an all-out effort to recruit more experienced clerks and pay as much as five to six dollars per hour to get them. Unlike Bloomingdale's, Macy's and Gimbels in New York, Saks is not unionized and is therefore not bound by a union scale. Saks pays experienced sales personnel top dollars, but is free to dip below union minimums for those it considers nonessential employees.

"I've worked here part time for four years, and I

now know Bloomingdale's thinking about customer service," says Mrs. M, a Bloomingdale's employee who prefers to remain anonymous. Mrs. M is a so-called floater, who fills in for ill or vacationing workers in various departments throughout the store. "If they lose one customer they don't really care because they know there are one hundred more ready to take up the slack." Mrs. M's appraisal of Bloomingdale's is interesting not only from her perspective as a current employee, but also because she spent most of her adult life in retailing. Together with her late husband, she built their business in a small Southern town into a substantial dry goods emporium. (The store is now managed by one of her sons.) "When I was involved in running our business, we took the exact opposite approach of Bloomingdale's. We always went on the assumption that by disappointing just one customer we could wind up losing twelve more. Good service was most important to us. Bloomingdale's acts this way only when it comes to returns. They will give credit for most anything— even if it's months old—if the customer demands it."

Mrs. M's comments about Bloomingdale's are revealing: "We are so understaffed that I often have to serve one customer while three more wait for me to finish. Sometimes the people lose patience and leave. This happened recently at the Polo shirt counter—customers were angry and complaining about the lack of sales help, but there was nothing I could do. Bloomingdale's tries to get by with as little help as possible. What's more, they often take inexperienced people—those with no knowledge of a particular department—put them alone on a sales floor and expect them to service customers properly. It is just impossible. Sometimes they have me selling goods I know nothing about. I don't know the sizes, the fabrics or the stock. No store with quality service would do that."

"Poor service is precisely the reason why Bloomingdale's cannot sell really top-of-the-line clothing," says Halston. "Those dressing rooms are cattle pens and every shopper is out for himself. Women who pay for my better dresses want personal attention and service throughout the purchase and Bloomingdale's just doesn't have the regular floor staff capable of doing this."

In spite of the critics, however, most Bloomie's people don't seem to let such negatives deter them. The old slogan for retail success, "Know your customer," gets turned around at Bloomingdale's. For millions of Bloomie's devotees, it is crucial to "know the store." For them, knowing what Bloomie's is up to is essential for them to stay hip to the latest styles, fashions and furnishings. Bloomie's is their lifestyle leader—the place they turn to for direction.

"People want life to be fun," Gordon Cooke likes to say. "Change and variety are part of this fun. We put our necks, as well as our time and money, on the line to spot the trends, bring the change and offer the variety before anyone else does. And this accounts for a large measure of our success: busy, active people need a source they can trust to edit what is good and acceptable in style. We do it for them and they love us for it."

A Manhattan newspaper editor puts it differently: "People who go to Bloomingdale's don't trust their own taste."

## 2

# Social Climbing

*On a raw winter evening in 1947, rising young executive Lawrence Lachman arrived at a fashionable New York town house for a formal dinner party. Dressed in natty pin stripes and a crisp blue shirt, he glowed with the pride of a man who knows he is on the way up. Weeks earlier, at the age of thirty-one, Lachman had been appointed treasurer of Bloomingdale's.*

*Circling among the guests at the smart Fifth Avenue soiree, Lachman found himself raising toasts with the wife of a Broad Street banker.*

*"What business are you in?" she asked.*

*"I've just been appointed treasurer of Bloomingdale's," Lachman declared, beaming.*

*"Oh, I know that place," she answered. "That's where my maid shops."*

No facts, figures or statistics could better illustrate the "then and now" of Bloomingdale's than the above anecdote. Nothing else so clearly reveals that the trend setter of today bears little resemblance to the Bloomingdale's of only three decades ago. In contrast to its current worldwide reputation as an elite and sophisticated store, Bloomingdale's spent the first seventy-five years of its existence as a price-conscious, sales-oriented, bargain-basement shop doing things the traditional way and catering almost exclusively to the lower end of the consumer market. It would probably come as a great shock to most of its current corps of devotees that Bloomingdale's was long regarded, as one national business editor puts it, "as a schlock store, a combination Korvettes and Orchard Street."

Only in the past thirty years has Bloomingdale's emerged from the cellar; only in the past fifteen has it surfaced as the prestige leader of an industry; and only in the past ten has it become Bloomie's—the adored tastemaker and fashion leader for millions. The recent history of Bloomingdale's is the saga of a retail revolution in less than a generation—a revolution that was in fact carefully and meticulously planned to the smallest detail.

Bloomingdale's roots go back more than a century, to its founding in the early post–Civil War period by two brothers, Lyman G. and Joseph B. Bloomingdale. Born and raised in New York City, and products of its public schools, the brothers took the daring and to some "foolhardy" step of opening a retail store on Manhattan's Fifty-sixth Street. At this juncture in New York's history, Fifty-sixth Street was a dividing line of sorts— a geographical marker representing the far point of the city's cosmopolitan section and the beginning of its outlying borders. In those days the great pocket of retail activity centered in lower Manhattan, from Second to Fourteenth streets. To the horse-and-buggy city dwellers of the time, the area around Fifty-sixth Street was the out-of-the-way home of small factories, warehouses and the working-class poor—certainly a place to be avoided by the "civilized" middle and upper classes.

It was here, in this "shanty town where goats ran free," that the brothers Bloomingdale landed their first retail venture. Choice of this apparently illogical site rested on two factors: money and confidence. The brothers lacked sufficient capital for the more attractive and costly downtown locations, and perhaps more important, they had confidence that they would succeed regardless of location.

Their confidence was based on more than just pie-in-the-sky optimism. The brothers were not newcomers.

to private enterprise when, in 1872, they opened what they then called Bloomingdale's Great East Side Bazaar. One had worked in a retail establishment on New York's Grand Street and the other in San Francisco. They were, in their own words, "thoroughly American in ideas and principles and thoroughly educated in the dry goods business in every detail."

Their first joint venture, manufacturing hoop skirts, had been successful but was viewed by the brothers as having limited long-term potential. Ironically (if one thinks about the current Bloomingdale's), Lyman and Joseph favored a business less subject to passing whims, and therefore turned their sights to owning a dry goods store. (The term "dry goods store" was commonly used in the 1800s and early 1900s, and is still popular in rural parts of the country, to describe retail outlets carrying textiles, ready-to-wear clothing and notions.) Living uptown, the brothers combed their home turf for a place where "a growing business would be successfully commenced and maintained." The search pointed to a shop on Third Avenue. Negotiations for the first Bloomingdale's location were described by the brothers in a souvenir booklet published when the Fifty-ninth Street store opened, on October 4, 1886:

At this time—early 1872—there was one store above Forty-second Street which rejoiced in two large plate-glass windows, but it was occupied by a shoe-dealer who held the lease on the premises. However, the Bloomingdales, having applied to all the local real estate agents, asking—almost begging—for a location, without success, visited this shoe store one evening with the intention of asking the proprietor if he would sell out, but were prevented from carrying out their project by the sudden appearance of a friend, whose presence precluded any confidential business talk. Negotiations were then opened for a store at the corner of Thirty-fourth Street; but happily, before arrangements were concluded, they saw an advertisement in the *Herald* of a fine store on Third Avenue for rent and fixtures for sale, and, upon making inquiries, were delighted to learn it was the shoe dealer who desired to retire from business. The lease and fixtures of that store changed owners with a celerity which astonished the shoe man, Bloomingdale Brothers obtaining the very location they desired. This store was No. 938 on the avenue, had two large plate-glass show windows and a depth which was regarded by everybody as too extravagant for any purpose. Indeed, the owner had been seriously "talked to" by his friends on the folly of building such a large store on Third Avenue, and the acquaintances of the Bloomingdales kindly advised them to have a partition put up and save on their rent by subletting the rear to someone. The brothers, having acted entirely on their own judgment in taking the store, concluded to carry out their own ideas; but, whether in deference to their friends or because of a weakening either in pocket or nerve, it matters not now, they caused extremely "liberal" shelving to be erected, large spaces being left between the sections, and the shelves themselves not being near enough to each other to mar the beauty of the large store.

Recognizing that advertising had been pivotal in their search for a store, the brothers decided right from the start to adopt this tool for their own commercial purposes. The combination of consistent advertising, well-stocked inventories of appealing products, and low prices could, they believed, easily overcome the limitation of their location and make a success of Bloomingdale's Bazaar.

They were right. In less than six months after the grand opening (first day's volume: $3.68), more store shelves and counters were required to handle the growing volume of business and to stock increasing quantities of merchandise. After eighteen months, the little store's seams were stretched to the limit and more space was mandatory. The brothers asked the owner of the building to extend the shop and to force out their next-door neighbors.

Here they had to pay the first price of success. Again, in the brothers' own words: "About this time the traditional greed of landlords exhibited itself in a marked degree. Content to accept $1,200 per annum from the shoe-dealer and see the upper floors vacant, he demanded $3,100 for the whole building from his successful tenants, and they, seeing no other course, accepted the new lease at this figure and converted the upper floors into store-rooms."

Still, space continued to be a problem. By the next year the business had grown steadily, and the firm was again faced with the question of what to do for room. Another appeal to the landlord resulted in his building an extension in the rear of the structure, thus raising the yearly rental to $4,300, double the going rate for other buildings in the neighborhood. But getting the extra space was most crucial at the time, so the brothers dug in, paid up, and increased their advertising. And by early 1875 they found themselves as badly cramped for room as ever before.

The next move came in 1877, when Bloomingdale's secured three stories on Third Avenue at the corner of Fifty-sixth Street. Believing they now had more room than they needed, the brothers sublet the basement to a dealer in china, glass and house-furnishing goods and left the top floors idle. By 1879, however, the old phantom of crowded salesrooms haunted them again, and they took possession of the second and third stories, converting the floors into stores practically overnight. They then took three adjoining stores and basements on Fifty-sixth Street, and added them to their many-times-enlarged establishment.

The brothers' runaway success provoked the need for further expansion in 1880. Fortunately, the furnishings merchant in the main store's basement moved out at this time, so Lyman and Joseph assumed ownership of the shop and turned it into a Bloomingdale's department. Shortly before the change in ownership, the former merchant had sworn under oath (the common practice then for making financial statements) to an annual sales volume of $25,000. In less than two years, the same department, now under Bloomingdale's management, was transacting $25,000 in sales on a monthly basis.

As New York's retail community moved uptown over the years—from lower Manhattan to Fourteenth Street, then to Twenty-third Street, and on to Herald Square—Bloomingdale's started attracting customers from well beyond its own neighborhood. Partly because of this, Bloomingdale's sales more than quadrupled, from $184,000 to $851,000, during the period 1877–1885. With this kind of accelerating growth, even the newly expanded store was too small to serve the crush of Bloomingdale's customers. So the brothers decided to purchase land for an even grander expansion three blocks away on Third Avenue and Fifty-ninth Street, site of the present flagship store (the store now occupies twice as much land as the original site). Hiring a well-known real estate agent, Lyman and Joseph gave the go-ahead to make the purchase at virtually any price. Unfortunately, the owner had set aside the land for his children and could not be prevailed upon to set a price. The property was not for sale.

Undaunted, the brothers refused to take no for an answer. The Fifty-ninth Street site seemed to be the ideal location, so they turned on the pressure. The pesty real estate agent was ordered to follow the owner to his vacation spa in Saratoga and not to leave his side until a deal was made. The ploy worked. To rid himself of the annoying agent, the owner named a price so high he thought no one would be foolish enough to pay it. He was wrong. Hearing the "good news," the Bloomingdale brothers immediately drew a check and told the agent, "If you cannot do any better, accept the terms—we must have it."

The deal, which was quickly concluded, left New York's business community openly laughing at the brothers' stupidity. The consensus was that the Bloomingdales had overpaid. The brothers, however, thought just the opposite: they considered the deal to be a coup of coups. What observers at the time had not known was that the brothers valued the newly acquired property at $50,000 more than they paid for it.

History has proved the brothers to be far-sighted

real estate speculators as well as extraordinary merchants. Better than anyone else, the Bloomingdales had tested the merits of Third Avenue and knew it to be an up-and-coming retail mecca—an area with an exceptional future. After all, they were among Third Avenue's merchant pioneers. Their very first dry goods store—and all the other Bloomingdale stores to follow —were located on the avenue. Lyman and Joseph were confident that retail trade was moving uptown. And of course, they were right. In less than five years, the purchase price was considered a genuine bargain by all knowledgeable observers.

It was in 1885 that the brothers authorized construction of a brand-new store to be built on the Fifty-ninth Street site. Two existing structures were razed to make room for Bloomingdale's first custom-designed store. The new building would match the size of the major department stores of the time, like Lord & Taylor and Arnold Constable.*

Construction of the Fifty-ninth Street facility began on May 1, 1885, with Schwartzman and Buchman as the architects and Tribune Builders in charge of construction. Bloomingdale's remained at its Fifty-sixth Street location throughout the year and a half of construction so that business could continue uninterrupted, while work proceeded on the new building. The new store had to satisfy the Bloomingdale brothers' orders for a "substantial, well-ventilated building, having every improvement and facility for promoting the health, comfort and convenience of both customers and employees." The resulting structure was a model of modern convenience and efficiency for its time, and its huge electric plant was then the largest ever installed by the Edison Company. There were wardrobes and dining rooms for employees, parlors and reception rooms for customers, and four elevators. The opening-day (October 4, 1886) souvenir book revealed the broad range of merchandise departments:

---

* Lord & Taylor and Macy's are now the only major New York stores older than Bloomingdale's; Arnold Constable went bankrupt in 1973.

In the front basement, 115 × 120 ft., extending under the sidewalks, is the China, Glass, and Queensware and House furnishing Departments, including trunks, Willow-ware and large Toys— the rear basement, 40 × 115 ft., being the Shipping Department.

The Store floor contains the Silk, Flannel, Blanket, Domestic, Dress Goods, Notions, Ribbon, Lace, Gents' Furnishing, Jewelry, Clocks, Books and Stationery, Passementerie and Hosiery Departments; a balcony between the first and second floors, a part of which is taken up by the parlor and reception rooms, affording an elegant view of this entire busy floor.

The second floor is devoted to the Trimmed and Untrimmed Millinery, Cloak, Suit, Fur, Corset, Ladies' and Children's Underwear, Infants' Wear, Boys' Clothing, and Shoe Departments.

The third floor is devoted to the Carpet, Rug, Upholstery, Bric-a-brac and Art, and Furniture Departments.

The fourth floor contains cloak and dining-rooms for employees; the gents separate from the ladies, each sex having its own suite of rooms. A kitchen is attached to the ladies' dining-room so that warm lunches can be had when desired, ample time being accorded the lady employees to provide their lunches as they deem fit. On this floor also are the manufacturing departments, comprising Dressmaking and the manufacture of Gents' Shirts, Bathing Suits, Lace Goods, Machine-knit stockings, and Plush goods.*

The fifth floor is the Receiving Department, reserve stock, and the extensive Mail Order Department.

The sixth floor is used for storage, repair shops, and employees' workrooms.

---

* The presence of manufacturing departments reflected the great popularity of custom-made clothing at that time. Bloomingdale's prided itself on quality custom clothing at reasonable prices.

Never humble, the Bloomingdale brothers seized the grand opening to boast of their success and to peer optimistically (and accurately) into the future:

> The same careful friends who predicted disaster in 1872 may not think so even in the light of the brilliant past; but the honest endeavor to please the public, combined with the knowledge how, when and where to buy, the possession of an enormous stock and a bewildering variety of styles, the contentment with a small profit, and the active belief in advertising exactly what can be at all times substantiated, must prove as successful in the future as it has been in the past.

Lyman and Joseph were, for the most part, traditional merchants in operating style and methods. Success came to them through adherence to the classic business laws: hard work, persistence, customer service, advance planning, ample inventories and competitive pricing. And they were thus able to expand the company's market area beyond its East Side home base to attract a solid middle-class clientele from the West Side as well as from downtown. Although never wild-eyed innovators, Lyman and Joseph did show flashes of promotional genius that Bloomingdale's current management would be proud of. Equipping the big new store with a newfangled invention known as the "escalator" (the first ever by a major American retailer), the brothers promoted the contraption as a "sky carriage" and invited the public to come in for a ride. (This may well have been the first time that Marvin Traub's "shopping here is an adventure" theme was put to the test.)

Most important, however, was the fact that the brothers recognized the tremendous power of advertising as a motivational tool, a way to develop instant recognition, a technique for building impulse sales and a magnet to draw customers to their still somewhat remote location. They proved that by being one of the first New York retailers to make a major investment in advertising, they could induce thousands to travel to the store from all parts of Manhattan, outlying boroughs and nearby towns in New Jersey and Connecticut. The store's reputation for service and merchandise simply proved stronger than the inconvenience of getting there. (In much the same way today, Barney's, the famous men's store, uses heavy advertising to draw customers in a realigned city to *its* now out-of-the-way downtown location.)

How well the Bloomingdale's advertising strategy succeeded was summed up in a guidebook called "Round-About New York," published by the brothers in 1902: "Bloomingdale's store is remarkable in as much as it is out of the so-called shopping trade center of New York. Shoppers do not drift to Bloomingdale's. They are drawn here. They go by choice. The store draws trade from every section of Greater New York and from miles around."

And the following was written by a reporter in New York's *Evening Mail* of April 8, 1909:

Does LOCATION have much of a bearing on THE RESULTS to be obtained from advertising?

The writer is so much of an optimist on advertising that he thinks PEOPLE WOULD SWIM FROM THE BATTERY TO GOVERNOR'S ISLAND to get anything good that might be advertised there—if there was no other means of getting across the stretch of water that separates the two places—

AND IF THE ADVERTISEMENT INSPIRED THEIR CONFIDENCE.

A striking example of building up a business in a locality that was very inconvenient twenty years ago is that of BLOOMINGDALE BROS. AT THIRD AVENUE AND FIFTY-NINTH STREET.

When this business was started, the location seemed to be FAR-REMOVED FROM EVERYWHERE.

It was hard to get to, but that did not deter the founders of the house from starting a business THAT HAS SINCE GROWN TO ENORMOUS PROPORTIONS.

. . . When the writer came to New York in 1892, BLOOMINGDALE BROS. WERE ABOUT THE LARGEST ADVERTISERS IN THE CITY.

Half pages in the morning and evening newspapers were a steady occurrence, and full pages
were always used in the Sunday newspapers.

They used FOUR FULL PAGES in the old New
York "Recorder," which, at the time, was the
LARGEST ADVERTISEMENT EVER PRINTED. Later on
they used EIGHT FULL PAGES in the New York
"Press."

THEY HAVE ALWAYS BELIEVED IN ADVERTISING
and the firm regards it as news. An expansive advertising department is maintained UNDER THE
ABLE MANAGEMENT OF MR. C. J. SHEARER, and
great care is taken to tell the store news invitingly
and entertainingly.

The advertising BRINGS VERY HANDSOME RE-
TURNS, because IT IS WELL DONE and because the
firm surrounds itself WITH ABLE BUYERS.

There is a steadfastness about the firm's methods
that is sure to make the business permanently successful.

One very excellent trait is the firm's loyalty to
its employees. There are men and women in the
store who have been there 20, 25, 30 and 35 years.

HOW CAN AN ORGANIZATION THAT PULLS PEO-
PLE TOGETHER EVER FAIL OF SUCCESS, ESPECIALLY
WHEN IT USES CLEVER ADVERTISING TO PILOT IT?

By the turn of the century, Bloomingdale's had developed into a full-line department store, featuring a
broad range of merchandise and services, from dry
cleaning to horse liniments. The following merchandise
selection is from the Catalogue and Diary for 1910:

- Forest Mills Ladies' Union Suits in Cotton,
  Wool and Silk—$1.00 to $1.50
- Our own direct importation, here in five differ-
  ent styles and all sizes, children's patent leather
  hats—$1.49
- Chiffon Panama Coats—$9.75
- Girl's Mixture Coats (Very Serviceable School
  Coats)—$3.95

The following jingle for the bath shop reveals an early penchant for home furnishings:

Keep it light
Keep it White
Keep it Nickel Bright
Bloomingdale's they have for sale
The "Palette Brand" that never fail . . .
250 kinds to choose from—towel racks and soap cups.

In the category of offerings long since banished from the store we find:

* Dry cleaning services—lace curtains and blankets—.50¢
* Powder Caps—.29¢
* Maid Aprons—.49¢
* Megaphones—.24¢–$1.49
* Pianos—$10 down, $10 a month*
* Hexagon bolts—.20¢ per box
* Albany Grease—.85¢ for 5 lbs.
* Frank Miller's Hoof Dressing—.45¢ per quart

Mirroring today's Bloomingdale's, the store made an isolated attempt in 1910 to associate with the city's cultural elite. The back of the catalogue was devoted to seating plans of New York's top theaters and included the following copy:

Theatre Goers—Everything in the way of concert dress, in fact every requirement of those who frequent places of amusement or whose social duties call them out often, may be secured at the store of certain satisfaction—Bloomingdale's.

This appeal was a radical departure from the store's established policy of catering to the city's lower and

---

* Bloomingdale's was at the time the world's largest distributor of player pianos, selling 7,000 annually.

middle classes and can only be viewed as an early attempt to attract a more affluent clientele.

Surprisingly, we find from the 1910 catalogue that Bloomingdale's was the only major store in New York with its own banking department:

A regular domestic and foreign banking business.
Deposits secured subject to check.
Foreign money bought and sold.
Drafts and coupons payable in U.S.
Canada or Europe promptly collected.
Travelers letter of credit issued.

A peek at the fashions of the times reveals this bit of vogue circa 1910: "The latest Paris shapes for the Women of Fashion—Low Bust, Long Hip, Straight Front."

But the dominant theme of the catalogue was thrift, and that image was spelled out from the start: "All goods described in the following pages are strictly high-grade and invariably most modestly priced. We are a store that provides for most every human want more expeditiously and at less cost than any other."

The publication of the Catalogue and Diary of 1910 coincided with a significant event in the store's growth and evolution. Completion of the Queensboro Bridge linking the borough of Queens with Manhattan had generated increasing use of the private automobile and of public carriages. The bridge virtually deposited its Manhattan-bound traffic at Bloomingdale's door, so the formerly out-of-the-way Fifty-ninth Street location was rapidly becoming more central to the city's traffic flow. And Bloomingdale's was quick to make note of its newly bustling environs in its promotional copy: "A word to our location. A big, busy store right at the threshold of thousands of New York's most substantial citizens—a great modern store that is reached by auto, carriage, car or afoot with less effort, annoyance or delay than any other store from any part of Manhattan, the Bronx, or Queens County."

\* \* \*

Much of the Bloomingdale's story in the period between 1911 and World War II was historically uneventful. The notable exception was the union with what is now known as Federated Department Stores. The *New York Times* of September 17, 1929, carried the story on the front page. Bloomingdale's (annual sales volume of $23 million) would take part in a major retail merger of its stock interest with Abraham and Straus ($25 million annual sales), William Filene's Sons Company of Boston ($46 million annual sales) and F. Lazarus & Company of Columbus, Ohio ($12 million annual sales). The new venture's total gross revenues of $106 million per year would make it a giant for its time. Lehman Brothers, which negotiated the merger for more than six months, announced that the purpose was to "bring under unified control, successful retail stores through their acquisition and affiliation." Paul Mazur, Filene's former chief of research, was the Lehman Brothers partner who organized the deal. Earlier that year Lehman had arranged for R. H. Macy's acquisition of L. Bamberger & Company, resulting in another retail giant, with combined annual revenues of $125 million.

The mechanism for the Bloomingdale's merger was a holding company in which stock control of the participating store corporations was exchanged for stock in the holding company. The bulk of Bloomingdale's shares were closely held by the sons of cofounder Lyman Bloomingdale. The three brothers agreed to the merger for personal and financial security, to diversify geographical risks and to simplify family tax problems when older members died. They announced from the start, however, that the merger would in no way change Bloomingdale's individual character or local identity. And history has borne this out: Federated Department Stores is well known for the wide operating freedom it grants its subsidiaries.

After the merger, Bloomingdale's continued to flourish as it capitalized on the northward movement of Manhattan's social and commercial activities, as well as the northeastward movement of many families to Queens. Lyman's sons, who had inherited the business upon their father's death in 1905, began to leave the scene. (The other cofounder, Joseph, had retired from the business years before Lyman's death.) Irving died in 1929, leaving an estate of $9.5 million; Samuel, who had served as Bloomingdale's president since 1905, retired in 1930 and was named honorary chairman of the board. Successive rounds of professional managers then took turns at the helm. For the most part, the original course charted by Lyman and Joseph was dutifully followed: maintenance of a full-line department store featuring copious inventories, wide selections and thrifty prices. The bargain-basement image proved ideal for the store's market area, composed at the time primarily of working-class, first-generation Americans. With the elevated subway towering over Third Avenue—and Irish bars, dingy shops and cheap restaurants crammed in the dark, noisy streets below—Bloomingdale's country became an early example of urban blight. The store made its home in a poor, blue-collar community and it clearly reflected the tastes and incomes of its closest neighbors, while simultaneously catering to more distant customers attracted to a thrift outlet.

With the end of World War II, winds of change began to stir throughout the nation. Strong, victorious, confident, Americans prepared for a burst of economic growth. The return to family life, to homes and jobs, occupied the minds of homecoming GIs. Throughout the New York metropolitan area there were plans for new construction, new ventures, new developments.

Enter the key triumvirate in the evolution of the modern Bloomingdale's: J. E. Davidson, chairman; James Schoff, Sr., president; and Lawrence Lachman, treasurer. "It was the year I joined the store, in 1947, that the three of us started the behind-the-scenes planning for the emergence of the new Bloomingdale's— the store the world knows today as Bloomie's," Lachman reveals. "What happened to Bloomingdale's was no accident: we purposely set out to transform a lower-middle-class, lackluster retail establishment into a chic, affluent fashion leader. I must admit, however, that we never dreamed we'd be as successful as we were."

The decision to make the transformation was based on the simple belief that Bloomingdale's could improve its gross profit performance by selling higher-priced goods. After all, selling a thirty-dollar item that shows a fifteen-dollar gross profit is obviously preferable to selling a ten-dollar item with a five-dollar gross profit, since the cost of sales remains more or less constant regardless of the price of the merchandise. This kind of financial planning came naturally to Lachman, an accountant by training. Although he rose to the chairman's office in 1969, he always remained the numbers man—a conservative money manager in a world of merchants. A summa cum laude graduate of New York University, class of 1936, Lachman had earlier held financial posts with James McCreery & Co., a former New York department store, and Citizens Utilities Company of Stamford, Connecticut.

Lachman's arrival was critical because it gave Bloomingdale's the financial expertise it needed at this critical juncture. The timing was right for the upgrading to more expensive merchandise for two reasons. In the first place, there had always been an affluent community nearby that Bloomingdale's had never reached. The wealthiest people in New York lived within walking distance (on Fifth Avenue), and yet the store had never catered to them. Secondly, management knew that the East Side neighborhood around the store would be undergoing vast improvements. There were plans to raze the old stores and bars, to tear down the Third Avenue El, and to construct commercial office buildings and luxury apartments in their place. It was clear that the market was changing and Bloomingdale's wanted to change along with it—even lead the way.

Credit for launching the upgrading must be given to J. E. Davidson, who as chairman of Bloomingdale's called the shots. It was really his decision to make the transformation, and he did it for personal as well as business reasons. He was, above all, a perfectionist——an aloof and domineering executive with a highly developed sense of taste. With his strong penchant for elegance, he actually felt uncomfortable with Bloomingdale's second-rate merchandise. The following anecdote is revealing:

"Davidson asked me to decorate his apartment on Central Park West and demanded that I obtain a certain antique French rug for the living room floor," says David Bell, former chief of design of Bloomingdale's furniture department and now head of Design Multiples, a New York interiors agency. "The rug did not perfectly match some other accessories in the room, so Davidson personally dyed it to the right color shade, using the staining power of two hundred tea bags."

The first store department to be singled out for upgrading was delicacies. Again, this was done partly for personal and partly for business reasons. On the business side, it would be the easiest department to change because it was the smallest; and it would be personally rewarding to Davidson, a dedicated gourmet. The year was 1948, and change came quickly under the supervision of food buyer Bob Gumport. Management's directive that Bloomingdale's food shop was to become the finest outlet in the United States for packaged gourmet foods led Gumport and his staff to a worldwide search for gastronomic delights that would be new to American palates. "For years, the store's food department was little more than a neighborhood grocery," says Gumport. "The main merchandise categories were the basics: milk, eggs and condiments."

The strategy under Davidson was to begin selling exclusive food products that were not sold in the supermarkets and were generally new to the U.S. consumer. It became Gumport's job to comb the world for unique foods and to secure them for sale at Bloomingdale's. Gumport and the store's four junior food buyers traveled to Europe more than a hundred times in the next twenty years, exploring for interesting delicacies. Once an attractive item was found, the hard work began. The manufacturer had to be located, distribution terms hammered out, and in many cases, Bloomingdale's then spent months or years convincing the U.S. Food and Drug Administration to approve the product for importation. Sometimes promising delicacies had to be abandoned in Europe simply because there was no hope of obtaining FDA approval to sell the products here. When Gumport stumbled on an unusual preserved fruit dish in Spain, he immediately tracked down the manufacturer and visited his small plant in the countryside. One look at the facility—which was run-down, filthy and infested with rats—and Gumport knew he could never sell the item in the States. This kind of problem, common when high U.S. sanitary standards are applied to foreign food-processing techniques, had to be overcome time and again throughout the building of the delicacies department.

Some of the items featured in the delicacies shop have never caught on big in the U.S. market. Truffles, edible fungi dug from the ground by trained dogs and pigs, have been pushed by Bloomingdale's for years, but with little success. Part of the reason is cost: truffles have always been wildly expensive even for Bloomingdale's customers.

Traub deserves the credit for one of Bloomingdale's most successful delicacies: its freshly baked international-style breads. During his many trips to Switzerland, Gumport noted that Globus, a fashionable department store in Zurich, was doing a high-volume business selling fresh bread. Gumport described the Globus operation to Traub, who was interested enough to send other Bloomingdale's officials to Zurich to take a closer look. Favorable reports flowed back to New York, and in 1971 Bloomingdale's opened its own bread department. It proved to be an outright winner from the start. Some of the store's 150 types of bread were originally imported—flown in daily from France and other European capitals—but now all the baking is done by twenty different ethnic shops located in the Greater New York area.

At this first phase of the Bloomingdale's transformation, several attributes were evident that have been present in subsequent changes: insistence on excellence, shrewd buying and a demanding attitude. They did not, however, always achieve the desired results. When Davidson found the store's Roquefort cheese to be too salty, he dispatched Gumport to the Roquefort caves in France. Bloomingdale's insisted that centuries of

French cheesemaking procedures be changed at its whim. The result: the French refused to even consider the idea, and Bloomingdale's learned an early lesson that its reputation and prestige had not yet reached earth-shattering proportions.

Bloomingdale's move to develop a gourmet's paradise was important mostly as a signal of more significant changes that were to sweep through the store during the next twenty years. It was a signal that Bloomingdale's was moving away from the familiar strategy of "being all things to everybody"—that it was changing from a middle-of-the-road department store to a fashion store aiming at young, affluent and free-spending consumers. In the process, washers, driers, automobile accessories and other solid middle-class trappings of stores like Macy's, Gimbels and Sears were banned from the selling floors. A retail transformation occurred, one that stripped away the old and built the foundation for a new and exciting concept of fashion merchandising.

"We chose to change delicacies first, because we knew it would be easiest," Lachman reminisces. "All the time, however, we were fully aware of the major obstacles ahead. That is, in most cases, we couldn't hope to get the kinds of big-name, high-fashion, prestige goods we wanted for every department. Bloomingdale's reputation as a bargain-basement store was so well entrenched that the first-class suppliers wouldn't sell to us. We represented the exact opposite of the highbrow-type showcase they wanted for their goods. This was especially true of Seventh Avenue's ready-to-wear women's apparel makers. The best names wouldn't touch us with a ten-foot pole."

Management knew that if this bias was ever to be reversed, the store would have to earn a top reputation in more than just delicacies. So the next department singled out for upgrading was one that seemed to be an easy target at the time: home furnishings. European manufacturers, hungry after the war, were willing to work with Bloomingdale's the way Seventh Avenue was not. The decision to completely revamp Bloomingdale's furniture line was made in late 1949, but Davidson and company recognized that the first step in building a great store is building great taste. Furniture buyers accustomed to dealing with mass-produced junk could not be expected to know their way around classic designs, period pieces and antique reproductions. Davidson relished the idea of making his people furniture connoisseurs—to instill in them the knowledge, the taste, the eye for quality. To accomplish this, he sent them on tours of European museums, to Scandinavia and Italy, conducted seminars with furniture experts, and even hired the curator of the Frick Collection to come on board to work with the buyers. Credit must be given to Davidson's management planning: the store did its homework before attempting to sell a single item of fine furniture.

The effort paid off. In terms of annual revenues, furniture became the second-largest merchandise category in the store and it remains so to this day. Even more important, the move to elegant furniture with a strong European influence gave Bloomingdale's its first real dose of panache. Suddenly the Bloomingdale's name carried with it the suggestion of class.

The plan was working. Slowly, but undeniably, the store's image was changing. And with it came a new type of Bloomingdale's customer—more affluent, better educated and willing to spend more for quality. These customers were attracted by the glowing press coverage the store was starting to earn and by word of mouth from friends and neighbors who stopped by to see for themselves.

As the transformation showed early signs of success, management started worrying about the future. The new image was fragile at this point, and it was important not to jeopardize it. This was especially true in terms of branch store expansion. The opening of the first two branches—New Rochelle (1947) and Fresh Meadows (1949)—was already a *fait accompli* when the transformation was launched; but management put an immediate freeze on all further expansion.

The reason for this was clear: Davidson did not want Bloomingdale's stores to be sitting next to Sears, Gimbels or the like, for fear they would all be lumped together in the public's mind. At this very delicate stage of image-building, Bloomingdale's could not risk losing some of its cachet by rubbing elbows with the lackluster, me-too merchants on Main Street. To be perceived as unique, Davidson recognized that he'd have to stand apart from the crowd.

Only when management believed its new image was firmly established did eyes turn once again toward branches. Starting with Stamford, Connecticut, in 1954, Bloomingdale's launched its full-scale expansion program, which now counts fifteen stores in seven states. Successful? Yes, but not without problems. The early concern over transplanting the Bloomie's "magic" to suburbia remains, and there is no doubt that the excitement of the Fifty-ninth Street store has never been duplicated at the branch level. Sales per square foot tell the story: not a single branch produces even half the flagship store's sales performance by square foot, and some do even less than a third of that.

Still, the early branches gave Lachman, the money man, no cause for concern. Expansion was producing satisfactory sales, and Bloomingdale's return on investment was good. The merchandise upgrading effort also continued on target, with men's wear, women's accessories, intimate apparel and children's wear departments following on the early success of delicacies and home furnishings. For the first time since the triumvirate had set its master plan in motion, an aura of confidence filled the executive offices on Fifty-ninth Street. The pieces of the jigsaw puzzle were coming together and taking on the intended shape. The Bloomingdale's name had status appeal.

But one significant element remained: the conquering of Seventh Avenue. "We looked up in the early 1960s and saw that the time was right to make those arrogant bastards on Seventh Avenue sell to us," Lachman says. "The women's ready-to-wear lines would be our last great growth market." The timing was perfect: Topname houses could no longer ignore Bloomingdale's, which now had the reputation, the customers and the money. They needed Bloomingdale's and they knew it. This new-found power was very rewarding to Bloomingdale's management—a true signal that their master strategy had succeeded.

Harold Krensky (who succeeded Davidson as Bloomingdale's chairman in 1967 and is now chairman of the executive committee of the parent corporation, Federated Department Stores) and Traub engineered the big push into designer ready-to-wear. Using the store's growing prestige and new sales clout, they picked off, one by one, the best in American and European designers. Early successes in the flagship store encouraged other designers to come aboard, and a true bandwagon was launched. Names like Saint Laurent, Halston and Blass became part of the Bloomingdale's appeal. Women's ready-to-wear is now the largest merchandise category and probably does more for the store's trendsetting image than any other.

A good measure of this success must be credited to Krensky's "subway interviews." To find out what kinds of apparel would turn on Bloomingdale's shoppers, the chairman would go down to the subway level and personally interview the straphangers who got off at Lexington Avenue to shop at Bloomingdale's. Getting to know what made their customers tick helped in the selection of new designers to promote.

"We had arrived—in every sense of the word we had arrived," Lachman gloats. "And I can't tell you the satisfaction in knowing that every damn manufacturer in the world jumped at the chance to sell to Bloomingdale's. It was a sweet, sweet victory."

All the pride in the store's successful transformation bubbled over with the champagne at Bloomingdale's gala centennial celebration—a roaring black-tie bash held in the store after closing hours on October 3, 1972. The seventh floor was cleared and converted to a dance floor; on the eighth floor, 130 dinner tables were set up; and informal bars were spread throughout the store. As is the store's custom for really special occasions, part of Bloomingdale's was actually converted into a temporary banquet hall. The guests, some thirteen hundred notables—including Anne Klein, Diane and Egon Von Furstenberg, New York's Mayor John Lindsay, Terence Cardinal Cooke, Bess Myerson, Calvin Klein and Mr. and Mrs. Ralph Lauren—were wined and dined and treated to glowing speeches by Bloomingdale's brass, past and present. In the humorous note of the evening, Lyman Bloomingdale, grandson of the founder, recalled how he had spent his boyhood making sodas in the food department and then running around the sales floor after the last customers had left.

Outside, in a special gesture intended to signify the store's management philosophy, Bloomingdale's raised banners depicting Janus, the Roman god of thresholds, who faces past and future simultaneously. The meaning: Bloomingdale's knows where it is and where it is going.

# 3

# Fifty-ninth Street and Third: The Flagship Store

---

*New York is a tourist mecca—a city of world-re-nowned sites and landmarks. Still, no matter where visitors come from—Pittsburgh or Prague—one of the must stops on their itineraries is Bloomingdale's. Shopping at Bloomingdale's ranks right up there with the Statue of Liberty on the all-time top tourist attractions. People the world over know of this store.*

        Lois Elias, spokeswoman
        New York Convention and Visitors Bureau

In a city stingy with superlatives, few deny that Bloomingdale's Fifty-ninth Street is New York's premier store. The willingness of New Yorkers to openly acknowledge this is striking in a town where the knock and the put-down have been honed to a fine art. Says a top editor based at *Business Week*'s editorial offices in Manhattan: "A lot of people in this town view that damn store as a local treasure—something equivalent to the Guggenheim and Central Park. It's a unique situation, to say the least. I know of no other establishment that just seems to escape the New York barbs, the home-grown bitching. When it comes to Bloomingdale's, hard-nosed native New Yorkers—the very models of cosmopolitan cool—act like Kansan 4-H'ers admiring the governor's mansion. There's a sense of awe about the whole thing."

    To most New Yorkers—and to people around the world who know of the store—the flagship branch on the corner of Manhattan's Fifty-ninth Street and Third Avenue *is* Bloomingdale's. The most innovative major store in American retailing for almost three decades, the Art Deco mistress of mid-Manhattan just keeps on churning out incredible statistics along the way:

- In a given week, more than 300,000 customers troop in and out of the Fifty-ninth Street store.
- On Saturdays alone, the customer tally exceeds 60,000.
- On a typical day, the store racks up more than 30,000 transactions.
- Gross sales for the flagship store alone are about $200 million annually (slightly less than Macy's Manhattan flagship, which, as the largest store in the world, is twice as big as Bloomingdale's).
- The bottom line is fat: pretax profit is estimated at more than $26 million for the flagship store alone.

The success of Bloomingdale's Manhattan flagship has been the exception rather than the rule for big-city department stores. In the years since the late 1950s, when downtown business all but dried up across America and moved, instead, to suburbia, Bloomingdale's built a retail dynasty in the heart of New York City. The triple plagues of urban decay, a fleeing middle class and skyrocketing costs battered other big Manhattan merchants. Even old-line names like Stern's, Klein's, and Abercrombie & Fitch succumbed to bankruptcy, and others, like Macy's and Gimbels' New York stores, became only marginally profitable. Bloomingdale's, however, flourished like an orchid in a greenhouse. As former board chairman Lawrence Lachman is fond of saying: "We built the healthiest downtown business in the U.S.—a business that put the shops in suburbia to shame."

Why this extraordinary success—this seeming immunity to the ills of urban commerce? Two key management decisions deserve most of the credit. First, none of the store's chief executives in the past thirty years—Davidson, Schoff, Krensky, Lachman and Traub —has ever wavered in his determination to keep New York the most important store in the chain. The move to branch expansion was viewed not as a substitute for New York operations but more as an extension of them. While other Big Apple retailers cut back on their New York investments and, like Macy's at the time, let their stores deteriorate, Bloomingdale's kept the faith in the city's vitality. Bloomingdale's never panicked, never felt it would be forced to flee from downtown in a mad rush to suburbia, and instead continued to invest in the flagship store.

The second key factor is that the store has never strayed from its established market of the young, the affluent, the fashionable New Yorker. This devotion to its special market has earned the flagship store an enviable position in the New York social scene. Bloomingdale's has evolved as a sort of commercial playground for the residents of Manhattan's upper East Side. Bloomingdale's entertains them. Says Marvin Traub: "Our store is a never-ending party. We have art exhibits, language classes, cooking demonstrations, fashion shows and an endless stream of the most interesting people in this city."

Bloomingdale's ability to keep the party jumping is its ace in the hole for attracting the free-spending East Siders. Good times are always at a premium, and Bloomingdale's serves them up like a hip social director at a chic resort. New York's upper East Side community—Bloomingdale's prime market area—is a thriving oasis of steel-and-glass office towers, European clothes boutiques, Continental restaurants, quaint brownstones, million-dollar town houses, ambassadorial residences, art galleries and luxury high-rise apartments. This small pocket of real estate is home to the richest inhabitants of the richest city in the world. Nicknamed the Silk Stocking district, it is also a long-time New York political power base that has been the launching pad for the city's present mayor, Edward Koch, and for a former mayor, John Lindsay, both of whom served it first as congressmen.

The demographics of the upper East Side (Fifty-seventh to Eighty-sixth streets, York Avenue to Central Park) reveal a community far removed from your basic American neighborhood: median income exceeds $40,000, 61 percent of the inhabitants are single, 70 percent are between nineteen and forty years old, 97 percent are white, less than 5 percent are over sixty-five, and perhaps as many as 25 percent are gay. A look behind the statistics shows a young, liberal, professional and managerial group, many of whom are unattached and deeply involved in the dating scene. Most have active passports, travel widely and are committed to a Continental lifestyle, with the accent on imported foods, fashions and fads. The United Nations is less than a city mile away from Bloomingdale's, and embassies, diplomatic residences and consulates are spread throughout the upper East Side. "The DPLs live like kings—they have all the time and money in the world, and they all shop here," says a Bloomingdale's executive. "Take the delicacies department, for example. Half the things we carry there are bought for the wives of diplomats. They demand exotic foodstuffs and we supply it. To tell you the truth, with the UN so close to us, we'd have had to be grossly incompetent to make the delicacies department anything less than the success it is."

The upper East Side lifestyle is loose, free and off-beat. Local movie theaters are jammed seven nights a week, singles bars jump until the early hours and the hot restaurants are booked solid weeks in advance. Waiting for two hours in the rain to see the latest Ingmar Bergman film at one of the twin Coronet/Baronet theaters is standard operating procedure. So is spending $110 for a pair of cordovan loafers at Valentino, $100 for an evening at Studio 54 (which is on the West Side but attracts an East Side crowd), and $200 for an all-day beauty work-up at Elizabeth Arden. Here two-bedroom apartments rent for $1,000 a month, ten-room co-ops sell for half a million, town houses go for a million or more. And dinner for two at the nearby Palace restaurant can easily cost $400.

Bloomingdale's at Fifty-ninth Street is unique, in part because its market is unique. And when describing the Bloomingdale's success story, one must distinguish the

Fifty-ninth Street store from the branches, for they are worlds apart. The Manhattan store is the kingpin—the powerhouse that gives the entire chain the special Bloomingdale's cachet. A high percentage of Bloomingdale's New York customers will spend beyond their means to achieve the dual objectives of beauty and style. From the $265-a-week secretary searching for a mate to the $120,000-a-year apparel executive wining and dining clients, these common denominators hold true. By recognizing that its Manhattan market would accept merchandise and services a step ahead of the general population, Bloomingdale's has been free to experiment; by accepting the risks and challenges of leadership, the store has earned the trust, affection and respect of its customers. In nine cases out of ten, Bloomingdale's customers are willing to accept the store's fashion decisions. When the midi skirt was proving to be the fiasco of a generation throughout the U.S., Bloomingdale's was moving as many of the skirts as it could stock. "I'm no Bloomingdale's worshipper, but they sometimes have an extraordinary ability to sell merchandise no one else can move," says Halston. "When everyone was screaming that the midi was killing them, we sold as many as we could produce, many of them to Bloomingdale's. They can't sell our most expensive lines, but they can sell the more daring numbers. Many of their customers trust the store and don't care what others think. Bloomingdale's gives its Manhattan patrons what they want most: symbolic affirmation that they are sexier, richer, faster and more fashionable than anyone else. And the customers return the favor with undying loyalty and adoration."

Going a step further, Bloomingdale's conducts a carefully cultivated program of advertising and promotion designed to identify the Fifty-ninth Street store with the East Side singles life. Management encourages use of the "Bloomie's" nickname and quietly positions the store as an ideal meeting place for on-the-make locals. "Our customers are often called Saturday's Generation, because that's the day so many of them flock to Fifty-ninth Street to make their dates for the night," says Traub. Cheryl Forshner, long-time East Side single, says, "You have to remember this: you don't necessarily go to Bloomie's to dress well—you dress well to go to Bloomie's. Just to be seen there is important. You want to look like you belong. You want to look the part of a Bloomingdale's Lady."

To enhance the store's image as a social leader, management frequently stages "spectaculars," like the Bloomingdale's Perrier Marathon Run of spring 1978. Launched as a timely takeoff on the jogging craze, it invited New Yorkers to participate in a 6.2-mile run through Central Park. On the strength of a single ad in the Living Section of the *New York Times,* the marathon drew 5,912 runners, mostly single men and women. The tremendous outpouring of interest made the Bloomingdale's/Perrier race the biggest marathon event in the nation, outdrawing the famed Boston Marathon. Not all the participants were pleased, however, with Bloomingdale's attempt to turn the marathon into a purely commercial event. When Traub, himself a devoted jogger, tried to address the crowd before the run, he was roundly booed off the speakers' platform. "There's a fine line between effective image-building and crass commercialization," says Bruce Nevins, president of Great Waters of France, Inc., the marketers of Perrier bottled water. "Runners, in particular, resent anything that smacks of exploitation of their sport."

One aspect of the Bloomingdale's social scene gets the hush-hush treatment from management: the fact that New York's huge homosexual community views the store as a popular meeting ground. The city's diverse sexual groups have, in fact, marked off specific store departments as their private preserves. Lesbians favor intimate apparel, transvestites float between cosmetics and furs; and for male gays, prime dating turf centers around men's shirts, shoes and ties—and, of course, the men's rooms.

While pretending to ignore the homosexual presence, management carefully caters to the gay market. Gay customers are viewed as tastemakers and fashion leaders and their buying power is well respected. Says a former Bloomingdale's employee: "New York's gay community has a sort of built-in intelligence network that keeps tabs on which stores, government agencies, politicians and the like are friendly to the gay people. When an institution gets thumbs up, the word spreads to favor it with gay dollars and votes. Bloomie's manages to subtly position itself as a friend of the gays, so it keeps all that heavy buying power on its side. Gays are among the biggest spenders in the city. They drop big bucks at Bloomie's. After all, they dress like Beau Brummel, have the most dynamite apartments in town and maybe a gorgeous cottage on Fire Island or in the Hamptons. Just selling them the furniture alone means a fortune for Bloomingdale's. One day I was up near the model furniture rooms display when a gay couple came in, admired a nine-piece ultramodern living room suite, found a salesman and casually bought the entire setting, rugs and all, for $12,300."

Publicity is vital to the flagship store's special place in American retailing. Bloomingdale's Fifty-ninth Street is a true media star which, in its own inimitable fashion, manages to command an exceptional amount of national news coverage, pulling off such PR plums as the cover of *Time* magazine, page one of the *Wall Street Journal* and a feature segment on TV's *60 Minutes*. The store, of course, actively seeks publicity, planting feature ideas with network producers and key publishers regularly. The *60 Minutes* segment, which was a fifteen-minute prime-time valentine to the flagship store, came as a direct result of Bloomingdale's request to CBS. Although thousands of stores compete for this kind of coverage, Bloomingdale's succeeds like no other.

"Bloomingdale's won over the press as soon as it started shaking up this country's standards of retailing," says the *Business Week* staff editor. "For the first time, a major department store shed the image of a grand old matron, kicked up its heels, and came down a loose, promiscuous young woman prowling the town for action. It was like breathing life into an industry that had been in a deep coma for years. Whereas in most stores you could memorize the floor plans in about a week—and know them for life—Bloomingdale's started switching around its shops and departments like musical chairs. The element of surprise was introduced and people loved it. Promotions were purposely planned to fizzle out in months, only to be replaced by others. You never really knew what was going to happen at Fifty-ninth Street—you still don't—and this is the store's most important contribution to retailing: the element of spontaneity.

"Bloomingdale's has proved itself to be an innovator and that's what the press eats up. In any dry and boring industry, the one company that dares to break the ice and move in new directions is the company every business reporter wants to cover. Add to this Bloomingdale's good fortune of being located in mid Manhattan —blocks away from the news headquarters of the major national wire services, the big three networks, the *Times,* the *News* and a host of business magazines like ours, *Fortune* and *Forbes.* Don't forget, this is concentrated media town—the heart of the nation's print and broadcast journalism—and a good story here gets national coverage while one in Akron, Ohio, may not. Bloomingdale's Fifty-ninth Street got the press it needed to build its reputation because it was an innovator, yes, but also because it was so close to the reporters and the cameras."

From the very first days of Bloomingdale's rebirth, management's pioneering efforts have always focused on the Fifty-ninth Street store. The concept of department store designer boutiques saw first light in the flagship unit, as did the personal visits by new designer talent. In fact, it's safe to say that Bloomingdale's Fifty-ninth Street has been largely responsible for the development of most of the hot apparel designers of the past ten years and has contributed substantially to their international fame and celebrity status. "In 1969 I went into business for myself, and Bloomingdale's gave my company its first boutique," Halston recalls. "I was a hat designer at Bergdorf's when Bloomingdale's first made the offer to feature my designs in the store. I had made a little splash in the business before my association with Bloomingdale's, but the Halston Boutique on Fifty-ninth Street was the real catalyst for my career."

Halston was lured to the store by Harold Krensky, then Bloomingdale's chief executive. The two met at the time Krensky was reorganizing the fashion floors to appeal to a more affluent clientele. Traditionally, the store kept its budget, moderate and high-priced women's clothing on the third floor. But Krensky believed that the presence of budget clothing detracted from the appeal of the quality merchandise. He ordered the bargain lines removed to lower levels and decided to use the extra floor space for designer boutiques. "It was then that I met Halston," Krensky reminisces. "Bloomingdale's executives used to eat lunch at the old Savoy Plaza Hotel, now the site of the General Motors Building. I was there one day when my vice president of ready-to-wear, Mel Jacobs, called me over to meet someone. It was a tall, handsome wig and hat designer who was experimenting with clothing and wanted a chance to prove himself. We talked that first day and we subsequently visited each others' offices. I had faith in Halston from the start and I offered him an in-store boutique. We designed it to be a replica of his working studio."

Krensky's concept of the Halston Boutique was a shop to bridge the gap between ready-to-wear and couture. The result was a top-of-the-line ready-to-wear that remains at the heart of Halston's marketing plan today. When Halston first came to Krensky's attention, the designer was working with Art Deco themes, incorporating them into casual clothing with a sophisticated look. Halston was concerned that women should look smart and well dressed without formal clothing. Bloomingdale's wanted this look for the store and backed Halston with the pledge to buy the entire collection for his new boutique. "We decided to move heavily into argyle sweaters and to make them one of the main attractions of the boutique," Halston adds. "I was terribly excited about the opening and I was running every which way to arrange the details. The people working for me had no titles, no fancy offices then. We were all catch as catch can, and we made every mistake in the book. Worst of all, the contractor we hired to produce the sweaters backed out at the last minute to take on another job. If you are not big in the apparel business and have no real clout, people step on you. That's what they did to me then."

To stock his boutique in time for the grand opening at the Fifty-ninth Street store, Halston and his small staff had to sit down at sewing machines themselves and stitch the sweaters together one by one. The great Halston, who now sits in a glittering mirrored office suite in New York's prestigious Olympic Towers—and who is served coffee by a white-aproned maid—had to work nights at a sewing machine to get his foot in Bloomie's door and his career in orbit.

Another well-known designer whose career owes much to her association with Bloomingdale's Fifty-ninth Street is Gloria Vanderbilt. A woman with questionable talent as an apparel designer, she has managed to build a successful career on the strength of her family name and a carefully cultivated image. She is a charming and pleasant woman of great inherited wealth who works hard to establish her own identity and who relishes the role of a celebrity. Vanderbilt is known to routinely confront women wearing her clothing and to thank them for doing so. A self-taught artist, Vanderbilt made a name for herself in art circles throughout the 1950s and '60s. During this period she had twenty-five exhibitions and four museum retrospectives. Her foray into the commercial world came after a guest appearance on the *Tonight Show*. Asked by Johnny Carson to show her paintings and collages on television, she held a televised art show. This led to a contract with Hallmark Cards to design a special line of paper products for the company. After that she applied her colorful designs to china, fabrics, glassware, place mats, bath accessories, towels and fashion. Her biggest venture is the current association with Murjani USA Ltd., a New York-based apparel outfit owned by Hong Kong business interests. For Murjani, Vanderbilt has designed a line of "status jeans" (priced at over $40 and sporting the Vanderbilt name), blouses and shirts. The line has been successful throughout the U.S., thanks in large measure to the showcase Bloomie's provided for it.

"At Bloomingdale's New York store, they know

exactly how to present a designer and a fashion collection to the public," Vanderbilt says. "The people who work there are thorough professionals who supervise every minor detail to the nth degree. For example, they have the art of the personal appearance down to a science."

Requests for a designer to make an appearance at Fifty-ninth Street are usually made by the buyer soon after a major order is placed. Details for advance publicity are then worked out between the designer's public relations agency (Jody Donohue Associates in the case of Gloria Vanderbilt) and Bloomingdale's promotion department. In most cases, joint press releases are issued and the store advertises the event a week or two in advance. For a well-known designer like Gloria Vanderbilt, a crowd of two hundred to three hundred is likely to show up for the visit. The celebrity goes out on the sales floor, introduced by a Bloomingdale's staffer, and gives a fifteen-minute talk on fashion and style. Questions are then accepted, informal chatter goes on for another twenty minutes or so, and the event is over in about one hour. "People love the contact with designers," Vanderbilt says. "They tell their friends, word spreads, and it really helps build a loyal following—a following of people who will buy your collections year after year. I started making personal appearances at Fifty-ninth Street in the early 1970s for my sheet line, and many of the people who saw me there still come back now. They bought my bedding, and now they buy my jeans. Personal appearances at the store generate great word of mouth, get exceptional press coverage, and do more than anything else to get the ball rolling on a successful collection."

"The flagship store sets the pace for the entire chain," says Ralph Lauren. "There's an avant-garde atmosphere that everyone in the industry recognizes. Bloomingdale's slogan 'It's Like No Other Store in the World' rings true when it comes to Fifty-ninth Street." Designer Calvin Klein agrees: "Bloomingdale's Fifty-ninth Street is the fashion showcase—the place where my designs get knocked off first. It's where the other manufacturers go to see what they want to imitate."

What does the flagship store look like? Viewed from the exterior, it is a grayish-white building with Art Deco touches. In terms of sheer size, Bloomingdale's is just run-of-the-mill big. Much smaller than its downtown rival Macy's Herald Square, Bloomingdale's has little more than 450,000 square feet of selling space. Eleven stories high, with some two hundred departments, the physical structure inside is rather plain. Walls are mostly white, muted gray or tan; lighting is harsh and unattractive; ugly pillars crop up annoyingly.

Among the departments on the main floor are women's casual blouses, stockings, sunglasses and handbags, as well as men's furnishings, including shirts, ties, belts and shoes. Some of the more interesting men's boutiques opened in recent years are Silvermine, featuring silver and gold jewelry; Calvin Klein's men's wear; Sasson fashion jeans; Trumper, a wood-paneled shop with an old-English look that sells British soaps, grooming accessories and travel bags. This mélange of different looks is indicative of Bloomingdale's merchandising flair: virtually every product category benefits from an interesting and inventive display treatment. And nothing remains static, with boutiques and shops being constantly changed, eliminated and replaced.

Part of the main floor was renovated in late 1979 with the opening of a dramatic new promenade called b'way. With its shiny black walls, floors and ceilings it is a radical departure from traditional department store design. Some applaud it as gutsy and innovative; others label it cheap, tacky and sensational. Employees are near unanimous in their appraisal; the mirrored effect makes them dizzy and they detest it. b'way is dominated by the largest cosmetics department of any of the world's department stores. Here all the greats of the cosmetics and perfume industries are represented: Chanel, Halston, Geminesse, Dior, Pierre Cardin, Calvin Klein, Ultima, Frances Denney, Revlon, Ralph Lauren, Nina Ricci, Estée Lauder, Helena Rubinstein,

Yves Saint Laurent, Elizabeth Arden, Fashion Flair and others. Most are limited to just six feet of shelf space, but they are happy to get that. When it comes to selling cosmetics, Bloomingdale's has no equal—it is a cosmetics mass merchandiser, racking up $20 million per year in perfumes, lipstick, powder and the broad spectrum of beauty aids.

Bloomingdale's cosmetics department is a battlefield, with every major and minor company in the business competing for space. The fiercest competition pits the old-line outfits like Revlon and Lauder (who together command about 45 percent of the nation's department store volume) against the latest upstarts in fragrances, boasting designer names such as Halston, Lauren and Calvin Klein. At Bloomingdale's Fifty-ninth Street, both sides are well represented, but the designer lines appear to be attracting the most customers.

Just how the new outfits get Bloomingdale's to bestow the prized six feet of space is interesting. Take the Calvin Klein story. In 1975 Revlon assigned one of its top executives, Stanley Kohlenberg, to convince Klein to license his name to Revlon. The giant beauty company wanted to use the designer's magic name to market a new line of perfume. Revlon had the rug pulled out from under it, however, when Klein persuaded Kohlenberg to leave Revlon and start a new company with him. Klein and his partner raised over $3 million and they were in business.

Although designers like Klein, Halston and Lauren claim to be deeply involved in their fragrance lines, they really do little more than lend their famous names. But that's more than enough. Big designer names give the cosmetics lines immediate entry to all the nation's major department stores. The stores vie for the designer collections, knowing that they add cachet to cosmetics departments and that the lines are presold to the public. In a store like Bloomingdale's especially, where the Calvin Klein and Ralph Lauren names are so prominent in ready-to-wear, the fragrance products are a natural addition. While cosmetics marketed under an unknown name have a hard time securing space at a prestige sales outlet like Bloomingdale's,

Klein/Kohlenberg and company can waltz right in and siphon off market share from the staid old names like Helena Rubinstein and Elizabeth Arden. Those who try to wedge their way into this battle without the big-name mystique have to spend lavishly—up to $10 million—on advertising, giveaways and promotions to earn even the smallest amount of sales space.

"The stores don't care if the manufacturer loses money," says Revlon's chief executive, Michel Bergerac. "Why should they? The department stores will bleed this new wave and pretty soon some will drop out. Then the department stores will wait for the next group of idiots to do the same thing."

Although Bloomingdale's does not have a traditional bargain basement, the fact that the lower levels are considered the least important is plainly evident, because they are among the most poorly presented parts of the store. Even the lighting is harsh and uneven. Two exceptions to the below-main doldrums are Saturday's Generation and men's suits and coats. The former is an outpost of relatively inexpensive and trendy casual clothing. Jeans, colorful tops, leisure outfits, T-shirts and the like are displayed amid neon lights, jukeboxes and rock music. Bloomingdale's has encouraged the use of this area as a meeting place by installing an espresso bar and a haircutting salon. Customers here are primarily the under-thirty crowd, with a large sprinkling of gays. The men's coats and suits department is a rather quiet and elegant section of the store, boasting apparel by Adolfo, Cardin, Lanvin, Burberry, Calvin Klein and others. Close by there is also a lively tennis boutique, featuring equipment, sneakers and colorful tennis wear by Izod, Fila and Head.

Steps below the main level, with its own street entrance, is delicacies. One of the store's oldest and most popular departments, delicacies has been at the center of a recent competitive battle with Macy's, now Bloomingdale's archrival. The sleeping giant on Herald Square came alive in the mid 1970s with the appointment of a new chief executive, Ed Finkelstein, who after a highly successful stint as president of Macy's San Francisco, was summoned to New York. Finkelstein had earned his stripes on the West Coast by developing imaginative merchandising techniques that attracted young and affluent shoppers, the precise market group department stores are after these days and one Macy's had been missing out on for years. Macy's had never taken part in the postwar fashion merchandising movement that made stores like Bloomingdale's so successful, and as a result, its image became dowdy and dull and profits plummeted. Finkelstein's assignment in New York was clear from day one: Transform the largest store in the world to the powerhouse it once was; attract the free-spending singles from the upper East Side; and for the first time, steal some of Bloomingdale's thunder with this group.

One of Finkelstein's first moves was to duplicate in Manhattan The Cellar department that had proved to be a smashing success in San Francisco. The Cellar is known in the retail trade as a "total selling environment." An updated version of the traditional department store food department. The Cellar combines delicacy foodstuffs with housewares, novelty items and a branch of New York's famous singles bar and restaurant P. J. Clarke's. More than just a delicacies department. The Cellar is a place to visit, to kill time, to spend a rainy Sunday afternoon eating and shopping. Finkelstein's brainchild proved to be a winner in New York from the opening day. "We have managed to siphon off many of Bloomingdale's customers because we have a far greater variety of goods, fresh fruits and vegetables, and twice the stock Bloomingdale's carries," says Steve Fass, a ten-year veteran of Bloomingdale's who now heads Macy's food merchandising. "Take cheese, for example: Bloomingdale's carries maybe sixteen display feet of cheese, and we have forty-five feet; we sell more caviar in one week than they sell in a year. Overall, our annual volume is at least twice that of Bloomingdale's delicacies shop. The Cellar has been the most successful part of Macy's upgrading program. It has added considerable excitement to the store and has attracted many of the East Siders who used to shop at Bloomingdale's exclusively."

Competition like this is forcing Bloomingdale's to

focus a high proportion of its management and financial resources on the flagship store at a time when the branch network is growing and becoming more and more demanding. Traub is obviously concerned with this. "The competition in New York is becoming tougher all the time. Stores that were asleep for decades are now awake and are giving us a run for our money in every merchandise category." Traub will not admit it, but Macy's is the biggest threat.

Up the escalators, on Bloomingdale's second floor, we find Plaza 2 women's accessories, featuring bags, hats and capes; a Young World of children's clothing and novelties; and the floor's main attraction—a big junior sportswear department, home of the trendy ready-to-wear Bloomingdale's is famous for. The area directly across from the second-floor escalator is reserved for promotions related to a current theme. One such treatment heralded the coming of the blockbuster film *Superman* with a flashy boutique called Supermania. Positioned to appeal to junior clothes buyers, the boutique featured see-through vinyl pants, gold lamé capes and rhinestone tops.

Floor three is the most elegant and exciting in the store. Definitely the preserve of affluent women, the floor is home to: Leather Trappings, a posh department of sumptuous leather and fur outerwear; Pure Jeanius, an oasis of designer jeans by the likes of Gloria Vanderbilt, Charlotte Ford, Calvin Klein and Giorgio Sant'Angelo; and the Perfumer's Workshop, where patrons can mix and match scents to custom-design their own fragrances. Top billing on this floor, however, is reserved for the individual designer boutiques. Clustered together like the exclusive boutiques along the Rue Saint-Honoré in Paris, the world-renowned designer shops glitter with chrome and glass displays of sophisticated fashions by Anne Klein, Calvin Klein, Sasson, Saint Laurent, Missoni, Perry Ellis, Cacharel, Ralph Lauren (the reigning king of Bloomingdale's designers, Lauren commands the largest boutique here as well as in the men's wear department).

No longer part of the high-fashion floor is the old Green Room, launched by J. E. Davidson in an abortive attempt to sell couturier clothing. This made-to-order shop never really caught on and was closed more than ten years ago. It did, however, serve as an early showcase for the then obscure designer Bill Blass.

"When I first started, right after the Second World War," Blass says, "designers were never allowed to leave the back room to meet customers. We were considered to be very dispensable." Beginning his career as a sketcher with the couture house of David Crystal, Blass got his first shot at original design work a few years later. Soon after, he started traveling across the nation, visiting the major cities to present his collections to local buyers. "This is how I started building a name for myself," Blass notes. "Most other designers stayed in New York exclusively, never venturing out to the nation's midsection. I was different, and this set me apart from the others. In this business, there's no substitute for exposure, and the exposure from my travels started giving some weight to the Bill Blass name. It was at this point in my career, in the early 1950s, that my relationship with Bloomingdale's began. My couture collection was sold in the Green Room of the Fifty-ninth Street store. Unfortunately, that boutique never caught on the way Bloomingdale's management hoped it would.

"Still, my relationship with Bloomingdale's customers is strong. The Fifty-ninth Street store is an amazing showcase. In 1970, I became the first U.S. apparel designer to do a line of sheets. Springs Mills manufactured it and Bloomingdale's was the first to sell it. They put on a tremendous promotion in the Manhattan store, and the whole line took off like a jet. It has been a big business for me ever since, and it started the whole trend toward designer bedding. New concepts launched in that store reverberate across the nation."

The fourth floor is rather dull, except for a great glassware department boasting elegant crystals from Waterford, Rosenthal, Iittala and Baccarat, and an exceptional women's shoe department, featuring designs by Joan and David, Maud Frizon, Charles Jourdan and Bruno Magli. Other merchandise groups on this level include silverware, lighting fixtures, maternity clothing, pillows and window shades.

The fifth floor houses the second most important merchandise category in the store: home furnishings. The top attractions here are the model furniture rooms, which range from the breath-taking to the gaudy. The rooms are set off, exhibition style, from the selling floor and are blocked from traffic by museum-type ropes. This is a favorite browsing area for native New Yorkers, especially those with an interest in interior design. Even the biggest names in the design industry, who like to put down Bloomingdale's for one reason or another, stop by to see the latest versions of the model rooms.

The sixth floor houses a relatively new department called The Main Course, which is Bloomingdale's answer to Macy's The Cellar. The look here is of an outdoor street scene, with a simulated marble sidewalk leading to a series of gift, cooking and housewares boutiques. There is a light, airy feeling about the place which comes from the liberal use of glass, polished steel and a real skylight. (Part of the sixth-floor ceiling happens to be a lower roof of the Bloomingdale's building, which makes the skylight possible.) The central theme of The Main Course is home entertainment. Virtually all the merchandise in the area revolves around activities like cooking a lavish meal, setting a lovely table and generally charming the pants off one's houseguests. The main boutique—called, appropriately enough, That's Entertainment—sets the mood for the entire floor with a glittering collection of serving pitchers, wine carafes, stemware and hostess trays. Other mini shops along the interior promenade include:

- A La Carte—A collection of modern-looking mugs in a wide variety of colors and sizes
- The Cook's Cloth—Aprons, dish towels and potholders galore, many with a French saying or motif

- Woodworks—Everything wooden for the well-equipped kitchen or dining room, including bowls, carving boards and cheese platters
- Party Times—Candles, candles and more candles; the accent here is on the unusual, with one twenty-dollar candle designed to resemble a fruit pie
- Turn-Ons—This appliance haven for the serious chef features the latest in blenders and food processors
- Cook's Kitchen—Featuring kitchen equipment from A to Z, this shop has all the gadgets you need to cook up anything from a great soufflé to beef Wellington; a computerized film projector provides instant demonstrations on the proper use of all the equipment in the shop

The Main Course also features gifts, a limited amount of fresh fruits and vegetables, and live cooking demonstrations. Most of Bloomingdale's food lines are, however, still sold exclusively in the delicacies area —an important distinction between The Main Course and Macy's Cellar.

The seventh and eighth floors are rather drab. Seven houses a bookshop, which also sells art supplies, an extensive linen and towel department, and a coffee shop called The Greenhouse. Eight has a surprisingly small bath shop, which features shower curtains, mats, soap dishes and the like; an American Express Travel Service office; and the Lancôme Institut de Beauté, a skincare, make-up and haircutting salon. The general appearance of these top two sales floors is not attractive. There is a lack of cohesion among the departments, the displays are often messy and the walls and floors appear relatively shabby. One gets the distinct impression that everything management could not find a place for on the lower floors was simply dumped on the top two.

Behind the fashions and the fashionable people, Bloomingdale's Fifty-ninth Street is the working office for the store's top executives. And in this case, contrary to the traditional corporate pecking order, the higher the executive rank, the lower the floor on which he works. The big brass—chairman, president and treasurer—are discreetly tucked away in a suite of offices on the seventh floor. Here the décor varies according to the individual. When Lawrence Lachman ran the show, the huge corner office reserved for the chairman was decorated in a conservative style, with furnishings suitable for the chief executive of a blue-chip oil company: oversize mahogany desks, red carpets and heavy floral drapes. The surroundings mirrored Lachman's stiff, formal personality. Traub, on the other hand, prefers the trendy look with which he has always been associated. He favors earth tones, and is inclined toward casual-looking furniture.

Floors nine, ten and eleven are reserved for internal functions, including employee and lower-level management offices, first aid, a workers' cafeteria, in-house advertising and sign-making shops. Nothing fancy here: the facilities are crude and cluttered. There's a bare-bones feeling about the place, something like a basement with desks installed. Middle management offices, for the likes of the VPs of public relations and promotion, are tiny and reflect the fact that these posts are subordinate to the merchandising brass.

Also found behind the scenes at Fifty-ninth Street is an element mostly missing from the sales floors below: poor working people, Puerto Ricans and blue-collar types. As in other prestige department stores, the very social classes priced out of Bloomingdale's market are those who run its cafeterias, man the boilers and scrub the floors. The work force is large: twelve thousand chainwide, four thousand at the flagship.

The Manhattan flagship is the only Bloomingdale's store that is unionized. It is a union shop, which means that every nonmanagerial employee must belong to Local 3 of the United Store Workers (a unit of the Retail, Wholesale and Department Store Workers Union). It has been this way for over forty years now, and although the union has tried to organize the other

Bloomingdale's branches, its efforts have not been successful.

In 1978, starting union wages at the flagship were $122 per week, or about $3.25 per hour for a 37½-hour week. This base wage increases to $126, $130 and $135 in six-month intervals. Floaters start at $2.75 per hour, which is increased to $3.25 after four months of employment. Fringe benefits include surgical and hospitalization coverage as well as voluntary participation in a Federated Department Stores pension plan. How much an employee earns at Fifty-ninth Street depends to a great extent on the department in which he works. In addition to salary, every full-time salesperson earns a commission, from one-half to six percent of gross sales, again depending upon the department. "This is the biggest determinant of individual salaries," says Ida Torres, a United Store Workers executive. "The best departments are ready-to-wear and furniture—that's where the best money is made. A good experienced woman working in the buttons department for thirty years may only make $10,000 a year while a relative newcomer in furniture or ready-to-wear can make $21,000. The highest-paid salesperson I've ever known of in this store worked in furniture and made $47,500. There is a lot of competition to work in these better departments and it is a management decision as to who gets the job."

In spite of their union wages and benefits, employees at the flagship store tend to be an unhappy and disgruntled group. Many feel that they are used and abused by their employer; they cite overwork and the need for better amenities such as decent cafeteria food and ample clothing lockers. The overwork issue, in fact, is echoed even in the middle management ranks, with some department heads bitterly complaining of seventy-to-eighty-hour weeks. Bloomingdale's is known in the trade as a sweatshop—a store that relies on a skeleton staff to handle an overwhelming work load. The result is a deep-seated employer/employee antagonism, especially in the lower ranks.

"The women here have a saying," says Mrs. M. "Don't work too hard for the store because the store doesn't care at all about you. Work here one week and you know that's true."

# 4

# The Bloomingdale's Blitz: Strike, Conquer, Retreat

*Jill Clayburgh and Cliff Gorman in a scene from the film* An Unmarried Woman:

**Clayburgh: "I'm getting divorced!"**
**Gorman: "No shit. What happened?"**
**Clayburgh: "He was buying a shirt at Bloomingdale's and fell in love."**

The flagship store serves as the staging ground for what is widely known as the Bloomingdale's Blitz. Most of the store's major promotions are launched at Fifty-ninth Street and brought to the attention of the New York press before they are exported to the suburban branches. New York is where Bloomingdale's likes to make news. For example, on the same day that the United Nations General Assembly voted to admit Red China to its international body—October 25, 1971—less than twenty blocks away from UN headquarters, Bloomingdale's unveiled a bamboo boutique, China Passage, crammed with traditional Oriental goods from the Chinese mainland.

After a generation-long trade embargo against mainland China collapsed in summer 1971, Bloomingdale's had managed in just a few months to cut through the bureaucracy and import a once contraband line. Predictably, the New York press flocked to Fifty-Ninth Street to capture the moment. Coverage of the China

Passage boutique's grand opening made the city's live evening newscasts and was picked up for feature material by the *New York Times* and the *Post*. The big press play confirmed Bloomingdale's ability to harness the drama of a major current event to further its own commercial ends. Marvin Traub—an old hand at press relations—has proved over and over again that he has good instincts for what turns reporters on. In an era of "happy news," he knows that upbeat human interest stories are considered essential for editorial balance and that every feature reporter jumps at the chance to cover the kind of "light" events Bloomie's serves up.

But there was more to the China boutique than the publicity it produced. The opening of China Passage typified the gambling instinct of a gutsy business willing to take chances to preserve its position as a trend setter. In a nation that propagandized for decades against the evils of the "Red menace," Bloomingdale's decided to break the ice and plunge headfirst into politically turbulent waters. Fears of controversy— which would have dissuaded more cautious retailers, such as Bonwit Teller or Lord & Taylor—were discounted in favor of the opportunity to once again demonstrate leadership in a fashion trend. For the chance to seize the limelight and to capture widespread attention, Bloomingdale's will accept a level of risk considered imprudent by many of its competitors. It is a likable and exciting quality of the store and one for which Traub is primarily responsible.

Bloomingdale's must gamble in this way because the store stakes its reputation on its ability to identify and popularize new fashion directions early in their development. In marketing terms, this is known as Bloomingdale's USP, or Unique Selling Point—the element of a product, service or company which distinguishes it from the competition.

A major characteristic of Bloomingdale's operating style is the wholehearted support it gives to its promotions. To Traub's credit it must be said that once a promotion gets the green light, the full resources of the Bloomingdale's organization fall in line to support it. In the China event, for example, Bloomie's did more than just stock the new goods and watch from the sidelines. Instead, all major departments took an active role in promoting the appeal of the "China look." After the Fifty-ninth Street boutique had opened, the interior environment of all the Bloomingdale's stores soon reflected the same theme. What's more, Chinese culture was put forward as an appealing influence for the American lifestyle: Bloomie's hosted Oriental cooking classes, Chinese fashion shows and exhibitions of mainland art. Before the two nations had even formalized relations, Bloomingdale's had begun to build its own bridges across the Pacific.

The strategy behind this kind of merchandising was clear: Bloomingdale's believed it could use its power as a fashion authority to "turn America on" to Chinese culture. And in the process, it could also open a new and lucrative market, sell exclusive merchandise at high markups and attract widespread publicity as an innovator. The store had the guts to stake out this virgin market because it knew that many of its customers would be ready for China if Bloomie's said they should be.

Decisions based on this kind of thinking are mostly Traub's doing. Of all the merchants who have run Bloomingdale's since its rebirth, Traub best understands the willingness of many Bloomingdale's customers to be led by the hand, to be taught good taste, to be told what is "in" and what is not. A native New Yorker (raised in Manhattan), Traub is the son of a corset maker. He was wounded in World War II, earned a Purple Heart, and returned with one leg shorter than the other. Today he wears a built-up shoe, but has no trouble walking or for that matter jogging daily near his Tudor-style home in Scarsdale, New York. Traub started his career with Bloomingdale's in 1950, at the age of twenty-five, a year after he graduated magna cum laude from Harvard Business School. After a brief stint as an assistant to Alexander's chairman George Farkas (he earned $100 a week), Traub moved to Bloomingdale's, literally starting in the basement (as assistant to the vice president in charge of that floor). Traub showed an early flair for merchandising and was moved quickly through the ranks: by 1956 he was named divisional merchandising manager for home furnishings; he became home furnishings vice president in 1960; executive vice president and general merchandise manager in 1962; president in 1969; and finally, chairman of the board in 1978.

Traub climbed the corporate ladder at a time when the store was learning to entice and manipulate its East Side customers, and he learned that for many of the Bloomingdale's devotees, the very fact that the store makes a statement makes that statement acceptable. "It's really kind of shocking, the influence that store has on so many people," notes former Bloomie's advertising V-P Doris Shaw. "From home furnishings to ready-to-wear apparel, Bloomingdale's calls the shots. When they introduce a new furniture style, as they did with the Chinese look, all eyes in the industry watch, note the reaction and then often reflect the Bloomingdale's statement. The store's power stems from two factors: first, they hold a leadership position in the furnishings industry. This comes from the hard work and financial risk they take in working with manufacturers from the start of production, testing new concepts and traveling the world for new ideas. The store's buyers are assigned to do this and they are well compensated for their efforts, with salaries ranging up to $60,000. Second, and equally important, is that they present their new styles so attractively that the whole thing becomes irresistible. As the *New York Times* is to journalism, Bloomingdale's is to retailing. Their power lies in the fact that they are so closely observed and so widely imitated."

Recognition of the store's ability to transfer its tastes and preferences to many of its customers gives Bloomingdale's managers the confidence to act quickly. They are willing to commit to substantial investments without the bureaucratic approval procedure required at so many corporations. Having a large pool of customers ready and willing to try almost anything new the store has to offer provides something of a cushion against devastating sales fiascos. For this reason—in what is highly unusual for a multidivisional organization

—Federated Department Stores give Bloomingdale's a long leash in running its daily operations. Major decisions, like launching the China promotion, do not require approval from headquarters; the store chairman can act alone.

"We thought the Chinese had interesting merchandise our customers would like," Traub recalls. "The Chinese have one of the world's great cultures and their goods reflect this: they are exotic, elegant and often ingenious. Our customers expect us to find treasures like these and bring them home." Traub took his cue to act when, in the summer of 1971, the White House ended the trade embargo against Communist China. He immediately placed a secret call to a well-known French importer of Chinese merchandise. Applying the considerable pressure Bloomingdale's can exert, Traub convinced the trader to detour to New York a major shipment of mainland merchandise already headed for France. Thus Traub's arm-twisting paved the way for the opening of the China Passage boutique on the day of the United Nations vote.

The coup proved to be a stroke of genius. It is widely considered as Traub's most successful promotion—one of those cases in which his instincts were on target. Through the China Passage shop, Bloomingdale's moved hundreds of thousands of cooking woks, rattan baskets, straw place mats, bamboo poles, ornamental ladders, vegetable steamers, coolie hats, silk fans, teapots and blue cotton Mao suits (four thousand of the suits sold out in spite of warnings that the blue dye might rub off on the wearers).

It would be easy to say that good timing and sound instincts account for successes like these, but that would be giving only half the story. Hard work, attention to detail and a responsive corporate organization deserve much of the credit. Essential to the store's operations is the position of fashion coordinator (there is one for every major merchandise category), which carries responsibility for implementing management's theme concepts. Fashion coordinators are paid high salaries to encourage (some say "force") Bloomingdale's suppliers to produce merchandise that reflects the current promotion. The system works like this: The store chief decides that the China look should prevail throughout Bloomingdale's. He calls a meeting of the fashion coordinators, explains his ideas about the theme and solicits their thoughts. Thus the broad guidelines of the theme are established: the new look will filter through all departments (except appliances), the accent will be on handmade Chinese goods, and prices will range from $5 for novelties to $4,350 for furniture. With these directives spelled out, the fashion coordinators, like mother hens, gather together the buyers to pass along the information. This process assures that virtually every buyer in the store will be moving in the same direction, and making purchases with the same theme and price ranges in mind. Once buyers have their marching orders, the word goes out to ready-to-wear designers to come up with such items as Chinese-style smocks; furniture makers are asked to add rattan and wicker to their lines. Thus, one by one, fashion coordinators work with buyers, who in turn work with suppliers to make sure that there is a representative sampling in most departments that reflects the latest theme.

Fashion coordination is the key to the store's unified look and explains, in part, why some of the world's great designers seem to come up with the same new look at the same time: Often it's because Bloomingdale's has asked them to. Although the designers contend that they are completely independent, virtually all of them are influenced by each other, by the trade press and by powerful buyers at stores like Bloomingdale's. Ralph Lauren—an exception among top designers because he manufactures his own collection rather than contracting it out—is also one of the few to admit to external influences: "The Bloomingdale's buyer comes to me from time to time with ideas she would like to see incorporated in my collection. I usually try to cooperate, to some extent, depending on my own feelings about the store's theme. For the China thing, I came up with appropriate shirts and blouses. It's all a matter of being nice to the hand that feeds you."

Bill Blass made a personal trip to the mainland to soak up the culture and to cultivate relationships with manufacturers and trade officials. His China-inspired collection was unveiled after the trip. Asked why the design community seems to move en masse to new "looks," Blass gives this confusing answer: "No one has any influence on what we designers design. It's just one of those sort of mystical things that we sense new styles simultaneously. We are all in the same business and, I guess, it's just a chemistry in the air. Of course, if a big customer like Bloomingdale's asks me to cooperate on a theme, I do it. Sometimes they ask and sometimes they don't."

Blass's confession that a major customer does have influence on the design process is important. One must never lose sight of the fact that the top designers have made it because they are entrepreneurs as well as artists. All who have achieved lasting success have a deep respect for the bottom line and for the compromises and sacrifices required to run a business.

The world of high fashion is a competitive arena, where highly charged egos and ambitions fuel the fight for top ranking. Many of the big names dislike each other, love to start nasty rumors and enjoy nothing more than watching the other fail. Most of the designer superstars are rich, but with the grand lifestyles they lead, the appetite for more and more money is constant. Halston, whose thirty-two corporations shovel in about $100 million a year in revenues, says, "I still live in fear of losing a single important client."

So when Bloomingdale's gets hot for a new theme, and asks for their cooperation, even the high and mighty designers try to please. And the fashion coordinator gets the cooperation Bloomie's needs to present a unified promotion to the public.

Getting the appropriate merchandise to make a theme promotion succeed is often far more complicated than simply making the rounds of the star designers. Quite frequently the search can range as far as the emerging nations of Asia, where exotic goods and cheap labor are still available. One of the annual stops on this route is China's Canton Trade Fair, a yearly presentation of items produced in the People's Republic of

China. Visits to Canton started during the China promotion and have continued to date.

Bloomingdale's approach to this event is indicative of its willingness to go farther than most of its competitors to get exactly what it wants. While other major retails are content to have agents and exporters look out for their interests at the Canton Fair, Bloomingdale's commits to the considerable expense of sending its own buyers, fashion coordinators and merchandise managers right to the source of supply—at a cost of roughly $2,000 per person per week. To Bloomingdale's, spending this kind of money is an investment in its own originality. Ever since J. E. Davidson demanded that his executives "travel the world and soak up the various cultures," store management has been willing to put money up front in order to get more imaginative merchandise on the sales floors. This is vital to the Bloomingdale's Blitz: while the others, who rely on central agents to do their purchasing, all come up with identical merchandise, Bloomie's grabs the exclusives.

Face-to-face buying is vital for a fashion-oriented store. It can be compared to the difference between a consumer who shops by mail and one who visits stores. The latter can inspect all the goods, feel the fabrics, try clothing on and see if the item is just right. And that is precisely what Bloomingdale's does when it goes right to the source of its supplies. When vice president of home furnishings Carl Levine visited the Canton Fair, for example, he eyed some lacquered boxes that he thought would be popular in the New York store. To make the boxes suitable for his customers' tastes, however, Levine asked the Chinese to reproduce them according to Bloomingdale's specifications. They refused: the idea of making the ancient boxes without the time-honored floral patterns (as Levine requested) offended local sensibilities. At first, there was no arguing with the Chinese. In spite of the fact that Bloomingdale's China Passage shop had opened a major market in the U.S. for mainland goods, delegates from the Chinese trading companies attending the fair refused to discuss the matter, prohibited Bloomingdale's executives from visiting China between fairs, and even ignored Levine's letters. Nothing could be done to break the deadlock until months later, when China's National Light Industry Group visited the flagship store; duly impressed with Bloomingdale's, the group's leader arranged on the spot for Levine to visit Peking. In less than a year, the Chinese were producing chairs, posters and boxes à la Bloomingdale's designs.

Chinese goods have remained popular at Bloomingdale's since the opening of China Passage. For this reason, Bloomingdale's executives have made numerous buying trips to China and learned that dealing in the People's Republic can be a fascinating but exasperating experience. Negotiations to purchase silk and cotton can take many hours, straining the patience of restless New Yorkers. Endless rounds of weak tea and strong Chinese cigarettes (everyone is expected to smoke) are required to get through the day. To the Chinese, the American fashion business is still new and intriguing, but they are clever business people and they learn quickly.

Bloomingdale's is willing to spend the time and money required to build a network of international business ties, to work in distant markets and strange cultures, because this is crucial to obtaining distinctive merchandise. As a former fashion coordinator reveals: "We start off with more or less simple ideas, then graduate so that we are challenging manufacturers abroad to produce more spectacular items." The underlying motive for this attention to detail is to develop goods capable of generating above-average profits. And Bloomie's delivers exceptional profits for a store of its size. As we learned from the now classic retailing report by Goldman Sachs, there is a direct relationship between innovative merchandising and great profitability. Fashion goods simply fetch higher markups than do widely distributed commodities. This is one of the reasons why Bloomingdale's zigzags from one promotion to another. The overall strategy—the Bloomingdale's Blitz—is at the heart of the store's business plan, and more clearly than anything else reveals how Bloomie's operates:

1. Start or discover a new fad, trend or style with potentially wide appeal.
2. Be the first to promote the trend.
3. Obtain unique merchandise associated with the trend before it is available to the competition and dominate the market.
4. Capitalize on this unique and exclusive merchandise by basing prices on extraordinary markups.
5. Retreat from the trend once widespread imitation sets in and competition applies downward pressure on prices.
6. Start the process over again with the promotion of a new trend.

Making the Blitz work demands an instinctive feel for fashion cycles. What is the most attractive and appealing new look to offer consumers at a given time? That question will always perplex retailers. Although scores of systems have been devised to figure this out, none is really accurate.

"We always relied on instincts rather than formal laws or principles of fashion," says Barbara D'Arcy, a delightful, bubbling executive and one of the great innovators in Bloomingdale's furniture department. "We have always believed that we had the talent and the experience to set chic and elegant fashions for our customers." D'Arcy, who decorated Bloomingdale's model furniture rooms for sixteen years until her appointment, in 1977, as vice president of store design, was instrumental in one of the earliest examples of the Bloomingdale's Blitz: the transformation of the furniture department in the early 1950s.

At the time, modern furniture was the predominant style at most of the leading stores. Fashion-conscious consumers in the market for something different were forced to accept the heavy Early American or classic French designs. "There wasn't much excitement in the furniture business then, and we sensed this," D'Arcy continues. "We knew that to satisfy discriminating shoppers and to build a top reputation for Bloomingdale's furniture department, we'd have to be the first to cultivate and promote a new look in furnishings."

As a junior decorator in the store's furniture department, D'Arcy made a name for herself by using mattress ticking as a chic alternative to traditional sofa fabric. As a result, she was called on by Davidson as one of the chosen few to tour Europe in the early fifties in search of new furniture ideas. Traveling through France, D'Arcy was impressed with the fine craftsmanship of the small local artisans scattered throughout the French provinces. She liked the light woods and the simplicity of design that were the hallmarks of the country furniture and she believed that the styles would be appealing to Bloomingdale's New York customers. This was a radical departure for American buyers, who, until D'Arcy changed things, had concentrated exclusively on the heavy-handed formality of Parisian furniture. Few Americans had ever dealt with the provincial artisans before, preferring instead to work with the big city-based furniture factories.

Displays of the "Country French" look D'Arcy and her hand-picked craftsmen developed were incorporated in Bloomingdale's model furniture rooms in the fall of 1954, and this went on to become the nation's most important furniture style for a decade—a success that did much for D'Arcy's career. (She is one of the few retailing interior designers who has moved from staff to management positions. Another in that select group is John Gerald, a former designer of B. Altman's model rooms who graduated to the presidency of W. and J. Sloane.) "As soon as the model rooms were opened for viewing, the press did glowing pieces on our Country French look," D'Arcy recalls. "Most important, the look proved to be a very big seller, generating the lion's share of our furniture sales for ten years. Since we were, at first, the only ones with this style, we earned an instant reputation for innovative furnishings. As soon as another store started to imitate what we were doing, we'd take a new tack in order to stay unique. If others copied the southern provincial look, we'd get into the northern styles. That's the way we kept the edge."

By being the first to promote a particular style, and

by selling exclusive merchandise long before the competition follows suit, Bloomingdale's usually has a year or more in which to extract exceptional profits from its trendy lines. Here the store can easily surpass the traditional 50 percent retail markup, going all the way to 100 percent or more above cost. The special breed of Bloomie's customers is willing to pay a premium for innovation—to be the first with a Mao suit or an electric wok. And when it's an exclusive at Bloomingdale's, there is no standard for price comparison and no way to buy the merchandise elsewhere. That is why Bloomingdale's views the first sign of widespread imitation as a signal to move to higher ground with a new promotion.

"They know there's nothing harder than hitting a moving target," says Richad Zolt, an executive with the prestigious Stark Carpet Company, which sells only to accredited interior designers and is considered by many to be the nation's foremost rug dealer. "The faster they are on their feet, the harder it is for other department stores to copy them and thus the longer they have the advantage of setting arbitrary prices at high markups.

"Take the case of a rug style Bloomingdale's promotes. It's called Tibetan dhurrie and it was originally a very fine cotton rug made in Tibet. Some years ago India learned how to knock these off and all the Tibetan dhurries now imported to the U.S. actually come from India. The difference is that they are now made in wool because this is an easier material to work with; the rugs can be turned out faster and cheaper. All the labor is done by informal village mills in India. Although the rugs are handmade and take a month to produce, Bloomingdale's buyers can pick them up there for about $280 for a six by nine. We know, because our buyers rub elbows with Bloomingdale's buyers in India. Bloomingdale's then turns around and marks up the rugs by almost three times what they cost, letting them go for $800. That's more than just about anyone else gets. Bloomingdale's gets away with these markups because it carries trendy goods long before the competition. It gets into hot items like Tibetan dhurries and sells them before most other stores even know what the name means."

Sometimes this emphasis on trendiness displaces other considerations. In the early 1960s Bloomingdale's furniture buyers were pushing Louis XIV desks as the elegant addition to a modern office or study. A substantial investment had been made in the desks, but hardly a unit was sold. The problem was that Bloomingdale's had failed to notice that the cutouts were too small for the sitter's legs.

But such setbacks are no deterrent, and Bloomingdale's actually performs best under pressure. When the opportunity presents itself to demonstrate leadership in the fashion world, Bloomie's is almost always up to the test. "Take the case of the Paris knock-off of 1977," says Gordon Cooke. "We did there in eight weeks what usually takes a year or more to accomplish. Why the rush? That's easy—we want to keep the lead." Returning to New York from the Paris fashion previews in October, Bloomie's ready-to-wear buyers were exuberant about the new look the big-name designers were showing for spring: natural-shaped blazers, straight-legged slacks and simple fabrics. Confident that this sexy look could edge out the peasant theme as the dominant fashion statement for spring '78, buyers pressed management to incorporate the new style into the merchandise line in time for the coming sales season. Because this involved even faster action than Bloomingdale's was accustomed to taking, Traub was called on to make the decision. He liked the new look, sensed the need for some pizazz in the spring line and okayed the knock-off. Buyers then moved fast. Final sketches were prepared, contracts were let to apparel manufacturers and in less than two months the line was ready for sale.

To assure consumer acceptance of the collection, Bloomingdale's launched its now famous "We Believe" advertising campaign. Backed by full-page ads in the *New York Times,* the campaign featured the new straight-from-Paris looks. Bloomie's promotion executives were confident that an official Bloomingdale's statement of "We believe in these fashions" would be all the motivation many of its patrons would need to buy the new styles. And they were right. The style caught on instantly, and once again, the Blitz had performed like a disciplined war machine.

One of the secrets of Bloomingdale's flexibility is its success in getting suppliers (called "resources" in the trade) to cooperate on fast-track projects. Bloomingdale's ability to sell great quantities of merchandise, and its position as a national showcase for fashion goods, give it considerable clout with suppliers. In what has become known as "partnership buying," stores like Bloomie's work with their resources to help each other. Suppliers consult with Bloomie's throughout the entire sales effort: in getting goods produced on time and in promoting them once they are in the stores. This is in contrast to the more usual so-called adversary buying situation, in which store and resource act on the premise that each must cheat the other or they'll wind up being cheated themselves.

Just how extraordinarily fast Bloomie's suppliers had to act to produce the Paris knock-off line becomes evident when we examine the traditional procedure for the design and delivery of new fashion collections. For a spring line, top designers like Bill Blass will start sketching a full year before the actual sales season begins. Work on the couture line—which consists of costly, limited production items used to build an umbrella theme for the full collection and to add a certain cachet to the designer's name—is done first, because this sets the tone for the ready-to-wear. Creating a line for the couture shows has always been the best way for designers to get their names and their collections widely publicized in newspapers and fashion magazines. The couture collections are presented at elegant fashion shows attended by the elite of the fashion industry and covered in full by the international press. Prices for couture clothes range from $2,000 for a dress to $5,000 for a formal outfit. Insiders call this "investment clothing" because it is designed to have appeal for several seasons, rather than passing in and out of style in a single year. This is true for most couture collections, not just those influenced by classic designs and styles. Wealthy patrons take pride in knowing that they are above the passing fads of seasonal fashions. They also are confident that they own something relatively exclusive because couture items are produced in lots of less than one hundred.

From a purely financial standpoint, couture lines have become unimportant to most designers. Bill Blass's couture collection accounts for about $4 million per year in revenues, less than 10 percent of his total volume. Couture is significant, however, because of the influence it has on the designer's mass-produced ready-to-wear lines. Promising styles in the couture line are later adapted for the much lower-priced read-to-wear collection. To take a couture design that costs $2,000 and turn it into a Blassport (the trade name for Blass's ready-to-wear line, which is carried by Bloomingdale's) dress, the designer uses cheap fabric, takes advantage of the economies of mass production and pays lower production wages (there are different unions for couture and ready-to-wear).

In most cases, spring ready-to-wear lines are contracted to manufacturers in late summer of the previous year, with the first sample goods coming off the production lines in September. For the next two months, buyers make the rounds, placing orders for shipment to the stores in January through March. The entire process usually takes about nine months. But Bloomie's managed the Paris knock-off in two.

The talk about Bloomingdale's speed, agility and trendiness thoroughly bothers Marvin Traub. He is, of course, proud of the store's performance, but worries that all this attention to designers and breaking fashions will make too many people think they can't afford to shop at his store. "People tend to talk about the more exciting part of our business," he says, "and this tends to be expensive because it is unique merchandise. We stress excitement more than we stress prices. It's part of our mystique, but we're very sensitive about this and don't want to have the reputation of being more expensive. We couldn't be the size we are if we really were. We sell a great deal of moderate-priced sportswear."

A comparative survey of major department stores

and independent retailers confirms that prices on well-known, widely distributed merchandise are virtually identical everywhere. National brands like Sony, Pierre Cardin, Izod, Danskin, Head, Texas Instruments, Bali and John Kloss are usually no more costly at Bloomingdale's than at competing stores (except for the discounters). In most cases, Bloomingdale's joins the pack with the standard markup.

Why, then, the big fuss over unique and exclusive merchandise? Why go to the effort and expense of multimillion-dollar promotions if so much of the merchandise is the same as in competing stores? Doris Shaw reiterates a point that we hear over and over again about Bloomingdale's—one that is crucial to the Bloomingdale's Blitz: "It makes all the sense in the world—it's a master strategy. The small increment of merchandise that is trend-setting builds a psychological showcase for the everyday stuff. It generates the excitement that makes the store special, builds traffic, and once that is done, everything on the floors has a better chance of selling out. Marvin Traub believes that a merchant has a greater responsibility than simply to unlock the doors of his store. To his way of thinking, the store can't just sit there—it must be presented. Like a starlet facing the press for the first time, Bloomingdale's must do something exotic, beautiful or outrageous in order to keep the limelight trained on its name."

And as we have seen, showcase merchandise can have a powerful impact on the bottom line. By freeing Bloomingdale's from strict adherence to traditional markups, showcase goods provide that extra cushion of profits that makes the store an exceptional performer and gives management the flexibility to take risks. As a whole, Federated Department Stores return about 4 percent (after tax) profit on total sales (in 1977, profits of $196,565,000 were earned on sales of $4,923,399,000). This is much higher than the average for department stores of comparable volume.* For Bloomingdale's,

---

* Macy's earned 3.2 percent, Carter Hawley Hale (owners of Bergdorf's) 3.3 percent and Associated Dry Goods (owners of Lord & Taylor) 2.9 percent.

which is at the top of the Federated profit curve, the after-tax return is even greater as a percentage of sales. But why are Bloomingdale's profits not higher still? Why in a store that engineers extraordinary markups on so much costly merchandise do actual profits come down to only pennies on the dollar?

The answer can be traced directly to Bloomingdale's operating style. The elaborate promotions, the art exhibitions, the Chinese cooking classes—all cost money. Add to that the above-average sums Bloomie's spends on lavish store design (like the construction of b'way), community relations and talented executives. Bloomingdale's invests heavily to generate its big revenue base and so there is considerable overhead to be covered before a profit can be earned.

An equally important factor, however, is that the Bloomingdale's Blitz sometimes collapses—that is, falls smack on its face and incurs heavy losses. There's often no way of telling how or why it happens: something the store promotes simply doesn't ring a bell with consumers. Temporarily, at least, the store's influence, power and instincts come to naught. A recent example of this involved one of Bloomingdale's early discoveries, Diane Von Furstenberg. Born in Belgium and educated in Spain, England and Switzerland, Diane came to the U.S. in 1969 and immediately set out to establish herself as an apparel designer. Her idea—to produce a line of smart, simple and highly fashionable dresses for less than $100 each—fell on deaf ears until Bloomingdale's buyers visited her small workshop in New York's Gotham Hotel. Katie Murphy, one of the behind-the-scenes powerhouses in the push to quality ready-to-wear, understood Von Furstenberg's concept, bought the line and suggested that the designer herself serve as the model for the collection.

"Bloomingdale's felt that a very special kind of face would be needed to sell my line," Von Furstenberg recalls. "They were screening models, tossing around ideas, putting out feelers to all the agencies, and then suddenly they stopped, looked at me and said I should do it." The mystique surrounding Von Furstenberg, her sexy good looks and marriage to a prince (Egon Von

Furstenberg) did, in fact, add immeasurably to the appeal of the dress collection. The feminine yet practical clothing sold well at Bloomingdale's, and the showcase treatment it received there propelled the line to national attention. At first, Bloomie's cornered the market for Von Furstenberg's line; later, when other stores gained distribution rights, Bloomingdale's still sold the lion's share of her collections in its market areas.

It was a perfect marriage of store, designer and customers. Until the fall of 1977, when for some inexplicable reason, Bloomie's customers turned off to Von Furstenberg's new collection and refused to buy the merchandise (an experience that, incidentally, was shared by other major department stores). The store's investment in her line turned to "red ink" very quickly. To move the merchandise off the floors, buyers had to institute 40 percent markdowns. This in spite of the fact that the new collection was not radically different from Von Furstenberg's traditional style. Consumers had either become bored with the look or were more interested in other lines. Diane, angry at any hint of such talk, blames it all on inventory problems. Her line has however rebounded from the bad season and is a respectable seller at Bloomie's once again.

And so it goes. Management recognizes that the ups and downs of trendy designers are a fact of life for the kind of business Bloomingdale's is. Just when one star will shine and another will burn out is always hard to predict. To stay highly profitable, Bloomingdale's uses the Blitz to extract maximum profits from its winners; and it relies on the checks and balances of the buyer system to make sure it is not left holding the bag with too many losers.

Every Bloomingdale's buyer functions practically as an independent merchant. Each department is a separate profit center and the buyer serves as chief operating officer of that department. The buyer is responsible for all costs incurred in running his department and for producing an even greater profit there. He is even charged for his share of advertising, displays and top management salaries. "This puts great pressure on the buyers to be sensible, prudent business people," Lachman explains. "They can't get too heavily into fringe merchandise, high-priced goods or untested goods. Instead, they must fill their departments with a broad range of variably priced items that will please their customers. People who shop here, after all, are not necessarily rich. Being a Bloomingdale's customer is a state of mind rather than a state of finance. We cater to the $15,000-a-year college professor, for example, but not the $30,000-a-year teamster. It's a matter of taste."

Developing taste is unquestionably the name of the game at Bloomingdale's, and it's up to the Blitz to find, establish and sell new tastes. So where does Bloomie's turn when the China look comes full circle? When rattan baskets, bamboo poles and all the other Oriental paraphernalia can be found in Alexander's, Korvettes and J. L. Hudson? Then it's goodbye Peking, hello Bombay. In search of virgin turf, Bloomingdale's sets its sights, of all places, on India. In the store's inimitable fashion, a subcontinent of hunger, disease and wretched poverty is termed "The Ultimate Fantasy" and is carefully packaged for sale to Bloomie's public. By the time the promotion is launched in the spring of 1978, it snowballs into the greatest array of Indian products ever assembled in the U.S.—a retail commitment of $8 million.

An examination of just how this promotion emerged provides a close look at the staging of a Bloomie's Blitz. The story goes back to the mid 1960s, when a growing interest in drugs, meditation and Eastern religions had led many American college students to view India as a spiritual promised land. This interest was also spurred by the Beatles' use of Indian sounds and instruments, principally the sitar, in their recordings, and by the group's association with guru Maharishi Mahesh Yogi. Head shops and clothing boutiques in college towns and major cities picked up on this trend by selling Indian artifacts, sandals and clothing.

By the late 1960s, bits and pieces of Indian goods started popping up in Bloomingdale's. Mostly the traditional items like madras shirts and handcrafts (Indian teas had been carried for many years), they accounted for less than $1 million in sales annually. Large-scale purchases were considered out of the question because Indian production facilities were backward and inefficient, and few local manufacturers could meet Bloomingdale's specifications for quality or speed of production. This concern with the reliability of suppliers is a nuts and bolts business consideration few consumers are aware of. Before contracts can be let for any goods, vendors must prove their ability to produce according to the terms of the deal. They must have the proper equipment, personnel and financial resources to deliver the appropriate goods as promised. This is a particularly troublesome problem when suppliers are not familiar with the U.S. market.

In Traub's early travels to Europe for the store's furniture department, he learned firsthand the difficulties of getting D'Arcy's provincial furniture artisans to institute quality controls. After a number of disappointing experiences with poor production runs, he demanded that the artisans produce prototype models before any big furniture orders were placed, so that all bugs in the procedures could be ironed out at an early stage. Even with these controls in place, some important lessons were learned through trial and error. Many of the local craftsmen were accustomed to using "green wood" for domestic furniture rather than the more expensive kiln-dried wood. When the cheaper product was shipped to the U.S., much of it warped on the long and soggy sea voyage.

Traub had this experience in mind when, in the late 1970s, he started exploring the options for a new promotion. He wanted something as daring and imaginative as the China boutique had been in '71. He was familiar with the subcontinent of India and believed it to have the right mix for a successful promotion: a built-in mystique, novelty and unusual merchandise. The question that remained was whether the inefficiencies of production could be overcome. Could Bloomingdale's work with local mills and factories to improve manufacturing techniques and install realistic quality controls?

Initially, the outlook was negative. Bloomingdale's executives had long regarded India as a poor place to do business. They knew that in many ways the subcontinent was way behind the times. Typical is the Indian government's approach toward containerization, the modern process of moving cargo in large marine containers rather than in clumsy individual packages. The efficiencies of containerization (which speeds cargo flow and reduces the costs involved) have enabled emerging nations like Malaysia to make great strides in industrial capacity. The big trading powers prefer to deal with nations that have embraced containerization by building ports to handle the new technology. India, however, has tangled container movements in so much red tape that the economies of the system are virtually lost there. As a result, the nation has lost millions of dollars in trade opportunities to other countries.

For Bloomingdale's, problems with its India-produced goods were minimal throughout the 1960s and '70s because of the small volume of merchandise carried by the store. Concern with India's production capabilities remained, therefore, on the back burner until Traub started exploring the idea of a major promotion featuring that country. As early as 1976, Traub dispatched executives to India to take a new look. Their assignment was to search for some indication of a responsible industrial sector that could be taught to produce goods suitable for sale to the store's demanding customers.

Among the first to touch down in Bombay and Calcutta were the buyers for men's and women's wear and home furnishings. Initial contacts were made through the Indian government. The buyers' assignment was to visit the supply resources recommended to them, personally inspecting each for its facilities, products and performance track record. To the surprise of many of the buyers, they found an aggressive, solidly capitalistic sector in India, run by young and wealthy businessmen blessed with sound instincts for what the American market required. Many had been serving the States for years and had developed a substantial customer base here. To prove their abilities to Bloomingdale's, they produced sample shirts, jackets, rugs and the like according to the buyers' specifications.

Early indications were therefore positive, and Traub flashed the green light to move ahead. By year end 1976, a secret decision was made to prepare India: The Ultimate Fantasy for introduction in spring '78. From development of the concept to the kickoff of the promotion on April 15, 1978, Bloomingdale's buyers made more than a hundred trips to India, working with thousands of suppliers, manufacturers and agents. Much of this travel expense was covered by a joint arrangement with Air-India. The airline agreed to fly Bloomie's personnel to India and to bring Indian performers, craftsmen and celebrities to the U.S. for the spring promotion. In return, Bloomingdale's agreed to promote an Indian tour in conjunction with American Express and to photograph the store's spring clothing catalogue in the subcontinent.

A total of sixty-five Bloomingdale's executives, including buyers, merchandise managers and fashion coordinators, visited the subcontinent, many for weeks at a time. For a full year before the promotion went public, they cultivated local production resources, let contracts for food products, furniture and clothing; sampled prototypes; ordered refinements; and then gave the go-ahead for full deliveries. By year end 1977, Bloomingdale's warehouse in New York was being stocked with the finished products, ready for movement to the stores in March.

At the same time that work went on in India, behind-the-scenes activities progressed in New York. Much of this centered around the eleventh floor, at Fifty-ninth Street, where Barbara D'Arcy and her staff laid the plans for in-store decorative devices to convey "the taste and feel of India." Silk ornaments, gauze wall hangings, vivid temple paintings, life-size stuffed camels, tents and ornamental costumes were designed and produced under D'Arcy's direction. For external publicity, Gordon Cooke's department prepared a series of special India ads backed by full-page spreads in the *New York Times,* the *Washington Post,* and *Boston Globe* and the *Philadelphia Inquirer,* and ten pages of the May issue of *Vogue* (the magazine conveniently made India the theme of that issue). In addition, Bloomingdale's arranged for a press conference, a black-tie in-store dinner dance to kick off the promotion, and a week of Indian festivals including a Festival of Lights, Festival of Music, Festival of Food, Festival of Spring and an Indian music program at Lincoln Center.

To be "true to the merchandise," all Bloomie's stores were fitted out with Indian silk banners suspended from the ceilings and large marble elephants. Kohl-eyed Indian women dressed in saris tended information booths, native artisans painted cloths in the aisles, small shops sold native crafts, and Mrinalini Sarabhai ("the Martha Graham of India") danced at the Fifty-ninth Street store. There was a series of live demonstrations to give pointers on the exotic arts of mehndi (henna painting of the hand), making enamel and filigree jewelry, threading flower garlands, drawing floor designs, Indian dancing, yoga and tie-dying. Model rooms, designed by Richard Knapple, reflected themes of major Indian cities: the Udaipur room all white, with walls covered in filigree sheesham wood; the Delhi room with deep-blue walls and dominated by the largest bronze Shiva in North America.

On kickoff day, the store boasted a rainbow collection of Indian goods, including jewelry, accessories, gifts, apparel, furniture, art, thirty-six different types of chutney, hand-painted Pichwai hangings for $2,500 each, and a three-piece solid-silver seating group ticketed at $80,000.

It was the Blitz in action. And in one sense it was extremely successful: as Traub had predicted, "India" became a media event, garnering big-league coverage on local television, radio and newspapers (including features in the *New York Times*). The world's leading store had managed, once again, to dominate the media and to get the concentrated press coverage it needs. A more basic question, however, is whether India: The Ultimate Fantasy succeeded financially. Did it move merchandise? Although Bloomingdale's refuses to reveal this kind of information, observers throughout the retail community contend that the promotion did not sell great quantities of Indian goods. The consensus is that the India promotion achieved mixed results. The problems of selling Indian merchandise as high fashion were brought into focus by *The New Yorker* magazine's comments that no promotion could camouflage the fact that the real India is "not fashion, yoga or curry but hundreds of millions of poor people, many of whom are nearly naked, inert and hungry, and having known only malnutrition, have suffered permanent brain damage. To think of them at all—let alone picture them flying Air-India or walking into Bloomingdale's—is to jeopardize one's sleep and peace of mind." "People just weren't enthusiastic about the goods and they met with only modest sales," says Halston. "Certainly Bloomie's didn't set off any kind of craze or a new fashion trend. I wouldn't say it was a failure, however, because they got that all-important publicity and kept the store's name associated with something new and adventurous."

What went wrong with the merchandise selection? "Who can really tell?" Halston adds, "I gave up trying to figure out what some people like years ago when I was a hat designer. Jackie Kennedy was on television at the President's funeral and she was wearing one of her pillbox hats with a wide crease down the middle. The next day, women all across the nation ordered those pillbox hats with the crease. What they didn't know was that Jackie accidentally made the crease with her hand by trying to hold the hat on her head against a stiff breeze. Sometimes you can't predict what people will want. That's the kind of business we're in."

# 5

# The Top Two:
# Apparel and Furniture

*When I first came to Bloomingdale's, I was a struggling tie salesman trying to make a name for myself with new fashion ideas and Bloomingdale's was trying to do the same. Like babes in the woods we came together, blazed new trails together, prospered together and grew to be tops in our industries. It was a perfect marriage from the start and it just keeps humming along, getting better every year.*

*Ralph Lauren*

The talent, energy and financial resources of the Bloomingdale's Blitz are always applied, first and foremost, to the store's apparel and furniture lines—known as the Top Two. Boil down the hundreds of departments, boutiques and shops at Bloomingdale's and you have these two major merchandise categories, which generate estimated combined annual revenues of $350 million, about two thirds of the store's gross sales. Bloomingdale's success in these two areas is interesting not only from the standpoint of raw sales volume, but also as a perspective for viewing the store's extraordinary accomplishments in the past three decades.

When it comes to illustrating just how much Bloomingdale's has changed over the years, and how powerful it is in many ways, apparel and furniture take center stage. Of the two, apparel brings in the most revenue and is still the store's fastest-growing merchandise category. Clothing manufacturers the world over vie for the chance to sell to Bloomingdale's, and the store is home to virtually all the world-class designers. From Seventh Avenue to Savile Row to the Rue Saint-Honoré, fashion superstars look to Bloomingdale's to sell their goods and to provide a showcase or springboard for them that will lead to substantial sales across the U.S. "Bloomingdale's moves designer fashions like no one else—they really sell the stuff," says Mary Merris of *Women's Wear Daily*. "And I'm not talking about low-priced Alexander's fashions or anything. I mean $50-to-$100 blouses and $100-to-$200 skirts. Moving this kind of fairly high-priced, trendy fashion takes merchandising expertise and a loyal following of affluent and fashionable people. Bloomingdale's has both. Designers know this and they want very much to count Bloomingdale's among their customers. The ability to pick and choose which of the great lines the store will carry is a real plus for Bloomingdale's. After all, the ability to sell this kind of merchandise is where the real profits are. There's no more profitable major line in a department store than high-fashion ready-to-wear designer clothes. Bloomie's makes a bundle on them."

"Today there is not a single manufacturer or designer who does not want to sell to Bloomingdale's," Lawrence Lachman says. Bloomie's power with the garment industry is one of the former chairman's favorite topics of conversation, and the glint in his eyes when he talks about it reveals a great sense of personal satisfaction. Perhaps that is because things weren't always this way. Just thirty years ago, Bloomingdale's was a dirty word in high-fashion circles—much as Korvettes or Mays is today. Prestige apparel makers avoided Bloomingdale's as a second-rate retailer with a bargain-basement image that could do more damage than good to their carefully cultivated appeal. In the late 1940s and early '50s, Bloomingdale's attempts to engineer a dramatic shift toward upscale, high-fashion merchandise brought little response from the nation's clothing industry (which has always been based in New York). Regardless of Bloomingdale's ambitious plans for the future, its schlock image would take years to erase and the big guns of

Seventh Avenue simply weren't interested in waiting. Davidson, Lachman and Krensky recognized immediately that they were up against a stone wall and that they would have to find some way to detour around it. To make the store's upgrading program a complete success, management needed quality apparel desperately. On the furniture front, Bloomie's buyers were making inroads with European manufacturers, persuading them to create stunning collections based on Bloomingdale's designs; something equally dramatic had to be done with ready-to-wear.

The solution was nothing short of brilliant. Rather than stubbornly continuing to knock at Seventh Avenue's locked doors, Krensky masterminded a plan to go around the fashion establishment, strike out in new directions, and develop up and coming talent as Bloomingdale's exclusives. The goal was to make the store a fashion leader in its own right.

The focus of the store's efforts was on the search for promising designer talents with good prospects for commercial success. Krensky was most interested in working with the kind of people who could achieve great popularity if properly packaged and promoted by a major store. The "Krensky combination"—new talent plus publicity hype—has proved to be so successful that Bloomingdale's is credited with playing a major role in developing the careers of most of the superstar designers of the past two decades. Just how Bloomingdale's engineered this coup and how it earned its stripes in the fashion world is best seen through the careers of some of the once obscure designers the store has brought to international prominence.

Take the Ralph Lauren relationship. A world-class designer of men's (Polo) and women's (Ralph Lauren) ready-to-wear, Lauren sits near the top of the fashion industry. His clothing companies generate extraordinary sales from the Polo and Ralph Lauren labels, and the balance from Chaps, a collection of moderately priced men's wear and colognes; he is Bloomingdale's best-selling designer resource; his fragrance division is a veritable money machine; and his apparel lines are sold in all the nation's finest shops, from Saks to I. Magnin.

A short, slightly built man with striking good looks, Lauren appears considerably younger than his thirty-eight years. With his penchant for cowboy clothing and an outdoor country look, Lauren comes to work looking like a sawed-off version of the Marlboro Man: Levi's, boots, khaki shirt and a Western hat. Pictures of the designer atop his favorite mount adorn the walls of Polo's business offices on Manhattan's West Side. Pleasant, congenial and soft-spoken, Lauren cherishes his dual roles as fashion leader and successful entrepreneur, and he is especially proud of the rags-to-riches story that ties him to Bloomingdale's. A native New Yorker, Lauren was born in the Bronx, studied business at City College ("I hated it") and worked as a young man at both Brooks Brothers and Bloomingdale's. "It's hard to believe that I was ever eighteen years old and getting less than a dollar an hour to sell sweaters at Bloomingdale's. It was the Christmas selling season; I was happy to get any job that I could. A few years later I made my first professional contract with the store. This was the late 1950s—the time Bloomingdale's was setting out to make a name for itself in men's fashions. No one was really doing much in men's wear at the time and Krensky saw a good opportunity to make some waves and to build a reputation for innovation. Few people know this, but Bloomingdale's made its fashion name in men's wear first, then in women's clothing. The success of Bloomingdale's men's wear innovations gave the store the push it needed to make inroads in womens' fashions. Men's wear was picked first because no one else was doing much in this area: there was a real opportunity for an innovator to take center stage."

Frank Simon, then Bloomingdale's men's wear vice president and now president of Filene's, was an early Lauren supporter and did much to propel him into the fashion spotlight. Simon loved Lauren's designs from the start and saw them as excellent vehicles for Bloomingdale's to launch its men's wear trend-setting movement. Lauren's wide ties got the full promotional treatment: they were featured in the store windows, displayed on the sales floor in a specially designed showcase and treated to extensive advertising. In a matter of months, they became the hottest men's wear accessory in the store. "Bloomingdale's—and Ralph Lauren—were on our way," the designer says.

This one-two-three punch of bold window treatments, special floor displays and heavy advertising became Bloomingdale's classic formula for launching new fashion statements. Still used by the store today, it is intended to saturate consumers and the fashion press with a new look and to establish the illusion of wide acceptance before a single sale has been made. If the look catches on quickly with only a handful of fashion leaders, a bandwagon effect develops, forcing the followers to join in. This is exactly what happened with Lauren's early tie designs: Bloomingdale's used its coolly calculated hype to get the young designer's look into the fashion mainstream. The store helped Lauren build an audience. Contrary to industry rumors, however, Krensky and Davidson never financed Lauren's exit from Beau Brummell nor did they offer to lend money to his new company. "What they did was give me the courage to break away from Beau Brummell and start Polo. Bloomingdale's was receptive to just about everything I did, so I had the confidence to go it alone. It's nice to get started in business with a big and eager customer behind you."

Eager to capitalize on the growing popularity of the wide-tie look, and on Lauren's emergence as a "name" designer, Simon asked his increasingly successful resource to develop a line of men's shirts, slacks and suits. As an inducement, Bloomingdale's offered to purchase most or all of his initial production and to afford it the same promotional blitz that had launched the ties. Lauren accepted Simon's offer; and about a year after the first "new look" ties had gone on sale, he was ready with a full Polo line of suits, sport jackets and slacks. Using the same bold, brassy, European-influenced theme that brought him his first taste of commercial success, Lauren produced a suit collection featuring very wide lapels and highly defined tailoring. The look was fresh, innovative and cosmopolitan, but not avant-garde. Before it launched Lauren and the whole move to trendy men's wear, Bloomingdale's had

had a strong Ivy League image—the conservative but-toned-down look. Lauren simply updated and modernized this look, producing clothing in tasteful fabrics and in the traditional blues and grays that young Wall Street stockbrokers and Madison Avenue account executives could be comfortable wearing. The collection had great appeal to diverse groups of consumers and, like the ties, met with almost instant success. In 1971 the entire Polo collection was housed in its own boutique on the main floor at Fifty-ninth Street. Almost overnight, Ralph Lauren became a leader in the U.S. apparel industry. It seemed he could do no wrong: everything he touched turned to pure gold.

Fueled with the earnings of a $10-million-a-year men's wear business, Lauren turned his attention to women's ready-to-wear in 1971. Again Bloomingdale's was a willing ally. "Just as I had done with men's wear, I recognized a need in the women's wear market for a significant change in current styles. There was just no class—no sophistication—in women's ready-to-wear at the time. Everyone was competing with each other to be kinkier, trendier and more glittering. I was put off by the whole look and believed there could be a substantial market for a tweedy, horsy, country style. I designed a line of blouses incorporating the look and Bloomingdale's loved it at first sight. They set up a separate Ralph Lauren boutique for them. The next year I came out with a full Ralph Lauren women's ready-to-wear collection. Today I have a men's boutique on the first floor, a women's boutique on the third, and cologne all over the place."

Bloomingdale's upgrading of its apparel lines took place throughout the 1960s, with the move in men's wear coming on strong at the beginning of the decade and women's wear a few years later. Much of the success of the latter project must be credited to an exceptional woman, Katie Murphy.

"The lady had sharper instincts for fashion than anyone I've ever known," says Ralph Lauren. "She encouraged young talents like myself to have confidence in our ideas; her advice was always solid and tasteful. She knew better than anyone else how to package the designer concept." An intelligent and gutsy apparel executive, Murphy had made a name for herself at Bonwit Teller before joining Bloomingdale's as vice president and ready-to-wear fashion director in 1967. Her elaborate title was another way of saying "chief fashion coordinator": it was Murphy's responsibility to identify fashion trends and to work with buyers to incorporate new looks into Bloomingdale's lines. This job required great taste, foresight, diplomacy, courage and self-confidence: Katie Murphy had it all.

"When I was president of Filene's, I used to visit New York from time to time for business," says Harold Krensky. "I got to know Katie then and we would have lunch whenever I was in town. We'd chat endlessly about the fashion business and I was very impressed with her ideas. So when I took over the presidency of Bloomingdale's, one of the first things I did was to hire Katie away from Bonwit's."

From the start, Murphy exhibited a sixth sense for emerging fashions and a limitless ability to merchandise them to the public. To accomplish this, she made imaginative use of the in-store boutique—a concept that in less than a decade became a merchandising classic, imitated by virtually every department and specialty chain in the nation. To Murphy's way of thinking, special goods deserved special presentation, and by isolating merchandise lines, a store could manipulate consumers' acceptance of them. Murphy knew that Bloomie's had to do more than simply develop new designers and buy their collections. It had to come up with merchandising tricks to turn people on—it had to put more flair into its merchandising and call attention to the new styles in a bold and imaginative way.

Putting her theories into practice, Murphy turned the public's attention to the hip and sexy European fashions she adored by starting a series of boutiques reserved exclusively for the works of Continental designers. She wanted to bring to a traditional retail environment the color, the feel, the excitement and the variety of the world's great fashion streets in New York, Paris and Rome. To do so, each boutique had to be different, distinct and bold enough to stand on its own—the way a small shop must do on the Boulevard Saint-Germain.

The first of Murphy's boutiques opened in 1968 with the dramatic new Mic Mac line of designers Michel and Chantal Faure of Saint-Tropez. Launched at Bloomingdale's Fifty-ninth Street, the boutique proved to be a powerful showcase for Mic Mac's then startling maxi coats, which sold out there and went on to thundering success in more than a thousand retail stores around the U.S. Murphy was also good at helping Bloomingdale's get exclusives on certain merchandise collections: by agreeing to minimum purchases from some of the lesser-known resources, she would get their authorization to let Bloomingdale's design the line and keep it for itself only.

The string of Murphy's big successes reads like a who's who of fashion superstars. Halston relied on her talents to help set up his Bloomingdale's boutique in 1969; Yves Saint Laurent, convinced by Murphy to produce clothes in the U.S., opened his first American boutique in Bloomie's in 1970.

The Saint Laurent story is particularly interesting. Few will argue against the contention that Saint Laurent is now the king of fashion. Born in Algeria to French parents, Saint Laurent was a child prodigy who entered the world of couture at age sixteen and was anointed five years later by Christian Dior to be his successor as head of the house of Dior. An intelligent and aggressive businessman as well as a remarkably gifted designer, Saint Laurent wanted even more than this: to build his own fashion dynasty under the Saint Laurent label. When the necessary financial backing was offered by a wealthy entrepreneur from Georgia, Saint Laurent left the house of Dior to strike out on his own. The year was 1962, and the change was more than one of name alone; basic differences in Saint Laurent's style and design were evident soon after the break. Dior's customers were traditionally the upper-crust, middle-aged establishment types in Europe and the States; once on his own, Saint Laurent showed a preference for the more liberated designs that appealed to a younger and sexier clientele. He soon became the darling of a small but powerful group of slim, beautiful young women blessed with lots of money and the willingness to experiment with fashion. Saint Laurent's fabulous financial success made him the world's most imitated designer: the couturier's lavish collections were routinely knocked off by ready-to-wear manufacturers on both sides of the Atlantic. Eager to beat his imitators at their own game and to cash in on this mass-volume side of the apparel business, Saint Laurent produced his own moderately priced line and sold it through a chain of boutiques called Rive Gauche, which he also owns. It was for this line of clothing that Murphy and Laurent signed their agreement to open a boutique in Bloomingdale's.

Murphy's value to Bloomingdale's extended far beyond her talents as a skilled merchandiser and negotiator. The woman's charm, compassion and kindness won the hearts and minds of a generation of young Bloomingdale's buyers and encouraged them to follow her lead in the highly risky practice of promoting new designers. This ability to lead buyers and to orchestrate a unified look for a major store is the hallmark of a great fashion coordinator. Buyers' careers, after all, are put on the line with every new season: one devastating sales fiasco can wreck their chances for promotion to merchandise manager (the supervisor of many buyers). Bloomingdale's is filled with aggressive, ambitious and talented buyers who are attracted to the store from all over the country. All are competing against one another for the same promotion. The politics at Fifty-ninth Street is hot and heavy, and just as soon as a young buyer falls out of favor, twenty others are there to bad-mouth him and to bid for his place in the charmed circle of those considered to be promotable. The buyer whose judgment goes awry or who simply makes a mistake cannot easily hide from it. Since all buyers have their own profit-and-loss statements, one bad season can put a buyer in the red. Every buyer must live with the knowledge that past accomplishments cannot carry him for long. Retailing is very much a "what have you done for us lately" business. Sales printouts are the bible.

It is in this pressure-cooker atmosphere that fashion

coordinators must work. They must convince buyers that a new look or fashion theme will be popular with consumers; that it will move merchandise at full prices, without steep markdowns or clearances. That Murphy was able to sway buyers without resorting to arm twisting or management pressure is testimony of her leadership qualities. "There is a risk for buyers in striking out in new directions," Lawrence Lachman explains. "Like buying the collections of European designers, which, at that time, were untested in this country. But the young people had such faith in Katie's skill and taste that they accepted her leadership and went ahead with her suggestions. She had a wonderful talent for human relations. You had to love her as well as respect her. When a young buyer made a mistake, Katie would take the blame. When they performed well, she gave them all the credit." Mary Merris of *Women's Wear Daily* adds: "More than anyone else, Katie Murphy made that store the fashion powerhouse it is. She put Bloomingdale's on the ready-to-wear map and she brought a sense of excitement to the store that everyone felt, including her customers, her buyers and her bosses. And, I must add, a good measure of that excitement left the store when she did."

Murphy died unexpectedly in 1975, but her merchandising concepts and innovations remain as a personal legacy in all the Bloomingdale's branches. The "swing boutique," which she started, is still the prime vehicle for presenting hot new fashions, and her emphasis on the use of designer boutiques grows stronger every year.

Murphy's boutique legacy has, however, opened a Pandora's box for Bloomingdale's executives. The fact that prestige apparel sells best when displayed in its own private showcase has not escaped any of the store's lesser-known fashion resources. They are all very much aware of the continued success of Polo, Rive Gauche and Calvin Klein and are demanding boutiques of their own. The pressure on Bloomingdale's merchandise vice presidents to allot space for boutiques is intense as one big-name supplier after another demands this status treatment. Given the reality of limited floor space, it is obviously physically impossible to grant separate boutiques to the thousands of companies whose clothing is sold at Bloomingdale's. Many are small suppliers, and their requests have little clout. But choosing among the major resources alone can be a very difficult assignment. Sensitive issues like quality judgments, sales appeal, good will and competition come into play. The truth is that those suppliers denied boutiques never take it well, especially if a competitor—or worse yet, a brand-new company—gets the royal treatment. In cases like this, long-standing relationships can turn sour overnight.

How do Bloomingdale's fashion executives balance supplier demands with the need to preserve the store's merchandising integrity? Who gets the nod and who gets thumbs down? The answer is based on two key considerations: one concerns pure business judgment and the other raw power. First, management tries to limit boutiques to those collections with famous labels, proved customer appeal or great publicity potential. (These criteria are founded both on Murphy's thinking that "special goods demand special treatment" and on Traub's concept of being "true to the merchandise.") Second, and even more important, many of the more successful resources, especially the big designer-name houses like Ralph Lauren, Calvin Klein and Halston, simply refuse to sell to major retailers unless the store grants boutiques. This is a power play that the super-stars can pull because stores like Bloomingdale's simply cannot afford to do without them. Brands like Polo add status, generate substantial traffic and account for heavy gross volume. "One way we solve this problem of boutique requests is to ask ourselves which resources we'd do just about anything to keep," Lachman explains. "There are some people, like Ralph Lauren and Calvin Klein, who are so crucial to our merchandising thrust, and who account for such considerable sales, that we would never deny them special treatment for their goods. We want them too much to say no—and that's what it comes down to."

For the less powerful of the world's fashion resources, getting a foot in Bloomingdale's door is a major coup.

Most will take the opportunity to sell to Bloomingdale's any way they can, boutique or no boutique. Getting the nod to be a Bloomingdale's supplier is no mean feat: of the thousands who vie for the honor every year, only a small percentage are selected. Bloomingdale's is important to apparel and furniture makers because the store is an incredible merchandise showcase that can propel an unknown line to national attention in a matter of months. Buyers for all the major retailers, leading fashion editors and top designers all browse the Fifty-ninth Street store regularly to keep tabs on what is current. A collection that takes off at Bloomingdale's gets gobs of attention, instant word of mouth and the stamp of approval from fashion leaders.

To get a new product or line of merchandise into the Bloomingdale's system—be it a shirt, suit, couch or rug collection—vendors must convince the appropriate buyers that the goods are right for Bloomingdale's and that they will sell. In clothing and furniture—categories of goods so crucial to Bloomingdale's reputation—the buyers have especially high standards. The goods must be fashionable, well made and priced somewhere between the high and middle ranges. And most important, they should have some angle, flair or innovation that promises to attract a high level of customer interest. While some prospective vendors try desperately for years to satisfy these criteria, others are sharp enough to give Bloomingdale's exactly what it wants from the start. The latter waltz right in without even working up a sweat.

One such smart cookie is Warren Hirsh, president of Murjani USA. A former vice president of the well-known apparel firm Ship 'n Shore, Hirsh started out at Murjani making and selling an ordinary, unbranded line of women's blouses. Getting distribution for this type of garment in the prestige stores is difficult because these so-called parity goods lack the angle or flair that attracts buyers. But sensing a void in the moderately priced blouse market (the $20-to-$30 range), Hirsh came up with a plan to market a blouse collection that would have instant appeal to almost every major store.

His idea was to find a well-known designer willing to lend a status name to Murjani blouses.

His problem was finding one of the few designers not already associated with a competing line. But Hirsh persisted and finally signed just the deal he wanted with Gloria Vanderbilt, who had established a good track record in designer linens and china and was well known to store buyers. What's more, her high-society name would lend an aura of elegance rarely associated with moderated-priced blouses. Backed by Murjani's ($120 million annual revenues) efficient plants in Hong Kong and Macao, Hirsh could produce relatively inexpensive blouses that had the look and the label of high fashion. This concept jelled perfectly with a key aspect of Bloomingdale's apparel and furniture merchandising: that is, the need to offer customers some moderately priced lines of tasteful merchandise that can balance the more expensive goods and widen the store's customer appeal. Traub wants very much to position Bloomingdale's as an "affordable" store; lines like "Gloria Vanderbilt for Murjani" make this possible.

Hirsh's strategy worked so well that more than three quarters of the nation's top two hundred stores purchased his collection the first year it was offered. With one fell swoop, he gained entry into most of the major retail outlets simply by playing by the rules of today's fashion merchandising. Hirsh also used clever promotional tactics, which are typical of behind-the-scenes activities in the apparel and furnishing industries. Vendors must do more than simply get their products into Bloomingdale's; they must also establish relationships with buyers and merchandise managers and help sell the line to consumers.

"One hot line doesn't make you successful," Hirsh says. "What the garment manufacturers need is a long-range marketing plan that supports the retailer." For Murjani USA, that means spending over $1 million a year in advertising and a lot more in promotional items. The advertising budget, which is invested in television ads featuring Ms. Vanderbilt, is used to sway store buyers as well as consumers. The more money a manufacturer is willing to spend in advertising his collection, the more confident the buyers are that the line will be presold to the public and that it will sell in the stores. One of the first questions buyers ask of prospective vendors is the size of the ad budget. "They may not refuse to buy our line if we don't advertise," Hirsh explains, "but they would certainly buy less of our goods. Knowing that we advertise heavily, the Bloomingdale's buyer can confidently order ten thousand of our jeans, let's say, and know they will not get stuck with much excess inventory." To promote good relationships with the many buyers who deal with Murjani and to play the flashy role expected of fashion executives, Hirsh also goes in for extravaganzas. The pressures of the business demand that a company look successful to be successful. For Murjani, the price tag for that look came to $50,000 for a one-night bash at New York's disco Studio 54. Hirsh rented the place and invited six hundred buyers to dance, drink and preview his new line of Vanderbilt blouses and jeans.

Here again, the buying relationship is a different ball game for the established vendors than it is for the relative newcomers. Top resources know that Bloomingdale's needs them as badly as they need Bloomingdale's; they know their lines are proved winners and that successful track records speak for themselves. There is no need to razzle-dazzle buyers with promotional gimmicks. What's more, heavyweights like Klein and Lauren are assigned their own Bloomingdale's buyers, who service only their accounts. All year round they have their buyers' undivided interest and attention. Buyers for second-tier resources handle several vendors simultaneously.

Bloomingdale's apparel and furnishings buyers are widely praised and are considered by many to be among the best in the business. They tend to be the top-ranked retailing graduates from the best colleges and universities, are put through an executive training program and serve an apprenticeship before assuming full purchasing responsibility. They also work in a store run by former buyers; they rub elbows daily with some of the great names in the field (like Traub, D'Arcy and Carl Levine); and they are employed by a company that has based its recent success on excellent and imaginative buying.

Just how a buyer works with an important resource is best described by Ralph Lauren: "The buyer acts as the store's eyes and ears. She is in the market every day, sensing new developments and learning early on where her resources are headed. I'll start working on a fall collection about nine months before the garments are produced. The buyer is right there from the start, visiting and calling me regularly to get a feel for the design themes as they develop. She rarely expresses an opinion about the collection at this stage and only tries to influence me if the store is planning a special fall promotion and wants some of my line to conform to the theme. Just how much the buyer gets to see of the line before samples are ready is up to me—and it's usually very little. In most cases they are presented a *fait accompli:* the buyer's only decision is how much to buy. Of course, that is a very important consideration. The buyer must use her instincts, experience and knowledge of the store's customers to determine the size of an order. A wrong decision here can mean either insufficient inventory to satisfy customer demands or excess goods that have to be junked at clearance prices. It's a delicate balance—and Bloomingdale's buyers are very good at it."

Bloomingdale's is extraordinary in that its furniture operations are similar to the apparel end of the business —sans the designer-label influence. Furniture buyers are so committed to trendy as opposed to traditional furnishings that the inventory has an extremely short life cycle for hard goods. Whereas the furniture departments of comparable stores, like Lord & Taylor, stress the classic French, American and Scandinavian designs, Bloomingdale's emphasis is on hot new looks that move in and out of style rapidly. For this reason, furniture (like most of Bloomingdale's apparel) must be turned over quickly or it will be dated and suitable only for clearance. Here again, Bloomingdale's willingness to take this chancy route is evidence of the store's gutsy approach and reveals the confidence it has in its own ability to quickly sell out furniture inventories. The store does a great job of this and makes an estimated $18 million profit (in furniture alone) in the process. Much of this success is due to Bloomingdale's superior promotions and merchandising efforts and to management's willingness to face its mistakes, cut its losses and move on to the next opportunity. Furniture that does not sell well is marked down in just six weeks. The real losers wind up in Bloomingdale's own furniture clearance center in New Rochelle. "Everything in Bloomingdale's furniture department is packaged so professionally and presented to the public with such finesse that the overall effect is irresistible," says Doris Shaw. "The buying is great, the advertising is memorable, and the publicity work is magnificent. They know just how to get exciting press coverage."

Bloomingdale's furniture is more distinctive and original than its apparel lines. Most of the pieces are produced especially for Bloomingdale's, with the store's buyers contributing substantially to the design process. The merchandise is considered to be well made, of good quality and premium priced, ranging from $30 for a simple director's chair to many thousands for an elaborate sofa or wall unit. A substantial percentage of the furniture is sold during Bloomingdale's annual summer sale months, when virtually everything on the floor is marked down. Unlike apparel markdowns, however, furniture reductions are often promotional gimmicks and not a sign of poor buying. The great flexibility in furniture pricing (consumers have a much harder time price-comparing furniture than apparel because of the lack of identifiable brand names) enables the store to order sweeping reductions and still earn the traditional 50 percent markup overall. Initial ticket prices are set with the full expectation of significant reductions at a later date, so some padding is built into the profit margin. This is a common practice in furniture retailing; when it comes to big-ticket items, every merchant knows that customers want a price break. Consumers are much more likely to write a check for a $2,800 dining room set if they are led to believe that the price is a bargain. So furniture dealers routinely put two tags on a floor piece: one designated as the list price and the other, in red ink, as the sale or clearance price.

Bloomingdale's furniture customers are treated to the best service in the store. Salesmen are attentive, courteous, and thoroughly familiar with the merchandise lines. Each Bloomingdale's branch has a designer department staffed with competent and talented decorators, and in-store consultations on decorating problems are completely free of charge. Decorators cheerfully dispense advice on the right color lamp for a green table, the perfect rug for grass-cloth wall covering. Those customers requesting the more extensive at-home decorator services must pay a deposit or retainer, which is later applied to purchases. In return, decorators will help with everything from elaborate floor plans to fabric selections. The staff is efficient and talented; many of them are young design school graduates out to build up a name and a loyal following. Bloomingdale's reputation has enabled it to attract the cream of the crop.

Much of the way the in-store decorator service operates bears the stamp of David Bell, Bloomingdale's director of interior design from 1961 to 1975. A would-be actor turned designer, Bell came to Bloomingdale's after an initial stint at Macy's Herald Square. The young designer had made a name for himself by doing some original work with American Indian themes and was soon identified by Bloomingdale's executives as a top talent to hire for the ongoing furniture upgrading program. Bell was eager to join such a dynamic and progressive store, so, he jumped at the invitation to come to Fifty-Ninth Street to head the design department. From the start, Bell proved to be a stickler for service. He demanded that every customer request, no matter how small or trivial, be treated in a thorough and professional manner. "I always told my staff that there are no small jobs; only small decorators. I didn't believe in making a hundred-dollar customer feel inferior to those who spent ten thousand dollars." Under Bell's direction, every customer received a personalized letter from the department, thanking him for his business. "It was my idea, however, to require a deposit for the in-home decorating assignments. People used to have my staff designers go to their homes, prepare complex floor plans and select dozens of fabric swatches. All too often, they would just keep the plan and the fabrics and never order a damn thing. We had to free up our staff from this kind of abuse so that serious customers could use the service."

The decorating staff is also involved in the design of the model rooms—the centerpiece of Bloomingdale's furniture operations. From the start of Bloomingdale's furniture upgrading, the model rooms played a vital role in building its reputation for interesting and innovative merchandise. The rooms are a series of roped-off display areas that are completely furnished as if they were separate quarters in a home or apartment. Each setting is developed around a theme or design concept, which can be anything from ultramodern to Oriental to Indian. All the pieces in the settings are for sale in the store, and prices for the goods are listed on wall plaques. In the New York store, the rooms are treated by Manhattanites and tourists alike as an artistic event—a designation they have proved worthy of throughout the years. The best rooms have been nothing short of design masterpieces, beautiful and enthralling to see. Observers usually want to move right in or to instantly transform their own homes to duplicate the Bloomingdale's vision, precisely the reactions management is after.

"Bloomingdale's knows just how to get people so excited they want to buy the whole room," says Doris Shaw. "You can hear people thinking: Oh, my, that is fine and wonderful and I must have it in my life." Customers have been known to order everything in a model room, regardless of the cost. Salesmen still remember the French tourist who had the contents of an entire room shipped to his home. Among his purchases were tapestries at $7,900, cushions for $190, a $460 fireplace and $3,000 worth of floor coverings.

The model rooms have served most nobly as incredible publicity makers. Ever since the unveiling of one of the first settings, which featured the works of modern-furniture designer Robsjohn-Gibbings, each new showing has produced great media coverage. Word of mouth and press activity intensified during the Barbara D'Arcy years, thanks in part to her immensely popular Country French look.

Designing and assembling the model rooms is an enormous job. In the flagship store alone, there are eight rooms, each decorated twice a year (additional rearrangements are made for sale merchandise). The biggest event of all is reserved for late September. This is the major model room showing, the one in which most of the time and talent are invested and the one viewed by Bloomingdale's decorators as the store's design statement. Work on the September rooms begins in October of the preceding year—eleven months before the actual showing. "The first step is a series of brainstorming sessions between the furniture buyers, the vice presidents and Mr. Traub," D'Arcy explains. "Here is where the major themes take shape—the countries and the kind of furniture the store will feature for the following year. Traub is great at giving direction to this kind of thing—he has excellent taste and knows how to translate ideas into merchandising concepts."

Next, in mid November, the buyers fan out around the world to work with furniture makers to refine initial themes, draw explicit designs and establish costs and prices. There is great give-and-take here, with buyers and vendors exchanging thoughts and ideas. At the manufacturer's suggestion, a sofa originally planned for velvet, for example, may be changed to velour—current prices for velvet may be too high to keep the product within Bloomingdale's market range. "The trips last about six weeks, with each of the buyers visiting several factories," D'Arcy adds. "Depending on the complexity of the initial discussions, prototypes or limited production runs are ordered. Buyers then return to the field in February, check on the work, and if all is well, the full orders are placed. Merchandise is shipped in May and June. Floor plans for the model rooms are started in mid June, preparatory work on the physical spaces is done in late August and the furniture is set in place in early September. Every October it seems as if we'll never get all the work done in time for the next September, but we always do and the curtain goes up on the model rooms. I should know; I did more of them than anyone else—about five hundred."

D'Arcy's appointment as vice president of store design in 1975 signaled the end of an era for Bloomingdale's furniture department. The truth is she was kicked, upstairs in a diplomatic move to strip away her responsibility for the model rooms. The consensus in the seventh-floor executive offices was that D'Arcy's emphasis on elegant European furniture was out of step with the times. Bloomie's furniture customers were becoming younger and more informal; most preferred a casual lifestyle and wanted their homes to be decorated for comfortable entertaining. Cost also played a key factor: to cater to the migration of younger people into Bloomingdale's market areas, slightly lower-priced lines would have to be added to the merchandise selection. D'Arcy's addiction to French furniture made the store and its customers subject to Europe's spiraling inflation, and prices were simply getting too high.

D'Arcy's promotion, and her eventual replacement by designer Ralph Knapple, has had a significant impact on Bloomingdale's furniture department. Knapple, a graduate of both the New York School of Interior Design and Pratt Institute, prefers a sparse, basic look. His furniture is toned down, and is cleaner, simpler and more modern in design. Knapple is no great fan of D'Arcy's, and he has made this clear in public statements. Referring to the Country French look D'Arcy favored, Knapple has said, "For some reason this line never appealed to me."

Many of Knapple's model rooms have appeared stark and barren; one bedroom had little more than a bed, a lamp and a plant. Under his direction, there has also been a decided switch from European manufacturers to the more moderately priced U.S. and Canadian resources. While Bloomingdale's insists that the change has had a positive impact on gross furniture sales, observers believe that the benefits may be short-term. They believe that in furniture as well as in apparel, Bloomingdale's is trading away its cachet, its elegance and its position as the world's greatest store in an attempt to achieve wider and wider mass appeal. As Bloomingdale's branch network grows and as it strives for the ever greater sales gains that Federated (and Wall Street) demands, pressure to succumb to current taste, rather than to stake out new positions and wait for the others to follow, intensifies. This is not to say that Bloomingdale's no longer innovates, The truth is, however, that management is not as willing to wait as long or as often for its apparel or furniture gambles to pay off. Gone are the days of building dozens of new talents from scratch and patiently supporting and nurturing them over a period of years. Bloomingdale's is far bigger now than it was in the aggressive and imaginative sixties. The payoff has to be faster. "I had fourteen great years at Bloomingdale's—years of growth, excitement and change," says David Bell. "It was an excellent experience working with capable people like Davidson and then Traub, both of whom knew the furniture business very well. But when I felt that the excitement and sense of challenge were gone, I decided to leave the store. I packed it in in 1975 because Bloomingdale's was getting tied to a set merchandising formula; there was little room for experimentation. There are areas of design I like to explore that they just don't do at the store. Let me sum it up this way: Bloomingdale's is getting too damn big. Suddenly administration and operations are taking over where art once held sway. Bloomingdale's is like an old movie."

# 6

# The Propaganda Machine

*Martha and I are happy enough. I have my work and she has Bloomingdale's.*

*From a classic* New Yorker *cartoon*

Maintaining Bloomingdale's image of originality at a time of growing conservatism is the unenviable task of its advertising and public relations department. Like a skilled magician, Bloomingdale's relies on illusion and sleight of hand to draw attention away from what is really happening and to what management wants to reveal. The feeling is that carefully executed promotional efforts can maintain the aura of excitement even at a time when Bloomingdale's is retreating from some of its more adventurous strategies.

Sophisticated promotions have always been a hallmark of Bloomingdale's merchandising style. But this, too, may be changing. The promotion staff is plagued by deep-seated problems that threaten to become even more serious in the years ahead. Most important, management is not quite sure who should supervise promotions or how the function should be managed. Part of the problem can be traced to the fact that Bloomingdale's advertising and public relations department is a paradoxical world within a world; it sits atop the main store at Fifty-ninth Street but is actually near the bottom of the corporate pecking order. Although it has been crucial to Bloomingdale's success, it is disliked and even despised by those who depend on it most. And while the excellent work it does is one of the major factors that distinguish Bloomingdale's from the competition, this fact is rarely recognized by the people who really run the store. To understand why this is so is to understand both the complexities of major market retailing and the attitudes of its top executives. For many of the problems that beset Bloomingdale's advertising and public relations department plague its counterparts at other major stores.

Virtually all of Bloomingdale's advertising and public relations activities are handled in-house by the store's salaried employees. The store's famous newspaper and magazine advertisements are planned, designed and produced by the staff, and its press releases announcing company events ranging from executive promotions to new store openings are written and distributed by its own public relations specialists. The advertising and public relations department also orchestrates such activities as celebrity appearances, special events (for example, the visit of Queen Elizabeth and the store's *60 Minutes* segment), black-tie parties (like the ones kicking off the India theme and the 1972 centennial extravaganza), TV tie-ins (Sandy Hill, cohost of ABC-TV's national show *Good Morning America,* wears Bloomie's clothes on the air, and the store gets a mention for this in the closing credits), promotional signs and posters, VIP store tours, shopping bag designs, catalogues, and franchise deals (Bloomingdale's has sold the rights to franchise its popular 40 Carrots in-store restaurants).

Most major nonretail corporations of a similar size would farm out all or part of such promotional work to outside agencies, particularly the advertising. Typically, an advertising agency would do all the conceptual work, design, production and media buying and would be paid a commission based on the clients' total expenditures (called billings in the trade)—usually 15 percent of the billings plus an additional 17.65 percent above the cost of related services purchased for the client. The 15 percent commission is actually deducted from the media bill by the agency. It works this way: a full-page ad in the

*New York Times Magazine* may, according to the *Times* advertising rate card, go for $8,000, but recognized agencies purchasing this space are granted a 15 percent discount, reducing the cost of the ad to $6,800; the client pays the agency the full $8,000, and the agency keeps $1,200 as commission. This makes up the major fee paid to agencies.

Why, then, do Bloomingdale's and similar retail operations insist on performing these services in-house? Why not hire one of the many top flight Madison Avenue agencies that are expert at this type of work? The answer is based on a number of factors that are peculiar to major market retailing. Most important is the incredible pace of advertising activities at a promotionally aggressive store like Bloomingdale's, for the heart of the business is the discovery and presentation of late-breaking fashion. Jogging suits, disco roller skates, wet-look casual pants, peasant dresses, midi skirts, hot pants, maxi coats, narrow ties, wide ties, Country French, steel-and-glass modern, China, India, England, Kenzo, Von Furstenberg, Cardin, Halston, backgammon, Cuisinarts, Bill Blass sheets, halter tops, velour tops, Nehru jackets, Calvin Klein sneakers: all had their day and all had to be hyped to the public through ads in the battery of media outlets Bloomingdale's relies on. Changes in fashion come quickly—season after season, month after month—and new ads and related promotional strategies must be designed to reflect these changes. In the past few years alone, Bloomingdale's has had to move quickly to keep up with the blur of style changes in jeans alone: from good old Levi's, to fashion flare legs, to hip huggers to high-waist, to bell bottoms, to designer label straight-legs to designer baggies. Each new statement in jeans fashion completely rejected the previous look and demanded full-scale advertising, public relations and window treatments to effectively hype the change. Making yesterday's styles quickly passé is the perpetual goal of the ready-to-wear fashion industry; it takes a constant promotional barrage to convince consumers to discard perfectly good garments and to shell out hundreds or thousands of dollars simply to be able to conform to the Blooming-dale's ideal and to avoid looking out of date.

The feverish pitch of high-fashion retailing puts great pressure on the merchants as well as the consumers. Whereas companies in as fickle a business as auto-mobiles can produce ads for a new model car and then run the same campaign for up to a year or more, fash-ion retailers can rarely enjoy this luxury. Every single day of the year, including some Sundays and holidays, Bloomingdale's advertising department is either pre-senting or designing at least one new ad, and it is not unusual for fifty new ads to be in the production pipe-line at any one time. What's more, many of Blooming-dale's major ads—announcing special promotions, de-signers appearances and sales—have a life span of no more than a week and sometimes only a single day. This type of advertising is extremely expensive and in-efficient, but it is part and parcel of high-fashion re-tailing and must simply be accepted as one of the cost factors.

Bloomingdale's ads require extraordinary invest-ments of time, talent and money to achieve their dra-matic, eye-catching impact—only to be discarded in a matter of days. But a store that prides itself on being unique, and stakes its reputation on the ability to set trends, must make heroic efforts to produce advertising that commands attention regardless of its life span. Largely because of a growing advertising menace called "clutter," it is becoming increasingly difficult to grab the consumer's attention. With the heavy traffic jam of competing messages in the advertising media—televi-sion news shows take at least four commercial breaks per half hour, and highly regarded newspapers such as the *Washington Post* are often choked with more ads than editorial material—advertisers worry about con-sumers remembering their company name or product. Thus those responsible for allocating advertising bud-gets are obsessed with producing ads that can break through the "clutter" and will be remembered at the point of purchase. To churn out as many ads in as short a time as Bloomingdale's must and score high "recall" ratings takes a determined, dedicated and talented group of people driven to the point of near exhaustion. And that is exactly what Bloomingdale's is blessed with.

Bloomingdale's reputation as the world's greatest store and its fame as a training ground for young merchants makes it the most sought-after work place in American retailing. For the opportunity to work there, professional-level employees in the advertising and public relations department are willing to accept drab and crowded office facilities and a schedule that often stretches to sixty and seventy hours a week. Although Bloomingdale's salaries are considered to be competitive with other stores in its category, it is widely known as one of the retail industry's great sweatshops, demanding at least ten-hour days and a good deal of weekend work from its career employees. Many bitch and complain about the mental and physical exhaustion, but they keep at it and would fight for their jobs if they had to because of the prestige that working at Bloomingdale's lends to their résumés. A stint at Bloomingdale's does for a retail career what a post at Procter & Gamble does for a young marketing executive or Harvard Law School does for fledgling attorneys: it opens doors. Advertising and publicity pros (and of course, those involved in the merchandising disciplines) routinely leave Bloomingdale's for top-paying jobs at premier stores across the country.

Bloomingdale's staffers are therefore willing to put up with the craziness the store's advertising activities demand. It is not the kind of account advertising agencies like to handle—or for that matter can service well. The daily crisis atmosphere, the constantly changing strategies and directives, the need for constant two-way communication to avoid costly delays and resolve conflicts of opinion all but demand that the function be performed in-house. Under these difficult conditions, advertising people must virtually "sleep" with the merchants they serve, working side by side with them on a daily basis; an arm's-length outside agency relationship just wouldn't do. Mostly for television advertising— which requires too much specialized equipment to be produced in-house—does Bloomingdale's, like other

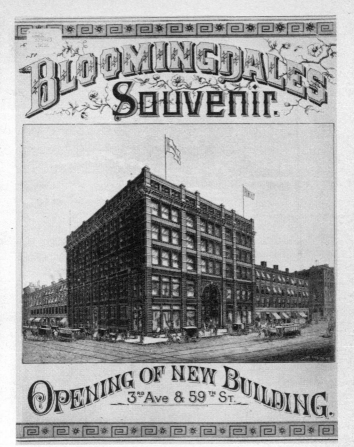

Cover of the souvenir booklet published by Bloomingdale's on the occasion of the opening of the new Fifty-ninth Street store in 1886. *(Courtesy of The New York Historical Society, New York City)*

Bloomingdale's once-famous advertising slogan "All Cars Transfer to Bloomingdale's" is prominently displayed in New York's Madison Square (over thirty blocks away from the Bloomingdale's site) after the turn of the century (1910).

The old Third Avenue El, long an eyesore on New York's East Side, used to run right above Bloomingdale's doors. This photo, taken in 1951, shows the downtown platform of the Fifty-ninth Street station. Bloomingdale's former chairman J. E. Davidson was correct in his assumption that the razing of the El would vastly improve the quality of the store's surrounding neighborhood. *(Courtesy of The New York Historical Society, New York City)*

The cursive logo, dropped from Bloomingdale's advertising and promotions in the 1970's , still adorns the façade of the Fifty-ninth Street store. The new logo features the store's name in lower-case lettering. *(Lawrence David Greenberg)*

The main (Lexington Avenue) entrance of Bloomingdale's flagship store. *(Lawrence David Greenberg)*

A bright neon sign on the lower level of the Fifty-ninth Street store proclaims the location of Saturday's Generation (a department featuring trendy casual clothes that is a popular haunt for young singles) and the Hair Place, Bloomingdale's in-store hair salon. *(Lawrence David Greenberg)*

Cul de Sac, a department devoted to designer handbags, one of Bloomie's many in-store boutiques. *(Federated Department Stores, Inc.)*

The Sleepwear Departmant, on the lingerie level at Bloomingdale's Fifty-ninth Street store, boasts an exotic collection of nightgowns and robes in a swank and sexy atmosphere. *(Federated Department Stores, Inc.)*

Mr. and Mrs. Marvin Traub, center and left, chat with another guest at a party. Chairman Traub, who considers himself to be an industry leader, likes to be seen at fashionable events. *(Lynn Karlin)*

Harold Krensky, former Bloomingdale's chief, is now Chairman of the Executive Committee of Federated. Based in New York, Krensky is still known to take the subway to Bloomie's, where he likes to go to catch up on the latest gossip. *(Courtesy of Federated Department Stores, Inc. Photo: Fabian Bachrach)*

Bloomingdale's White Plains branch, a sleek glass and steel facility in suburban Westchester County, New York, has attracted a loyal following from the very day of the grand opening. Its popularity proved to be the kiss of death for the aging New Rochelle unit. *(Courtesy of Westchester Rockland Newspapers. Photo: David Goldberg)*

*Opposite:* The only Bloomingdale's branch to fail as a traditional retail outlet, the New Rochelle unit has been converted into a furniture clearance center. The declining community surrounding the store was one of the principal factors for its demise. *(Lawrence David Greenberg)*

The Garden City branch, considered by some to be Bloomingdale's most attractive store, was designed by famed architect Edward Durrell Stone. It has proven to be an extraordinary success, attracting many of Long Island's affluent consumers. *(Lawrence David Greenberg)*

Bloomie's successful branch operation in Chestnut Hill, Massachusetts, is the first to combine an existing furniture outlet with a new (completed 1978) addition featuring fashion apparel. *(Federated Department Stores, Inc.)*

Cathy Cash Spellman, Bloomingdale's former vice president for advertising and public relations, led the store to its first television ad campaign. She is now a principal of Spellman & Co. (with husband, Joe, left) a small PR and promotion agency specializing in the fragrance field. *(Pierre Scherman)*

Yves Saint Laurent's Opium fragrance was introduced to the U.S. market through a dazzling black-tie bash held on an Oriental boat in New York's East River. Bloomingdale's and Saks were the only New York stores selected to sell the fragrance in its first year in the states. *(Lynn Karlin)*

*Opposite:* Yves Saint Laurent, the acknowledged master of international fashion, is seen here fitting a model with one of his lavish couture designs. Saint Laurent, who works in Paris, is known to be an intense and extremely private man. *(Lynn Karlin)*

Gloria Vanderbilt at the Studio 54 party and fashion show presenting her blouses and jeans for Murjani. *(Toni Palmieri)*

Zandra Rhodes, whose apparel and negligee collection is the most avant garde carried by Bloomingdale's, is a flashy and exotic woman in her own right. She is pictured here at the Opium party. *(Lynn Karlin)*

Bill Blass, one of the
few American fashion
designers who still
produce a couture
line, had some of his
earliest works
displayed and sold in
Bloomingdale's
Green Room. (This
lavish boutique,
featuring custom
clothing, never
succeeded and was
closed to make room
for ready-to-wear.)
Blass is pictured here
in his huge, cluttered
office lined with
photographs of
famous models and
assorted versions of
the Blass look. *(photo
© 1978 Barbra Walz)*

Diane Von Furstenberg, who credits Bloomingdale's with propelling her to national prominence, has been having difficulties of late with her apparel lines. Still, the designer's jet set reputation and sexy good looks make her a significant force in the design community. *(photo © 1978 Barbra Walz)*

*Opposite:* Halston's three favorite activities are smoking, sketching, and seeing himself in mirrors; here, he does all three simultaneously.
Notorious for his all-night socializing (especially at New York's Studio 54 disco), Halston is also an aggressive and ambitious businessman whose corporations rake in more than $100 million a year. *(photo © 1978 Barbra Walz)*

Ralph Lauren, whose relationship with Bloomingdale's helped him to graduate from tie salesman to Coty Award winning designer, is one of the few super stars in the fashion business who manage to maintain a successful family life. Lauren is pictured here with his wife and three children at their Long Island retreat. *(photo © 1978 Barbra Walz)*

major retailers, use an agency. For this Bloomingdale's
relies on Grey Advertising, one of the nation's largest.

Bloomingdale's advertising and public relations department is organized to simulate, as closely as possible, an independent agency. The staff, whose number
fluctuates between seventy-five and eighty-five people,
boasts a full compliment of standard agency professionals:

- Writers—responsible for the copy for print ads,
  promotional fliers, catalogues and executive
  speeches.
- Art directors—who develop the visual concepts
  for the ads, catalogues and shopping bags (Bloomie's was the first department store to produce
  professionally designed shopping bags; it gives
  them away liberally—more than ten million a
  year).
- Artists and photographers—responsible for
  fashion graphics and illustrations (for example,
  a wool skirt and blazer selected for a full-page
  ad in the *New York Times* is photographed or
  sketched by these professionals before the art
  director lays out the final ad). Bloomingdale's
  switched its visual emphasis in ads in recent
  years from photography to original artwork—a
  decision that stemmed from technical as well as
  aesthetic considerations. Most of the store's advertising is placed in newspapers, which are
  notorious for poor reproduction of photographs.
  Artwork simply comes out better than photography in the printed format and is therefore preferred by store executives. What's more, the use
  of artwork allows for a more inventive approach
  to ad design. Photography is making a come-
  back, however, as the fashionable stores turn to
  shadowy, sensual shots reminiscent of motion
  pictures of the 1940s. To get some of its best
  effects—in photography and original artwork—
  Bloomie's occasionally hires the services of big-
  name talents like Richard Avedon, who has
  served as a consultant to the store.

- Media buyers—who study the demographics of newspapers and magazines, and select those publications most suitable for Bloomingdale's ads. The publications most likely to get the nod for the heaviest ad spending are those with affluent, educated, fashionable readers. That is why the *New York Times* is chosen over the *New York Post*, the *Washington Post* over the *Washington Star*. The aim is to select the papers with class, the ones that can deliver the upscale, higher socioeconomic readership the store caters to.
- Press relations specialists—who serve as direct intermediaries between Bloomingdale's and the news media. The PR "flacks" keep Bloomingdale's name in the news by releasing both trivial tidbits and major news scoops about the store's multifaceted activities. Because so much of Bloomingdale's business involves glamour, wealth and famous names, the store has a relatively easy time getting good press play. Most of the really big coups—like the *Time* and *Wall Street Journal* stories, as well as the *60 Minutes* segment—come as a result of top-level contacts between Bloomie's promotion vice president and the news media.

Sitting at the head of the entire promotion department is the senior vice president for advertising and public relations (now Gordon Cooke). The job pays about $70,000 a year, reports directly to the store chief and enjoys considerable prestige in New York's advertising community. It also appears to be something of a hot seat, having been occupied in the past five years by four different executives—Mary Joan Glynn (who has since returned to the store as a vice president reporting to Cooke), Cathy Cash Spellman, Doris Shaw and Gordon Cooke. This is a store well known for its management continuity. Part of the problem stems from Traub's indecision on which kind of background is more important for the job, retailing or advertising agency; he keeps fluctuating between the two choices.

Cathy Spellman, for example, had no store experience before joining Bloomingdale's; Gordon Cooke, on the other hand, was hot off a very successful stint at Macy's. Traub's dilemma is clear: retailing pros are no doubt familiar with the mechanics of the business. They know the strengths and the shortcomings of retailing; and they are aware in advance of the frustrations and sticky politics that come with the vice president's job. All too often, however, those who have made a name for themselves in retailing try to transfer their former employer's advertising style to Bloomingdale's. Bloomingdale's, however, cannot tolerate widespread duplication. An agency pro is more likely to bring Bloomingdale's imaginative and original strategies for its public communications, but can he survive the backbiting world of department store advertising?

Cathy Cash Spellman, hired as Bloomingdale's advertising and public relations chief in 1975, could only take a year of it. An extremely talented, vivacious and charming woman, Spellman has achieved considerable business success without losing the warm human touch that is integral to her personality. An accomplished job hopper, she earned a glowing reputation working for the world's largest ad agency, J. Walter Thompson, as well as for the Celanese Corporation, Fieldcrest Mills, J. P. Stevens, and most notably Revlon, where she contributed to the fabulously successful promotion for Charlie perfume, now the best-selling fragrance in the U.S. Spellman's lack of retail experience proved to be one of the swing factors in her selection as Bloomingdale's top promotion executive. "By going outside retailing," Traub said at the time of her appointment, "we are trying to bring an infusion of new ideas and approaches to retail advertising." From this standpoint alone, Spellman's appointment proved to be a wise move: she did bring fresh ideas to the store and led it in imaginative directions. But Spellman resigned in January 1976 to become president of a small, $1-million-a-year advertising agency, McGlone, Nightingale, Reingold & Spellman (which went out of business about a year later). Her replacement at Bloomingdale's, Doris Shaw, also lasted about a year.

Spellman's abrupt departure came as a result of her distaste for working conditions at the store. Hard work was not the problem: as a successful alumnus of Revlon, considered to be one of the few employers more demanding than Bloomingdale's, she was used to that. Spellman's real bitch was with the abusive and demeaning treatment dished out by Bloomingdale's middle and upper management executives. Having built her career at agencies and at corporate organizations that respect the value of promotional talent, Spellman found it difficult to accept the stepchild status of department store advertising executives. "Stores are run by merchants," Spellman says, "and they believe that the world is divided into two classes: merchants and nonmerchants. If you are not one of them, you are not part of the club. Merchants have a brand of chauvinism all their own and it is very hard to break through the barriers they put up all around.

"Merchants define themselves in a very limited way. It's not good enough to work for a retail store to be considered a merchant. You have to be directly responsible for producing sales; you have to be responsible for selling merchandise. If you are not saddled with that pressure, they think your life is a breeze. Only they work really hard, the thinking goes, only they are responsible for the success of the store. People involved in promotional work alone are thought to be on perpetual vacations. Merchants look down on the advertising and public relations departments and this attitude is revealed in their treatment of the pros who work there, including the vice president. You get a lot of cold shoulders and piles of nasty memos. Everything is just the opposite of teamwork. It's an 'us versus them' feeling. Bloomingdale's merchant group is a very capable and talented bunch, to be sure, but what they dish out is a lot to take from anyone." Spellman did, however, leave the store on cordial terms and stays in close contact with her former employers. Now a partner with her husband in a small advertising/publicity agency, Spellman and Company, she beats the drums for a number of clients whose products are sold at Bloomingdale's.

The conflict between Bloomingdale's management

and its promotion staff stems from the nature of their corporate relationship. The advertising and public relations department is organized as an in-house agency, with buyers, merchandise managers and controlling vice presidents considered to be clients of the department, who give it assignments as they would an outside agency. Each merchandise group must pay its share of the costs. A $50,000 project to design and place a series of late-breaking ads featuring leather jeans is, for example, billed against the ready-to-wear budget. That expense becomes part of the department's overhead and is used in calculating its quarterly and annual profits. Although this arrangement is designed to duplicate traditional agency/client relationships, it does not. One of the crucial aspects that is missing here is the ability of the agency to resign the account. This parting of the ways is a daily occurrence in ad land; although agencies hate to do it, if an account becomes excessively demanding, unreasonable or abusive, most agencies will drop it. But Bloomingdale's advertising and public relations department can hardly do that. The store is its only account; the store owns the agency and controls the payroll. All the department heads know this, and therefore they know they are free to call all the shots. There is no fear of antagonizing the agency or losing its services.

Also complicating the relationship is the tremendous number of clients the department must serve. The hundreds of Bloomingdale's executives responsible for the vast array of merchandise the store stocks are all considered to be paying clients. "Most of the executives are in competition with each other for glowing sales results," Spellman explains. "That means they all want the promotion department to serve them faster and better than anyone else in the store. Let's say we are doing the big Christmas catalogue and we put out the call for suggestions from the merchants. There's no doubt that ten of them will demand that their goods be featured on the catalogue cover or on the first few choice pages. The politics and the infighting are intense and the ad people have to weed through this constantly. You wind up finally selecting one merchandise category to feature on the cover, and that means *bam*—you have nine new enemies."

In many cases, battles over how and where to advertise what go all the way up to Traub, who is the final arbiter on these issues. Traub has highly developed tastes in layout design and advertising copy, and his opinion is respected by the promotion executives. More than any past Bloomingdale's chief, Traub takes a very special interest in all the store's promotional activities and is often involved in the planning from the earliest conceptual stages. Also, every major ad is signed off by the chairman before it is released to the newspapers.

Theoretically, the advertising and publicity department works on a monthly cycle. Although projects are rarely completed on schedule, the monthly routine does give some order to the work load. By establishing artificial end-of-the-month deadlines, managers can help to assure that the work is finished in time to meet newspaper and printer closing dates. Phase one of the typical monthly cycle is the planning sessions attended by Traub, top merchants and promotion executives. Here discussions center on the kinds and categories of merchandise slated for advertising or other promotional support. Many of these choices are dictated by seasonal demands—for example, swimsuits for May or novelties for Christmas—but there is considerable give-and-take as to how the ads should be handled, the best media to use for the promotion and the size of the budget. The purpose of the meetings is to discuss all possible approaches, agree on a general direction and provide the rough framework on which the ad department can build. Once this is accomplished, the advertising vice president assigns an art director/copywriter team to produce the ad.

"There is usually a date set for the finished ad to be presented for approval to the responsible merchant," Spellman adds, "but something goes wrong to postpone the work at least 40 percent of the time. Garments that have to be photographed arrive late from the manufacturer and when they finally show up, they are the wrong styles or colors. Or, as so often happens, we get the right dress beautifully photographed on a lovely model —everything seems to go perfectly. Then, horror of horrors, the merchant decides he really wants to promote a different item that month, so we have to start all over again.

"There's no question about it: being the ad director at Bloomingdale's is like launching the Normandy invasion. Or better yet, it's like being in business and having five hundred unruly clients. Every merchant has the right to say yea or nay on a project, and they don't care at what stage of the process they choose to change your work."

What makes the job tougher still is that many of the merchants consider themselves to be highly capable copy editors and artists blessed with sound instincts for producing successful ads. This egotism characterizes some of the most abrasive personalities in the store. Convinced that they can do the job better than the pros, Bloomingdale's merchandise managers love to add their personal touch to or completely revise layouts before returning them to the advertising department. Worse yet, some write nasty remarks ("This is the worst piece of shit I have ever seen") across the face of the ads. Of course, this kind of obnoxious attack only fuels the antagonism between the merchants and the promotion staff.

The dollar amount of Bloomingdale's annual advertising and promotion budget is, like almost all the store's operating data, a closely guarded secret. An estimate puts the figure at $15 million—but only part of that actually comes out of Bloomingdale's pocket. The established tradition in the retail business holds that merchants should be reimbursed by manufacturers for one half of the costs of advertising the vendors' products. This so-called advertising is an incentive given by vendors to encourage wider advertising of their goods. For example, Murjani, the maker of Gloria Vanderbilt's blouse and jeans collection, offers its retailers co-op funds equal to 3 percent of their total order. So a store ordering $100,000 worth of blouses is entitled to $3,000 in co-op money, provided the retailer puts up

50 percent of the cost of the ads. Co-op money serves as an inducement to the merchants to order the manufacturer's goods and also helps to build demand for the merchandise once it is in the stores. What better way for Murjani to sell its line in key markets like New York and Washington than to be associated in advertising with Bloomingdale's prestigious name?

The percentage of gross sales on which co-op advertising credits are based reflects, in part, the strength, and status of the manufacturer. Generally speaking, the more successful a resource is and the wider its customer base, the less it needs to offer its merchants. One of the most successful clothing lines in the U.S. is Izod, the big maker of men's and women's casual wear. Launched in 1947 by founder Vincent de Paul Draddi, Izod got started when Draddi began selling men's shirts cut from dress fabrics. Draddi also owned the house of David Crystal, an elegant dress-making establishment, and he needed a merchandise line to make up for the cyclical nature of the dress business. The soft and comfortable knit fabrics used in the Izod shirts, and the intriguing alligator emblem that is their trademark, made them very popular with a select group of consumers, including show business celebrities and politicians. This popularity soon snowballed and Draddi found that his new business was bigger than David Crystal.

Izod has grown steadily, and today it is one of the real powerhouse resources, blessed with a strong consumer franchise. People know the brand name and demand it in vastly different types of stores across the country. The product's appeal transcends age, income and social distinctions; it is popular with college students and senior citizens alike. This kind of market strength gives Draddi great clout with the merchants: they need his collection more than he needs them. The loss of Izod can make an unmistakable gap in a store's merchandise selection, while for Izod, the loss of revenue from any one store is minor since the manufacturer has thousands of customers, from Bloomingdale's to Gimbels. Secure in its position and dependent on no one customer, the company is able to limit its co-op spending to 2 percent of sales. This 1 percent difference between Izod and the less established resources can amount to savings of $1 million a year.

For big, powerful major-market stores like Bloomingdale's, the co-op subsidies are especially sweet; and in fact, in many cases manufacturers pay for the entire cost of the ads. In a typical arrangement, Bloomie's assumes responsibility for advertising production costs, but the vendors pick up the tab for the far bigger media bills. In cases where individual vendors are too small to pay the freight alone, Bloomie's ad department puts together package deals combining several manufacturers' goods in a single ad, and the media costs are then shared. This tactic was used for the highly successful "We Believe" campaign. A typical two-page "We Believe" ad in the *New York Times* featured, by name, the garments of eight different resources: Bill Haire for Friedricks, Richard Assatley, Betsy Gonzales for Sonata, Helene Sidel, Morning Lady, L'Zinger, DBA Ltd., and Roselon Industries.

Although manufacturers are required, by law, to offer the same co-op deals to all their merchants, there is considerable flouting of this rule. The reasoning behind the law is that small stores should not be put at a competitive disadvantage, and the Federal Trade Commission does keep a close watch on this. Still, vendors are said to find ways to get around the law in order to satisfy top customers: some simply ignore the rule; others do not require that matching funds be put up for the co-op grants, so that the merchants get use of the money to pay the full cost of his ads. The truth is that the 100 percent co-op policy is offered mostly to the heavy-hitter merchants like Bloomingdale's. These powerhouses are worth catering to because they can sell mass quantities of merchandise and can build a popular base for products throughout their market areas. It is therefore in the manufacturers' own best interest to come up with the big bucks where it counts most. The only major stipulation vendors insist on is that the ads they pay for feature their merchandise by name. For this reason, Bloomingdale's rarely commits to so-called institutional advertising, which promotes the store name only. No one pays co-op money for institutional ads, so Bloomie's has stayed away from it. This policy may soon change in light of Saks Fifth Avenue's highly successful institutional TV campaign stressing the store's increasing emphasis on trendy fashion. Beautifully produced, using striking models and sumptuous location photography, the Saks commercials clearly signaled the store's reawakening as an aggressive fashion merchandiser. Saks's great strength is in its "carriage trade" image, which can attract the growing ranks of middle-class consumers eager to align themselves with elegance and prestige. Bloomingdale's recognizes Saks as a serious competitor and may therefore be forced to start an institutional campaign of its own.

The look of Bloomingdale's advertising has changed over the years, along with the strategy behind it. Postwar chief executives from Krensky on have introduced modern marketing disciplines to complement the store's merchandising practices. Much like banks and insurance companies, retailing is an old-line business with a conservative bent. Merchants are usually among the last business groups to adopt new developments in management science and technology. Use of sophisticated marketing tools, for example, was postponed by most major retailers until the dual pressures of growing competition and escalating business costs demanded more accurate methods of promotion and selling. Only then did many retailers turn to such modern marketing procedures as comprehensive analysis of proposed store sites, computerized direct mail programs in key market areas, and demographic selection of advertising media. Bloomingdale's has been at the forefront of this marketing thrust, and other merchants, impressed by Bloomie's success, have followed suit. Most of the better-managed stores in the industry—Saks, I. Magnin, Rich's, Macy's—are now using these marketing tactics to attract and maintain customers and to generate greater sales through credit card holders.

Bloomingdale's advertising of the past twenty years has been influenced by these marketing disciplines. Advertising concepts and strategies—from the central theme to the fashion photo—have been based on the popular truism "Advertising is good only if it sells." What's more, the adoption of modern marketing principles has meant that the store's advertising has had to conform to two major criteria: first, the ad must reach a clearly defined target audience, and second, the sales message must reflect consumers' current needs and aspirations. Simply put, advertising must be more than pretty, cute or dramatic. It cannot be art for art's sake. It must be designed to sell *specific* products to a *specific* audience.

Through the years, different tactics have been used to achieve these ends. The first of the marketing-oriented ads broke in the 1950s, in what is widely regarded as the "product era." Bloomingdale's ads produced during this period focused on merchandise specifications including price, durability and fabric content. The goal was to sell the public the "better mousetrap": the concept that Bloomingdale's current merchandise was better than the past year's and superior to that of the competition. To make this point, the store borrowed a page from advertising great, Rosser Reeves, who developed the classic marketing strategy, the Unique Selling Point (USP). This involved isolating the very specifications that differentiate or distinguish a product from its competition, making that difference seem crucial, and then hammering it home to consumers. Commonly known, USPs are the American Dental Association's recognition of Crest as a "decay-preventive dentifrice," the lack of caffeine in Sanka, Ralph Lauren's name on a tie and Halston's label in a dress. In the early fifties, Bloomingdale's relied on low prices as its most powerful USP, but it graduated later in the decade to more substantial features, such as brand-name labels and the new wonder fabrics. Bloomie's ads at this time used straightforward, descriptive language; they were designed to inform. Blouse ads stressed not the trendiness or the sex appeal, but the Dacron blend of the fabric. Headlines like "Dacron with a difference" called attention to the blouse's no-iron easy-care feature, and another headline read, "Arnel, carefree and bared." Both are perfect examples of the "better mousetrap" strategy.

This advertising approach changed drastically in the

sixties, as America entered a volatile period in politics, science and art. Madison Avenue reflected this by moving away from the hard-and-fast reliance on product specifications to a new exploration of the psychological and sociological factors in marketing. Many call this the "image era" or, in honor of one of the great practitioners of image advertising, the "David Ogilvy era" (Ogilvy is one of the founders of the huge advertising agency Ogilvy & Mather). With the growing popularity of this kind of advertising, the focus moved from what a product was to how it could enhance the consumer's self-image. Classic campaigns of this era featured the urbane Commander Whitehead for Schweppes mixers and a macho eyepatch-wearing spokesman for Hathaway shirts. In each case, the product representative upstaged the product itself as the main attraction. Schweppes sold an "image" of worldliness, wealth and sophistication; Hathaway aligned itself with masculine good looks.

For Bloomingdale's, which has always borrowed its advertising strategies from developments started on Madison Avenue, the move to image advertising coincided perfectly with the store's upgrading. From the start, management recognized that a new image was necessary to wipe away its reputation as a bargain-basement store. Designed to change the public's opinion of Bloomingdale's and to properly market its new departments, ads of the sixties read like this quarter-pager in the May 19, 1967, *New York Times:* "More French than les blue jeans; more American than a discotheque. That's Fonssagrives-Tiel." Featuring the French-made Fonssagrives-Tiel dress collection, the ad stressed Bloomingdale's involvement with the growing French-American fashion exchange. Young people in both countries were turning on to each other's apparel and Bloomingdale's was leading the way in the States. By the end of the decade, this kind of image advertising had worked its magic, and Bloomingdale's had won its much-sought-after reputation as an innovator and a tastemaker. On to the seventies: Bloomingdale's campaigns of the past decade have been developed to solidify and enhance the gains achieved in the sixties. For the most part, this meant doing everything possible to bolster the store's reputation as a dazzling and inventive fashion leader. Once again learning its lessons from the big package goods marketers, Bloomingdale's adopted the widely used "positioning" strategy—that is, the attempt by a marketer to sell a product or service on the strength of a central theme.

Seven-Up, for example, is positioned as the Un-Cola —the clear, fresh image as an alternative to the dozens of colas; Avis is positioned as the up-and-comer, the hustler, the "try harder" company. Bloomingdale's "positioning" in the 1970s has been built around its motto: "It's Like No Other Store in the World." That phrase is the heart of the positioning effort: the portrayal of Bloomie's as the ultimate shopping experience, as a store in a class by itself, and as *the* source of information on what is "in" and what is not.

From the very beginning of the decade, Bloomie's ads were expressing clear-cut opinions on matters of fashion, from home furnishings to hair length. A typical ad, from the April 30, 1970, edition of the *New York Times,* supports the midi look in hair styles, recommending that customers purchase wigs that are "not too long, not too short." Some years later, the advertising department invented the "Bloomingdale's Man" and the "Bloomingdale's Woman," strikingly handsome models who adorned the store's ads, dressed and styled according to the Bloomie's ideal. The underlying message was clear: "You, too, can—and should—look like this. We declare this to be the epitome of current taste and fashion."

Bloomingdale's ads of the seventies feature the store itself as the ultimate product. Campaigns such as "We Believe" reinforced this theme over and over again. Although the ads were full of merchandise illustrations, the real focus was the bold "We Believe" headline—the expression of Bloomingdale's opinion on emerging fashions. Again the store was "positioned" as a fashion leader, showing its customers what to buy, not what others were buying. " 'We Believe' works because people want us to edit the right fashions for them," Gordon

Cooke says. "They look to Bloomingdale's as a source of information, and they expect this from us."

This positioning strategy has proved to be immensely successful. By establishing Bloomie's as the supercool, up-to-the-minute fashion leader, management has found that it can indeed manipulate consumers, stimulate sales and exert a powerful influence over all aspects of the marketplace. The advertising and public relations department is incredibly effective because it makes the store's followers afraid to contradict its fashion statements, embarrassed to fall out of step with the current look. Bloomingdale's propaganda makes people want to discard perfectly good apparel and furniture in order to replace it with the latest looks featured in the store's ads and show windows. This is precisely the way a carefully cultivated image can translate into dollars and cents. Bloomingdale's put many of its customers in a bind in a recent fall season, for example, by promoting lines of dramatically redesigned casual clothing. In women's wear particularly, the changes were sweeping. Jeans and casual slacks shrunk overnight from the popular bell or flare bottom to a skin-tight, straight-leg design. Fabrics also changed from pre-washed denim to a dark-blue no-fade material, from fine gabardine to corduroy. Ads, catalogues, windows, mannequins, floor displays and swing boutiques showed nothing but the new look. Within a matter of weeks—from the end of summer to early fall—it was apparent to Bloomie's fans that, as usual, to stay in style required substantial investments in new clothes.

"It even works on Bloomie's employees, even though we should know better," says a chic-looking young administrator in Bloomingdale's own advertising department. "I promised myself last summer that I wouldn't buy any new clothes for the fall. My husband and I are saving for a house, so there's very little extra money in the budget. Also, I bought a load of clothes last year that are still in excellent condition, and I wanted to get some more wear out of them.

"But forget it, forget it, forget it! The house had to wait; last year's clothes went to the Salvation Army. As soon as the summer was ending, the new look was evident. I was on the sales floors every day at lunchtime and all I saw was straight-leg pants, designer jeans —a lot of great-looking stuff that I wanted and didn't have. Bloomie's made me feel embarrassed to put on those old bell bottoms, really embarrassed to go outside in them, or heaven forbid come to work in them—so I spent over $600 getting my wardrobe back into style.

"The sickness of the Bloomie's addiction is really evident when you work here. A lot of East Side girls like myself who make only $150 a week spend just about every penny on clothes. And many of my married co-workers admit to spending more than they make here; others who are single and have to support themselves build up tremendous charge account balances so that they can buy now and pay later. Bloomie's advertises everything so attractively that people who love clothes just feel they can't live without the stuff. You know you are a slave to fashion, but you just can't break the bonds."

Bloomingdale's hold over its customers—its recognized mastery of advertising and public relations— makes it a highly sought after ally for national promotion campaigns. More than any other store, manufacturers crave Bloomingdale's cooperation in launching new products. The consensus is that a product pushed by Bloomie's has a good shot at success—and that early success at Bloomingdale's can lead to a smash hit nationally. This was precisely the thinking behind the carefully planned introduction of Yves Saint Laurent's new fragrance line in the U.S. Charles of the Ritz, owners of the Saint Laurent license in the States, knew that the line had all the marks of a winner, and they wanted to handle the introduction with the great class it deserved. The fragrance's name alone—Opium— was a stroke of genius, the kind of imaginative label that says nothing and everything simultaneously. Priced substantially higher than Saint Laurent's first fragrance, Rive Gauche, Opium perfume sells for $40 a quarter ounce, and the cologne for $40 for two ounces (more than twice the price of other prestige colognes). The market for Opium was clearly defined from the start:

the young, daring, sexy and affluent upper middle class —just the group who are turning more and more to "party" drugs such as opium and cocaine. Thus by naming his product Opium, Saint Laurent developed instant rapport with the very people he hoped to sell to.

First introduced in European markets for Christmas 1977, Opium set sales records throughout the Continent. Initial revenues were running at the annual rate of $30 million—an extraordinary accomplishment for a new entry in the crowded and competitive fragrance market. Armed with glowing sales reports, Charles of the Ritz started its U.S. marketing effort in the spring of 1978. Executives here were intent on establishing an exclusive image for the product by purposely limiting its distribution to a select group of prestige retailers— a classic marketing ploy reserved for those very special products that thrive on snob appeal and that consumers will go out of their way to get (the Gucci and Louis Vuitton lines are good examples). Merchants selected, by Charles of the Ritz to carry Opium were Marshall Field, Filene's, Foley's, Garfinckel's, I. Magnin, Neiman-Marcus, Robinson's, Sakowitz, Sanger-Harris, Woodward & Lothrop—and for the all-important New York market, Bloomingdale's and Saks. The launch stores were guaranteed exclusive use of the product for the crucial fall-to-Christmas sales season.

The excitement surrounding Opium—stemming from its outrageous name, the Saint Laurent association and the early European success—made it one of those select products the major stores beg to be allowed to sell. Products with a rich and glamorous image add cachet to a store, build traffic and are often highly profitable. For these reasons, every name retailer in the U.S. wanted a shot at Opium—and Charles of the Ritz's job was to pick and choose those outlets that could do the most for the product. Once Ritz's executives had decided on their choices, presidents of the selected stores were invited to a full-scale product presentation at the company's board room in New York. Here the sales and promotion plans for the fragrance were laid before its prospective distributors. Again reflecting the increasing influence of marketing in the retail business, the presentations were detailed projections of Opium's positioning, advertising and public relations.

"The advertising and publicity is crucial to a product like Opium," says Cathy Cash Spellman, whose agency, Spellman and Company, was assigned to handle PR for the fragrance. "If handled properly, there is an opportunity to present an irresistible image and to make it a genuine status symbol. To pull this off, however, you must surround the product and its promotion with thorough professionals, those who know how to advertise, sell and present a glamour item. That's why we chose Bloomingdale's and Saks as exclusive distributors in New York: Saks has the carriage trade and Bloomie's has the magic. Bloomingdale's advertising and publicity is the best, bar none. Resources like Charles of the Ritz expect more from Bloomie's than any other store. That's why Bloomie's is always on everyone's product launch list."

Major promotions are often cooperative affairs, with the retailer and the resources playing complementary roles. To set the stage for Opium's official introduction to the U.S., Charles of the Ritz and Yves Saint Laurent threw a dazzling black-tie party aboard a ship docked at New York's South Street Seaport (attended by the author). For the event, Saint Laurent completely renovated a four-masted Chinese bark, the *Peking,* fitting it out with striking Oriental appointments, silk banners, wicker chairs, elegant sofas and huge lounge pillows. The guest list included Jackie Onassis, Andy Warhol, Truman Capote, Diane Keaton, Bill Blass, Halston, New York's Governor Hugh Carey and Mayor Edward Koch, Candice Bergen, John Lennon and Yoko Ono, Leonard Bernstein, Cheryl Tiegs, and Jack Nicholson. To entertain the partygoers, Saint Laurent hired famed fireworks expert Zambelli and Chinese sword dancers. The menu included mountains of beef and veal tartare, oysters, roast duck, champagne and caviar. After a night of reveling on the boat, the guests were invited, en masse, to a champagne breakfast at Studio 54. The one-night price tag, picked up by Charles of the Ritz, was $250,000.

The festivities made for a national media event, covered in full by the local television stations (WNBC and WCBS) and by the make-shift newspapers filling in for the big New York dailies, which were shut down by a major strike. "Parties like the *Peking* affair are useful for generating wide consumer recognition almost instantly," Spellman says. "In one night of newscasts, virtually the entire New York market learns of our product and sees it associated with the likes of Cheryl Tiegs and Candice Bergen. The stage is then set for the retailers: customers know of Opium, know they want to try it, and start looking for it. Savvy merchandisers like Bloomie's capitalize on this by designing dramatic displays for the product to keep interest high, giving it good real estate* and featuring the product in a window treatment. Bloomingdale's went one better: they gave Opium an entire window."

Throughout the Opium planning cycle, Spellman worked closely with Gordon Cooke and his subordinates—especially the PR staff. Bloomingdale's advertising and public relations departments is responsible for coordinating the store's role in major promotions of this type. Store displays in all Bloomingdale's branches, newspaper ads and window treatments are readied months before the product goes on sale. Traub is a stickler for excellence here: He wants everything from the floor displays to the full-page *Times* ads to have that special Bloomingdale's glitter. The store's professionalism in this regard is very much a mark of Traub's management.

Bloomingdale's has never extended its mastery of the print media to radio-TV. Top management feels most comfortable with newspaper advertisings, and least so with television. Bloomingdale's has been a major newspaper advertiser ever since Lyman and Joseph Bloomingdale opened the first shop in 1872, but it has only dabbled in television and has never harnessed the tremendous power of that medium. Bloomingdale's contends that promotions for chic, image-oriented products

* The term used in the fragrance business for sales or counter space.

do not translate as well into television advertising as they do in print. This is arguable considering the highly successful television campaigns for Mercedes, Cadillac and Perrier. The truth is that Bloomingdale's is not well staffed with broadcast experts, and the amount of money required for a major-market television campaign is staggering. And Bloomingdale's resources, who must pay for the ads, are reluctant to come up with the heavy budgets required to make any real splash in New York.

"Bloomie's can't afford to do anything in a half-hearted, cheapie way," Spellman says. "It must get enough money from the vendors to buy substantial quantities of air time. It would be counterproductive for Bloomingdale's sales efforts and for its image to mount a nickel-and-dime broadcast campaign. When Bloomie's does anything public, it needs a lot of exposure. Many of the vendors just don't want to come up with the kind of money that requires."

Spellman actually pushed Bloomingdale's into its first real test of television during her reign as the store's vice president of advertising and public relations. She believed that as a live news medium, TV could be used to bring the feeling of spontaneity to Bloomingdale's ads, that it could reinforce Bloomie's positioning as a fashion leader by delivering ads with the impact and immediacy of breaking news stories. "I wanted people to think of Bloomingdale's as an idea place where news is happening," she says. Spellman's persistence, combined with the persuasive arguments of the media salesmen who had hounded Bloomingdale's for years, finally convinced Traub to give the go-ahead for a 1975 Fathers' Day television campaign. Also involved as a strong supporter of this decision was Joseph Schnee, then senior vice president and general merchandising manager for men's wear and home furnishings. A real powerhouse in the management ranks, Schnee joined the store upon graduation from Syracuse University in 1953. Starting in the executive training program, he moved up through the organization, always just a few years behind Traub.

The Father's Day campaign was viewed by Traub,

Schnee and Spellman as a test of the medium. The concept they developed called for a series of ten-second ads, called IDs, to appear on local television news shows. Because of the brevity of the IDs, Bloomie's would be able to run them frequently enough to create the impression of a media blitz. With this plan in hand, Bloomingdale's rounded up its men's wear resources to present the concept and to get their thinking on it. Almost unanimously, they supported the idea and pledged the money to get the campaign off the ground. The reaction of Izod president Vince Draddi was typical: "Anyone who doesn't support this is crazy," he said at the time. "It will work. I am in total support of any imaginative advertising approach." Vendors were willing to bet their money that wide exposure backed by the Bloomingdale's name would be successful—and they were right. Sales for Father's Day 1975 increased significantly compared to the previous year.

This was not, however, the start of something big. Surprisingly, Bloomingdale's reverted to its traditional reliance on print media. The participating resources were pleased with the results, but not ecstatic. Most believed that the improved sales figures were due primarily to general economic conditions, consumer confidence and natural growth in the market. They simply could not justify the greater cost for television advertising over print. Many are as conservative about television advertising as their merchant customers. "I haven't contributed to big television campaigns since that one time," Draddi notes. "I just think that newspapers are the best medium for advertising my products. People see the ads in the paper in the morning and stop in to buy the goods that day. The reaction is spontaneous and immediate."

Internal factors also stalled the move to greater use of television. Schnee, the highest-ranking supporter of the television strategy, died in October 1976; Spellman had already left the store in January. The new ad chief, Doris Shaw, was not as committed to television and the thrust in that direction lost its steam. Still, Bloomingdale's does do limited television advertising, usually tied to seasonal promotions such as Christmas, annual white sales or the opening of new departments like The Main Course and b'way.

In one development, Bloomingdale's has made some imaginative use of the medium by participating in a series of live feature broadcasts with local television and radio stations. Typical of this were the *Morning Break* programs produced by Washington, D.C., television station WTOP and broadcast direct from Bloomingdale's stores in White Flint, Maryland, and Tysons, Corner, Virginia. Arranged by Bloomingdale's former vice president Arthur Cohen and WTOP's program director, Tim McDonald, this represented Bloomie's first ongoing TV commitment in a local community. The deal called for WTOP to bring its cameras into the stores for fifteen-minute live broadcasts on Tuesday mornings. Programming featured Bloomingdale's model rooms, new fashions, housewares and the like. In return for this showcase publicity, Bloomie's agreed to purchase thirteen thirty-second spot commercials on WTOP. A similar arrangement was worked out with local Westchester radio station WFAS, which broadcasts live segments from Bloomingdale's White Plains store. This combined advertising/publicity vehicle comes closest to Cathy Spellman's proposal for developing Bloomingdale's as a news source.

"It will be a top responsibility of the new generation of management—the post-Traub era—to really move Bloomingdale's into full-scale use of television," says a former Bloomie's advertising executive. "All the imaginative developments in communications are taking place not in print but in commercial television, cable and videotapes. In the near future, there will even be complete home information centers with every residence getting its news, stock reports, features and advertising on a compact printout terminal. Bloomingdale's will have to get in on all this—and get in before the competition—if it wants to retain its lead. Bloomie's has a reputation as a promotional mover and shaker: vendors expect it to stay on top of things. Getting first crack at all the best products—and getting all the big co-op money—depends on keeping this reputation. The advertising and public relations department is crucial to the store's continued success. It has helped to make it 'like no other store in the world' and it can help to keep it that way. But unless management continuity can be brought to the function, there will be trouble."

# 7.

# As Bloomie's Goes,
# So Goes the Nation

*Bloomingdale's influence on the American lifestyle is nothing short of staggering. We know from firsthand experience that they've been one of the prime movers in developing the national craze for health and fitness. The store's influence extends all the way to personal philosophy. Our research shows that Bloomingdale's has prompted people to develop a "me" attitude. That is, "I" come first—"I" have to do healthy things to take care of my body.*

George Chapdelaine
Product manager, Hood Dairies

In a nation of merchants—a land dotted with competing retail establishments, large and small—Bloomingdale's has, in recent years, been the most influential of them all. Bar none. For roughly two decades, a single store has captured the imagination and earned the extraordinary loyalty of millions of customers. What's more, Bloomingdale's fame has spread to places many thousands of miles from its nearest branch. Beverly Hills celebrities shop Bloomingdale's by telephone and catalogue; French teen-agers sport Bloomie's T-shirts at Paris's Le Drugstore. There is no denying that this retail institution, which had remained virtually obscure for nearly a century, has in its senior years surfaced as a true phenomenon.

The fascination with Bloomingdale's is one of those

rare developments that defy a simple explanation. Like Coors beer, the Chevy Corvette and Frank Sinatra, Bloomingdale's attracts a large following that just cannot get enough of it. No flash in the pan, either, Bloomie's has stayed popular, garnering new devotees as others have faded and passed away. Although critics may claim that Bloomingdale's is merely the product of a thunderous hype, that explanation, although partially true, just doesn't tell the whole story. Granted, Bloomingdale's has made clever use of the promotional arts, but as political campaigners have discovered, a multi-million-dollar media blitz is not always enough to win the hearts and minds of discriminating people. Other retailers outspend Bloomingdale's many times over, but no other has achieved its superstar status. No business can simply *make* itself loved and adored the way Bloomingdale's is. This kind of devotion to a commercial entity comes from a combination of natural and spontaneous forces. Bloomingdale's set out to achieve great success; it got much more than it ever dreamed possible.

Given this foundation of remarkable popular appeal, everything that Bloomie's says and does carries tremendous weight. Bloomingdale's uses this credibility to expand and secure its great popularity and to dictate the fashion changes that keep merchandise flowing through its branches. Again, the "We Believe" campaign is a perfect example of this. The main thrust of the ads focused not on the fashions themselves but instead on Bloomingdale's *belief* in them. That belief alone apparently convinced Bloomie's customers to spend millions of dollars to buy a new fashion look just weeks after the "We Believe" campaign broke.

This proved fashion leadership, this raw merchandising clout and ability to consistently generate exceptional profits, make Bloomingdale's the object of widespread imitation and duplication. In U.S. retailing, the store takes center stage: customers obey it, the press studies it and the competition copies it. This, in turn, produces Bloomingdale's greatest power—its tremendous influence on the nation's fashion, lifestyle and commerce. Even those who disdain current fashions—who resent the "New York establishment" or may have never even heard of Bloomingdale's—are affected. The truth is that Bloomie's touches almost every American, many without their knowing it.

"There are certain institutions which, by their very position or prominence, are copied by everyone else in that business," says an editor at *Business Week*'s New York headquarters. "The power Bloomingdale's exerts over retailing is similar to that which the *Wall Street Journal* has over business news. Just about everyone in financial reporting regards the *Journal* as the best source of business news around. So every day, in the editorial offices of newspapers, magazines and broadcast stations across the U.S., editors are checking the *Journal* to see what's important and what they themselves should report on.

"Because the *Journal* runs a page-one feature on something, that's reason enough for scores of editors at other publications to consider the topic important. So they assign a local reporter to follow up on the *Journal* piece or to simply paraphrase it. Here's the real devastating aspect of the *Journal*'s power: since everyone else imitates what it says, the *Journal*'s thinking on something becomes accepted fact. Let's assume, for example, that the *Journal* goes with a 'Your Money' feature quoting 'leading financial' experts that the next three months will be a bad time for buying stocks. When the *Los Angeles Times* or the *Miami Herald* picks up on this story and runs with it, a few million more people are led to believe the 'experts' that, for now, extra income should go to savings rather than securities. The casual advice of a few men sitting around a bar in New York comes to national attention and actually influences the way the nation behaves simply because the *Wall Street Journal* carries their comments. The eerie thing is that even people who work in factories in Iowa and who would never dream of reading the *Journal* come under its influence. They follow a story about stocks in the *Des Moines Register* and *Tribune* and never realize that the *Wall Street Journal* is the source of that story.

"The same chain reaction is responsible for Bloomingdale's pervasive influence. Men who suddenly find very narrow Bill Blass ties for sale in their favorite shop in Kansas City never realize that the new-style skinny ties are there because a resident buyer in New York saw them at Bloomie's, thought they were the coming thing and placed an order for her Kansas City clients. Apparel, furniture and housewares buyers shop Bloomingdale's the way business editors read the *Wall Street Journal:* both Bloomie's and the *Journal* are powerful because they are viewed as prominent and because they are widely copied."

Many in the fashion industry—and this applies to fashion furnishings as well as apparel—talk about Bloomingdale's influence in terms of a "ripple effect." Thus if one views the retail industry as a pond, with Bloomingdale's at the center, products dropped into Bloomingdale's create waves or "ripples" over the entire surface. Those parts of the pond (or industry) farthest from the center (New York) are the last to feel the effect of the splash. Though this analogy is somewhat distorted (Los Angeles, one of the farthest points from New York, certainly reflects current fashions faster than does a closer city like Indianapolis), it presents a generally accurate illustration of how fashions move into the mainstream. As the trendiest and most daring major store in the U.S., Bloomingdale's has played a pivotal role in the way merchandise is produced and presented for sale to the nation's consumers. That role is to serve as a "test market" for new and innovative products.

Virtually all consumer products are test marketed before they are widely distributed. Sophisticated marketers like Procter & Gamble and Colgate-Palmolive rarely introduce a new soap or toothpaste nationally without first testing the product's appeal in small, representative markets like Syracuse, New York, or Sioux City, Iowa, whose demographics reflect that of the nation as a whole. By monitoring all aspects of the product's promotion, packaging, performance and price on a limited basis, the manufacturer can respond to and correct problems while distribution is still on a small scale. Test markets are thus like laboratories for the companies, enabling them to sample real consumer reactions and to make products more attractive before the investment is made in national distribution. What's more, if testing reveals that a product does not have strong enough appeal to consumers regardless of the changes the company makes, it will likely be dropped.

It is of course better to find this out when forty thousand units of toothpaste have been produced for Syracuse rather than after fifty million have been produced for the entire nation.

In much the same way, makers of trendy and innovative high-fashion goods view Bloomingdale's as a test market suitable for their kinds of merchandise. Will satin baseball jackets take off as a hot casual item for young women? Will fashionable career women accept western style suits for office attire? Will platform beds with built-in stereo sets, priced at $3,500, appeal to young marrieds? Can the sophisticated housewife be made to believe that her kitchen is incomplete without a clay casserole for $75? The feeling is that if products such as these can be made to sell, Bloomingdale's is the one store that can get the ball rolling. No other store has such a large following of adventurous customers actively trying to be the first to adopt a new food, furnishing or fashion. And no other store has the credibility, the cachet and the national spotlight required to transform innovations into widely accepted staples. "Bloomingdale's is definitely a trend setter," says Murjani's Warren Hirsh. "They introduced our Gloria Vanderbilt jeans and made other stores and hip consumers aware of them. Many buyers from other stores shop Bloomingdale's regularly and pick up ideas there."

There's a saying popular in marketing circles that "nothing happens until a sale is made." This truism underlines the importance of Bloomingdale's to its major resources. Until that first sale is made, until a new product or style gets into the hands of consumers, it is nothing more than an idea. Bloomingdale's uses its influence to get those first sales made, to put the product into circulation and to get for it the attention, the word of mouth and the press coverage it needs to achieve national distribution.

"When I designed my first line of bed sheets back in the late sixties, this was considered a rather radical departure for the linen industry," says Bill Blass. "It was a time when most of the sheets sold were plain white—the more daring consumers were pretty much limited to solid pastel colors. We take designer sheets for granted now, but the introduction of fashion to so basic a merchandise line as sheets was considered revolutionary at the time. Surveys showed that many consumers thought it silly and unnecessary to have any kind of designs on their bedding. I was the first American apparel designer to do a line of sheets; I knew that it would be the ground-breaker—the one to open the field to a host of imitators. Since we were the first, however, we recognized the need to cultivate, among consumers, a taste for extravagant sheets. The manufacturer, Springs Mills, believed from the start that Bloomingdale's could do this for us better than any other store. Bloomingdale's could sell the concept, get it into fashionable homes and help to establish it as a status item. The line did not sell well at first, but Bloomingdale's hung in there, promoted it heavily and eventually built up very substantial sales.

"Bear in mind that Springs Mills was not in business to sell exclusively to a small, chic group in New York. To be successful in the sheet business, you must sell millions and millions of them across the country. Bloomingdale's is important because it does help to get this *national* momentum going. Once other stores noticed how well Bloomingdale's was starting to move our sheets, they jumped on the bandwagon and placed orders too. Designer sheets are now the most important part of the linen business, thanks in good measure to Bloomingdale's. People in Ohio who make their beds at night with Bill Blass sheets may not know it, but they've been influenced by Bloomingdale's."

Many people who are deeply involved in the fashion industry are continuously amazed at Bloomingdale's lopsided impact on national tastes and trends. A good measure of this stems from Bloomingdale's willingness to serve as a test market or, as one ready-to-wear manufacturer put it, a "fashion guinea pig." Bloomingdale's accepts this role because, as noted previously, this assures it the leadership image so crucial to its success. "The key thing to remember is that they are willing to listen to new ideas and new concepts," Hirsh adds. "They are open-minded." By this very willingness to take chances, to gamble on new and unproved fashions, Bloomingdale's naturally comes up first with more of the hot new fashions than any major competitor. This is the big payoff from the store's successful gambles; on the other side, however, are the heavy markdowns it must take on the losers.

"Other major retailers do experiment with new concepts, but this is usually limited to in-store boutiques set up just for this purpose," says Elizabeth Gutner, fashion director of *Seventeen* magazine. "Bloomie's is the only large-volume retailer that experiments storewide. Because they are willing to assume the risks, Bloomingdale's frequently sets the trends nationally. We know that a great many of our young readers in places far from New York wear junior clothes that first came to national attention through Bloomingdale's. Odds are that if Bloomie's didn't take a chance and promote these fashions, they never would have seen the light of day."

This is certainly true for new-wave French designer Kenzo. A great favorite of young women in their late teens and early twenties, Kenzo produces a collection that has been called "costumed" and "amusing." The line is known for its casual, fresh and original look, sporting baggy pants, full-cut tops and soft, comfortable fabrics. Bloomingdale's believed in the look at first sight and became the first major store in the U.S. to promote Kenzo and to grant him a separate boutique. The collection proved to be extremely popular, became a big favorite with Bloomie's young customers, and was subsequently picked up by savvy retailers across the nation. This in spite of the fact that Kenzo keeps no marketing arm or sales offices in the U.S., so buyers must go to his place in France to place orders. "Young women in the Midwest, the South and other regions far removed from New York now wear and adore Kenzo clothes," Gutner adds. "Fashionable retailers have been carrying the designer's line for several years now. I daresay, however, that none of them would have done so if Bloomingdale's didn't take the first step and prove that the line would be successful."

The press plays an integral role in developing and magnifying Bloomingdale's national influence. The store's proximity to the powerful New York news media makes it a center of attention for fashion and feature editors based not only at the city's dailies but at such national publications as *House Beautiful, House & Garden, Esquire, Seventeen, Cosmopolitan, Time, Newsweek*. Often, photo spreads on fashions in these magazines are shot at Bloomingdale's, and leading editors call on their contacts at the store for inside information on buying trends and emerging fashions. It is a matter of habit and convenience. Let's say the fashion editor at *Esquire* gets a call from Ralph Lauren's public relations agency hyping the prediction that Lauren's "Western look" will be the significant apparel design statement for the fall. Lauren's line is loaded with suede jackets, cowboy boots and ranch shirts, and the agency wants to get the collection moving by trying to create a bandwagon effect. A positive story in *Esquire* could do just that—make readers across the nation believe that the Western look is the ticket to high fashion for 1978. Well aware that PR agencies are often hyping products and styles that have no strong appeal, the *Esquire* editor is experienced enough to check on the "Western look" story with an objective retail source to find out whether the suede jackets and the boots are really moving. Journalists like to maintain a few trusted contacts whom they can call on regularly to verify stories, and virtually every New York-based fashion reporter has numerous contacts at Bloomie's. And because of the store's premier position, they often turn to Bloomie's first (and sometimes *only* to Bloomie's) to document their stories.

Here again we see the staggering impact of Bloomie's influence on the national fashion scene. A young buyer who happens to be a cooperative and quotable press contact may become a major authority on the popularity of emerging fashion. If the buyer raves about the early success of the "Western look" (which the buyer may do to help move his own inventories), chances are the story of this "hot new fashion" will go national. Although many responsible reporters check more than one source, few bother to call on more than two or three, and Bloomingdale's is almost always on the list. "I find that my personal appearances at Bloomingdale's are always covered by the press," says Gloria Vanderbilt. "When I travel out of New York, people know me from the publicity I get at Bloomingdale's."

"You could draw a straight line between Bloomingdale's furniture promotions and the house furnishings press," says former Bloomie's advertising VP and *House Beautiful* editor Doris Shaw. "Bloomingdale's is the most exciting furniture merchant in the country; it presents its collections better than anyone else. Add to this the fact that major magazines are only blocks from Bloomingdale's, and you understand why so much press coverage centers around that store. *House Beautiful*, for example, routinely sends reporters and photographers to Bloomie's to cover the model rooms, special theme promotions and the like. What Bloomingdale's is featuring gets more national attention than any other store. That leads to imitation."

Most of the nation's interior decorators are small-time operators, working out of their homes and serving a limited clientele. A far cry from the big-name New York and Los Angeles designers in terms of money and talent, the vast majority are duplicators rather than innovators. Constantly on the prowl for decorating ideas, they scan the professional journals and furnishing publications for concepts they can use on the job. Quite often, the pictorials they see in the periodicals are shot at Bloomingdale's or are Bloomingdale's-inspired. "A lot of the small-town decorators also browse through Bloomingdale's when they are in New York or near one of the branch stores," says Rick Zolt of the Stark Carpet Company, which sells to interior designers only. "The ideas they pick up go home with them and find expression throughout the country. Sooner or later,

Bloomingdale's furniture statements, such as the steel-and-glass look, are found in furniture stores and living rooms everywhere."

Bloomingdale's influence goes beyond its traditional strongholds in apparel and furnishings and extends all the way to food, lifestyles and personal philosophy. A dramatic example was Bloomie's crucial role in almost single-handedly launching the frozen yogurt craze, which has changed the eating habits of millions of Americans.

A relatively new product concept, frozen yogurt dates back to 1971, when The Spa, a popular student restaurant near Cambridge's Harvard Square, was searching for a health food substitute for ice cream that could be served from a traditional custard machine. The Spa's owner asked Hood Dairies—the big New England milk, cheese and yogurt producer—to come up with a suitable product. Sensing a new marketing opportunity, Hood's technicians accepted the challenge and developed frozen yogurt—a cultured dairy product that has many of the physical properties of ice cream but is made with allegedly healthier ingredients. "Frogurt" (Hood's trade name for its product) proved to be a great favorite at The Spa, which promoted it as an ice cream substitute and sold it in a cone. Encouraged by the product's popularity, Hood tried to expand Frogurt's distribution in the early 1970s. Positioning it as an ice cream substitute, Hood salesmen made their rounds at Boston's coffee shops, Dairy Queen–type drive-ins and fast-food restaurants. The results were discouraging: few outlets liked the concoction enough to place an order. To many, Frogurt seemed like a parity product—just another ice cream in an already crowded field.

A few years later, in the mid seventies, a fundamental change in department store retailing emerged, which to Hood's surprise vastly improved the outlook for Frogurt. Until this time, department stores had viewed their in-house restaurants as customer conveniences; most of them lost money, and the others were only marginally profitable. But Bloomingdale's, always the innovator, decided to change this by merchandising, for the first time, the one part of its store that did not produce ever greater profits—the restaurants. Bloomingdale's former food service director, Jack Terporten, won management approval to strip away the stodgy tea sandwich shop, typical of most department stores, and replace it with a trendy restaurant designed to appeal to the free-spending eighteen-to-thirty-five-year-old customers who are so important to Bloomie's. This age group is less sensitive to food prices and is less likely to dawdle for hours over coffee and a muffin. By building a chic and hip-looking restaurant, Terporten believed he could enhance Bloomie's image as an exciting place to shop and could turn food into a consistent profitmaker in the process.

After considerable planning and behind-the-scenes experiments, Bloomie's unveiled 40 Carrots, its version of the modern department store eatery. As fresh and natural-looking as the old restaurants had been old-fashioned and musty, the 40 Carrots restaurants are decorated in a Country French motif with plants, earthtone fabrics and wood beams. The menus, also radical departures from the old standards, feature fresh salads, quiche, and pita bread sandwiches. 40 Carrots has the general appearance and feel of a health food shop without being limited to traditional health foods. It has served as the model for what are now known as "healthy restaurants."

Impressed with the 40 Carrots concept, executives at Hood believed that the new restaurants could be excellent vehicles for getting Frogurt off the ground as a widely distributed product. Bloomie's was approached with the idea, liked it immediately, and agreed to put Frogurt on the 40 Carrots menu. The rest, as they say, is history. Bloomie's 40 Carrots became the rage in the branches as well as at Fifty-ninth Street, attracting big lines of customers willing to wait an hour or more to sample Frogurt. The eateries were extremely profitable from the start, made Bloomie's freaks even more adoring of their store, and attracted new customers on the strength of the Frogurt alone. "I was always a Saks and Bendel's shopper almost exclusively, until, believe it or not, I got turned on to Frogurt," says fashionable career women Nancy Stern, a resident of Manhattan's upper East Side. "The stuff is so great and I became so addicted to it that I would go to Bloomingdale's just to get it. While I was in the store, I started picking up a skirt here, a blouse there. Before I knew it, I was shopping more at Bloomingdale's than at Saks."

But the real point is that Bloomingdale's imaginative handling of Frogurt fueled the product's success from coast to coast. "Bloomingdale's even taught us a marketing lesson," says George Chapdelaine, Hood's product manager for Frogurt. "While we had been trying, unsuccessfully, to sell the product as an ice cream substitute, Bloomingdale's recognized that it should be positioned, instead, as a 'healthy food'—a meal rather than a snack. Rather than serving Frogurt on a cone, Bloomingdale's put it in a small bowl, covered it with fresh fruit, nuts, and other toppings, and called it 'lunch.' People loved the idea: it was healthy, refreshing and inexpensive. Positioned this way, it was definitely a product whose time had come."

Hood's marketing staff used what it saw as the magical appeal of the Bloomingdale's name to convince other department stores and small food shops to carry and promote Frogurt. Working through a so-called seeding process, Hood's salesmen moved from major city to major city, focusing first on the big, prestige retailers. Since word of Bloomingdale's success had already spread throughout the industry, the more aggressive stores were easy targets for the Hood spiel. Virtually all the Federated units fell into line; so, too, did Lord & Taylor, Jordan Marsh, Bon Marché and Neiman-Marcus. Once these powerful merchants introduced Frogurt in their marketing areas, getting the smaller food shops to follow suit proved to be relatively easy. "But Bloomingdale's really started the ball rolling in a big way," Chapdelaine adds. "Our studies show that before Bloomingdale's started positioning Frogurt as a lifestyle food, only 3 percent of the public ate any kind of yogurt; now 25 percent do. For us, the difference has been overwhelming: sales of Frogurt have increased from less than 100,000 gallons per year before Bloomingdale's became a customer to more than one million gallons a year now."

Frogurt's success depended, to a great extent, on the image developed for it. And developing images is Bloomingdale's forte. "Bloomingdale's has taught every other retailer how to package, promote and sell an image," says Nancy Benson, fashion editor of *Cosmopolitan* magazine. "In the process, they've turned the whole country on to everything from designer clothes to store-name underwear."

Not everyone agrees. A minority of powers in and around the retail business believes that Bloomingdale's has peaked as a fashion influence—or never really had much clout at all. One former Bloomingdale's vice president, now a high-ranking executive with a financial services outfit, believes that Bloomingdale's has a reverse impact on current trends and styles. He insists that much of Bloomingdale's merchandise clashes with middle American tastes and values and that this leads out-of-town buyers to move in an opposite direction from Bloomingdale's. "Some buyers and manufacturers visiting New York shop at Bloomingdale's to see what *not* to do," he says. "They believe that if it's selling at Bloomingdale's, it will probably be too way out for their middle-of-the-road clientele. This reflects their experience with items like the midi skirt: Bloomingdale's did just great with it while most retailers took a huge bath."

Bill Blass, although a great admirer of Bloomingdale's, believes the store's influence is on the wane. "When it comes to New York, especially, Bloomingdale's influence is less now than it was just five years ago. This is a sophisticated town and other retailers are catching up and setting trends themselves. Bloomingdale's is still a major influence outside New York, however."

Ralph Lauren, whose career is so closely intertwined with Bloomingdale's, is the most cynical of all: "No store has everlasting power over anyone or anything. No one can make winners out of losers. Merchandise has to be good and the people have to decide that for themselves."

Halston, who likes to relate questions about Bloomingdale's to his own experiences, puts it this way: "Does Bloomingdale's influence this country? Sometimes yes, sometimes no. It's that way with all of us who are so-called fashion leaders. People say that the Halston look has been widely imitated, but there have been times when my work resulted in negative influence. Like Bloomingdale's, which fell on its face in its effort to sell couture, I've had my ups and downs.

"When I was first establishing a national reputation for myself, Ali McGraw was becoming a hot property in Hollywood. Soon after completing the film *Love Story,* she was asked to be at a command performance for the queen of England and to meet the queen on stage. Ali asked me to design something special for her —something great to wear. I put a lot of work into it because I wanted to get as much attention from her appearance as she did. After all, the fashion page always notes who did the clothes—it was my chance to make a big splash in the right circles. Anyway, Ali came on stage and looked like a clown. Her tits were hanging out and the dress was all out of sorts with her body. Her husband, Bob Evans, wanted to punch me in the mouth. The real fault, however, was Ali's: being nervous she put the dress on backwards. I don't think I had much influence on the fashion industry from that experience. We all take our lumps now and then."

# 8

# Transplanting the Magic

---

*Scene from the television show* Rhoda:

*Brenda Morgenstern: "Rhod, look at this story in the Times. A woman went berserk in Bloomingdale's yesterday and charged twenty thousand dollars' worth of panty hose and cheese."*
*Rhoda: "I wonder how she broke it down."*
*Brenda: "Five dollars for cheese."*

The flaming love affair that binds Bloomingdale's and its upper East Side worshipers is not a New York exclusive. Since the late 1940s, when management first set out to conquer suburbia, Bloomingdale's has won a loyal following as it slowly snaked its way north and south of Manhattan's Gold Coast.

In many ways, the Bloomingdale's customer relationship is even more intense outside the city limits. For many suburban dwellers, the store is viewed as an oasis of "city chic"—a dose of cosmopolitan style and a welcome change from the double-knit boredom of the local landscape. "There's a sense of desperation about it—you simply have to get to Bloomingdale's at least twice a week," says Mrs. Roslyn Bloom of Yonkers, New York. "The need is compelling—almost undeniable. For women like myself, it's an urge to touch base with city life, to keep up with the real world beyond the suburbs. Many of us are reluctant suburbanites, here for business reasons or for the better schools. We miss the hustle of the city, the variety, the sharp-looking people, the museums, and most of all the great places to shop. We hate Sears, Korvettes, Altman's and all the other stores that try so hard to be vanilla ice cream. That's for dyed-in-the-wool suburbanites, not us. We are suburban people with city heads. We are Bloomingdale's people. When the children are out of college, most of us will probably move back to the city.

"I waited twenty years for Bloomingdale's to open a modern store out here. We always had the New Rochelle Bloomie's nearby, but that was a small, half-baked Bloomingdale's. Every time I heard rumors that a brand-new Bloomie's was going to be built here, I called the New York store and cheered them on. I had to wait until 1975 for the White Plains store to open; and when it did, I was standing in line for three hours before the opening. Now I'm perfectly content. Who could ask for more: I have a new car, all the free time in the world, and a Bloomie's minutes away."

Development of the Bloomingdale's branch network has been characterized from the start by an extraordinary phenomenon: wherever Bloomingdale's breaks ground, its reputation precedes it. Two related forces are at work here: The store's powerful propaganda machine and its position as a national trend setter combine to spread "the word" long before the branch is built in a new community. Pent-up demand builds like steam in a pressure cooker, virtually assuring profitable business from the day the ribbon is cut. Witness the hoopla greeting the grand opening of Bloomingdale's Tysons Corner, Virginia, unit in 1976. The first-night black-tie party on the store's selling floors turned out to be one of the social events of the season in the Washington area, attracting a roll call of big-name pols and bureaucrats.

More important from a pure business standpoint, almost seventy thousand Washington area residents signed up for Bloomingdale's credit cards before the doors were opened and management was able to confidently predict $30 million in sales for the first year. This kind of instant customer base is unheard of in the retail industry; and it is largely responsible for Bloomingdale's ease in obtaining expansion capital from its parent company, Federated Department Stores. A branch store's ability to by-pass the traditional incubation period and start generating profits soon after opening is the envy of the industry. When retail chieftains at any of the store chains like Lord & Taylor, Macy's and Saks sit around the board room pondering branch construction, one key factor gets the closest scrutiny: return on investment. Prove to decisionmakers (for Bloomingdale's, the board of directors of Federated Department Stores) that new branches will produce a healthy return on investment, and the green light is flashed for construction. The best way to convince top management that return on investment will be good is to develop a track record of successful branch development. Since Bloomingdale's branches are known to be highly profitable, there is little difficulty in obtaining the necessary cash. And a lot of money is required. A site as large as 20 acres (at $30,000 per acre) is required for a good-size branch; that can amount to $600,000 for real estate alone. Construction costs, which average $50 to $60 per square foot for most department stores, zoom up to $75 for the kind of exotic units Bloomingdale's builds. Add it all up, and you can figure about $20 million for a modern 250,000-square-foot department store.

For Bloomingdale's, interior store design is the most important, and costly, aspect of branch development. It's an area on which Bloomie's works harder and spends more than any other major retailer to produce stores that have a striking, modernistic appearance and interesting yet functional layouts. The planning for this falls into the bailiwick of Barbara D'Arcy, now vice president of store design; but Marvin Traub also takes a personal interest and is involved in every key decision from the choice of overall themes to color patterns.

Interior design work begins shortly after the launching of a new branch is officially announced to the public.

(Traub and the senior vice presidents may review the prospects for a new branch for a year or more before that announcement is made, but nothing is released to the press until a deal is signed.) As soon as the architects have completed plans for the physical structure, D'Arcy and her staff of about thirty draftsmen and designers are presented with drawings of the interior. What they see is a huge physical shell, containing only escalators, fire stairs and mechanical devices such as air-conditioning units. Everything else—"Whatever the customers can't buy," D'Arcy likes to say—is planned and designed by her department.

Step one is to produce a "block plan": working directly with D'Arcy, Traub allots an exact amount of square footage for each store department and then selects that department's location in the store. Once this plan is complete, interior designers are assigned to prepare a full visual blueprint for each department, including plans for wall coverings, merchandise presentation, lighting and colors. "This takes considerable talent because, in the early stages, the designers have to work with space, color and texture and do it all on paper," D'Arcy explains. "There is no chance to test out ideas as we go along, because we have to present a finished plan to management months before the store is built."

The final visual, which is a very detailed blueprint for the interior of the store, goes through a lengthy approval process. Vice presidents, buyers and merchandise managers get to see the plan and to suggest changes in it. The idea is to make certain that the interior design is valid from a business as well as an aesthetic standpoint. Only a buyer may know, for example, that the Washington market is not a good one for cloth coats and that floor space in that branch would be better utilized for dresses. Since sales per square foot is, as we have noted, a key yardstick in retail financial performance, management must be sure to allot every type of merchandise the precise amount of space it needs for the most efficient and productive sales.

The approval process is always rife with political infighting as arguments arise over space allotments, departmental locations and merchandise presentation. In planning the White Plains store, for example, D'Arcy designed the men's shoe department around a raised and carpeted platform that served as a built-in showcase for the shoes. But the shoe buyer objected to this approach, claiming that D'Arcy's treatment was too unorthodox for the relatively conservative Westchester consumers. D'Arcy took her case to Traub—and won. As usual, he was the final arbiter, and his decision turned out to be sound.

Once the internal disputes are settled and the interior blueprint is approved, D'Arcy signs off and turns the plan over to Bloomingdale's construction department. Staffers here arrange for the labor and materials, contracting some of the work to outsiders and doing some of it at Bloomingdale's own carpentry shops, located in the flagship store and at the warehouses. "It's a mammoth job, going from blueprint stage to finished store," D'Arcy says. "When we first start, it seems as if we'll never get done, but somehow we do, and the results are usually quite pleasing."

For competitive reasons, many aspects of Bloomingdale's branch development programs are never publicized. How close, for example, to another Federated store can a new Bloomie's branch be built? No one outside the corporate inner sanctum really knows. Sometimes the divisions compete head on: Bloomingdale's Garden City, Long Island, branch, for example, was built only blocks away from another Federated unit, Abraham and Straus (a similar situation now exists in White Plains, N.Y., with Bloomie's and A and S competing against one another.) Observers believe that in cases like this, the divisions are allowed to open branches near one another if the local market is big enough and if the stores have distinct merchandising strategies. "All of the stores are competitive in our trading area and naturally there will be some dovetailing with A & S," Traub said at the opening of Bloomingdale's Garden City branch. "But then, it's not so bad if there's competition in the company." Federated will not even comment on this. As is the case with most major retail organizations, secrecy is its corporate byword. The retail business is so intensely competitive that management is reluctant to release any more information on internal policies than is required by law.

Although most of its Fifty-Ninth Street loyalists view the Manhattan flagship as the one and only Bloomie's, a substantial branch network has emerged and is integral to the store's overall operations. In fact, branch operations now account for more than half of Bloomingdale's revenues—close to 60 percent of total volume. (This milestone was first reached in 1977 and clearly illustrates the strength of the flagship unit, which for years matched the combined revenues of more than ten branches.)

The location, year of opening, and size of Bloomingdale's full-service branches are shown below:

| | | |
|---|---|---|
| New Rochelle, N.Y. | 1947 | 110,000 sq. ft. |
| Fresh Meadows, N.Y. | 1949 | 149,000 sq. ft. |
| Stamford, Conn. | 1954 | 228,000 sq. ft. |
| Bergen County, N.J. | 1959 | 274,000 sq. ft. |
| Short Hills, N.J. | 1967 | 250,000 sq. ft. |
| Garden City, N.Y. | 1972 | 260,000 sq. ft. |
| White Plains, N.Y. | 1975 | 263,000 sq. ft. |
| Tysons Corner, Va. | 1976 | 235,000 sq. ft. |
| White Flint, Md. | 1977 | 263,000 sq. ft. |
| Chestnut Hill, Mass. | 1978 | 117,000 sq. ft. |

In an attempt to capitalize on the popularity and profitability of its home furnishings departments, Bloomingdale's embarked in the early 1970s on a long-planned mini network of specialty stores limited almost exclusively to furniture. Much smaller than the full-service branches (which made it easier to get zoning approval to build the stores), Bloomingdale's home furnishings units average about 85,000 square feet. They are located in Scarsdale, New York; Chestnut Hill Massachusetts; Manhasset, New York; and Jenkintown, Pennsylvania. All were built between 1971 and 1973.

Although Lachman and Traub prefer to put it another way, the home furnishings chain is Bloomingdale's first large-scale disappointment—that is, in the sense that the stores have never approached initial sales projections. Observers believe they have been profitable, but only marginally so, a fact that Bloomingdale's management has admitted, although indirectly. Traub states that no additional furniture stores will be built, but elaborates only to the extent of saying that Bloomingdale's now prefers to build full-service stores. The truth is that top executives at Bloomingdale's and Federated are not satisfied with the record of the home furnishings venture, but in typical corporate fashion, no one wants to accept blame. The alternative is to hide behind a veneer of success. Bloomingdale's brass want to manage the news about their stores—and they want it to be good news only.

A bright spot in these furniture branches is the unit in Chestnut Hill, Massachusetts. Located about seven miles from downtown Boston in the Chestnut Hill Mall, the store emphasizes modern, trendy furniture, which appeals to customers in the area who were bored with the more traditional styles featured at Paine's and other home-grown outlets. "Speak to anyone in this town about furniture, and they are likely to mention Bloomingdale's," says Julie Hatfield, fashion editor for the *Boston Herald American*. "The store has very attractive furniture—a lot of unique pieces you don't see elsewhere—and they keep bringing in new stuff all the time. The interest level stays very high. Boston didn't have a furniture store like this until Bloomingdale's came along."

The popularity of the Boston store led Bloomie's to break tradition by opening, in the fall of 1978, a branch devoted almost exclusively to apparel. The unit was built adjacent to the Chestnut Hill furniture store, and the move actually turned the operation from a small specialty outlet into a full-service department store. The location met the prerequisites for Bloomingdale's expansion: Chestnut Hill is in an affluent suburban market; Boston's suburbs are experiencing steady growth; and Bloomie's, by way of its furniture store, had already established a solid reputation there. The market was presold.

Here again, Federated was allowing sister stores to

compete in close quarters. Filene's, also a Federated division and for years the most famous store in Boston, has a major store in the Chestnut Hill Mall too. Observers believe that the opening of the new Bloomingdale's unit in the same shopping center is an attempt by Federated to tighten its grip on a growing, lucrative market by controlling more of the retail space.

Except for the Boston unit, Bloomingdale's home furnishings centers have suffered from poor sales volume because they have never generated substantial traffic. Armed with furniture alone, store managers seem unable to duplicate the excitement of the full-service Bloomie's. Moreover, two of these units compete head-on with full-size Bloomingdale's branches in the same market areas. This frustrating situation exists in New York's major suburban outposts. In Westchester County, the Scarsdale home furnishings unit competes with the White Plains store; on Long Island, the Manhasset home furnishings branch competes with the Garden City store. The Manhasset store, the first of the Bloomingdale's home furnishings units, is located on a fashionable shopping strip called the Miracle Mile. Sales at this branch, which opened in 1971, got off to a good start and stayed strong until the 1972 christening of Bloomingdale's full-service branch (which carries the full spectrum of Bloomingdale's merchandise, including furniture) in nearby Garden City. Soon after the stores started competing, the big Garden City branch (260,000 square feet) began to draw customers away from its furniture-only Manhasset sister (119,000 square feet), and sales in the latter plummeted. The Garden City branch proved to be too formidable an opponent. A bold and handsome store, designed by the noted architect Edward Durell Stone, it is a block-long, four-level structure of precast concrete. Said Traub at the grand opening, "In an effort to offer the excitement and diversity of our Fifty-ninth Street store, the new unit has shops within departments, most with different décor and architectural concepts." Here, too, Bloomie's reputation presold the market, generating forty thousand new credit card customers before the store opened.

Interstore competition is also one of the factors that

plagued Bloomingdale's branch in New Rochelle, New York, the only Bloomingdale's store to actually cease operations as a traditional retail outlet. It was transformed into a furniture clearance center in 1977. Plans for the store, the oldest branch, were set in motion in the early 1940s, several years before management's decision to upgrade Bloomingdale's from a second-rate retailer to a high-fashion merchandiser. "It was 1947 when we started planning the rebirth of Bloomingdale's —and at that time the New Rochelle store was already being worked on," Lachman notes. "This kind of branch unit did not fit in with our new plans because it was to be rather small and ordinary-looking, but it was too late to apply the brakes. If we had had the benefit of hindsight, we never would have opened the New Rochelle store."

The store was located on the main shopping drag in New Rochelle—then a bustling and affluent town about fifteen miles from midtown Manhattan. The branch held its own through the first two decades of operation, but started facing serious difficulties in the 1960s. As a transitional neighborhood located close to the Bronx, New Rochelle became a haven for working blacks seeking to move up to the promise of suburbia. Predictably, as some whites fled, more and more blacks moved in and the demographics of the community changed drastically. Although pockets of middle-class Jews and Italians remained (and are still there today), the first newcomers—solid, middle-class blacks—were soon joined by working-class and poorer groups. The main business district deteriorated rapidly as fast-food shops, cheap clothes stores and discount drug outlets replaced the established merchants who had catered to New Rochelle's affluent community for years. Litter was piled in the streets, rowdy youths challenged passers-by, and the fear of crime kept customers away at night. Reflecting the seediness of its surroundings, the Bloomingdale's branch was dingy, poorly lit, cluttered and generally neglected. It was clearly not flattering to Bloomingdale's image.

Recognizing that New Rochelle was the weakest member of the Bloomingdale's family, the United Store

Workers (organizers of the flagship store) tried to make it the first of the branches to be unionized. "We had our eye on the branches for years," says Ida Torres, a union executive. "New Rochelle was a prime target because the store was a mess and working conditions there were not good. Our efforts forced the store to hold an election, but we lost. Not because there was no need for a union—only because management duped the workers, raised some salaries and made limited improvements in order to turn the vote against us." (Bloomingdale's denies this, insisting that the vote was a clear indication of the employees' satisfaction with their employer.)

For years Bloomingdale's executives in New York put the mounting problems of the New Rochelle branch on the back burner; it was somehow like a black sheep in the family that no one seemed to know how to handle. Allocating capital for needed physical improvements was out of the question. Why invest in a dying neighborhood? Boarding up the store was also unacceptable. Management feared the action would hurt Bloomingdale's reputation and would damage Federated's image with the investment community. In a major public company like Federated, which is widely followed by Wall Street analysts, every management move is tempered by the impact it will have on the company's stock. Even the slightest sign of failure can make Wall Street turn sour on the company, causing selling pressure on the stock. As a result, the price of the shares can drop precipitously. "We tried to hold on to New Rochelle because the store remained in the black until the end," says Lachman, who was then running Bloomingdale's. "It is a painful experience to close down a branch, and so we held off as long as possible. We analyzed the situation regularly, trying to perceive some clear sign of what to do. After a while, we realized it would have to close—exactly when to take the action was the question."

The death knell came in 1975 with the opening of Bloomingdale's dazzling new branch in nearby White Plains, New York. Attractive and commanding in appearance—sporting an ultramodern design that resembles a huge steel-and-glass mirror—the White Plains store proved to be an instant winner. Soon after the grand opening, Traub remarked that the White Plains branch ranked near the top of the list of Bloomingdale's most successful stores. Bloomie's loyalists who had long supported the New Rochelle branch in spite of its sorry appearance quickly abandoned her in favor of White Plains.

"The writing was now clearly on the wall," Lachman says. "We realized that New Rochelle could no longer hold its own. Also, we now had a sparkling new presence in a part of Westchester County that was experiencing solid growth and that had a promising future. It was time to draw the curtain on New Rochelle. That's when we decided to turn the unit into a furniture clearance center." Although management refuses to say flat out that the New Rochelle branch failed, that is exactly what happened. The combination of changing social conditions in the store's market area, procrastination by top management and the success of the White Plains store joined forces in a one-two-three punch that KO'd the New Rochelle unit after almost thirty years of operation.

For the most part, Bloomingdale's evolution as a branch store organization has been successful. All the full-service branches are known to be highly profitable, most chalk up substantial annual sales gains and all are rooted in strong markets. "The Bloomingdale's branches are all winners," says Frances Blechman, a retail-industry analyst for Merrill Lynch, Pierce, Fenner & Smith. "They bring excitement to communities that have never experienced this kind of retailing before."

This is certainly true of Bloomingdale's foray into the Washington, D.C., area. When Bloomie's moved near the nation's capital in 1976, in the affluent suburb of Tysons Corner, Virginia, it took over a structure previously occupied by the then bankrupt Landesberg's store. The battle to break into the Washington market had been a tough one, encompassing seven years of site planning and zoning battles. Tysons Corner marked Bloomingdale's first full-store opening away from the New York metropolitan area, and the venture was considered a test of its ability to transplant the New York style to a different part of the country. Management's fears about this were evidenced by its cautious approach to store design and merchandise selection. A conscious effort was made to present a toned-down Bloomingdale's.

"They obviously wanted to take a conservative approach when they opened here," says Jerry Knight, a business reported for the *Washington Post.* "Management was a little scared about how people here would react to the Bloomingdale's emphasis on way-out goods and displays, so they purposely designed the store with much less electricity than the famous New York version."

But early success at Tysons Corner encouraged Bloomie's to move closer and closer to the New York look. By the time Bloomingdale's was ready to open a unit in nearby White Flint, Maryland, in 1977, management felt confident enough to design a flashy and exciting store, considered by many to be the best of the branches. White Flint is located in the wealthy, WASP country of Maryland's Montgomery County. "Outsiders think all the money in Washington is in Georgetown, but that's not true." Knight continues, "Montgomery County has the really big bucks and the people there have become Bloomie's fans. Also—and this seems to be a Bloomingdale's phenomenon wherever the stores are located—the White Flint branch has become a tourist attraction. Many of the visitors to the nation's capital now want to see Bloomingdale's as well as the Washington Monument."

Bloomingdale's success in the Washington-area market has come at the expense of two established stores there: Lord & Taylor and Garfinckel's. Both are known to have suffered since the arrival of the showy newcomer and both are stepping up their fashion merchandising strategies to try to compete more effectively. They may, however, be in for more bad news: the retail rumor mill is predicting that a third Bloomingdale's store will be built in downtown D.C. in the early 1980s.*

*     *     *

* Bloomingdale's refuses to comment on this.

Throughout Bloomingdale's suburban expansion, management has plotted each move with pinpoint accuracy, leaving nothing to chance. Once the decision was made to transform Bloomingdale's into a high-fashion merchandiser, all branch planning was put on ice for almost six years. (The New Rochelle and Fresh Meadows outlets, planned in the early 1940s, were completed in 1947 and 1949 respectively.) No new stores were opened until 1954 (Stamford, Connecticut). The purpose for the freeze was to utilize all executive talent in the process of making Fifty-ninth Street into a retail showplace.

"At a time when we needed every bit of skill and effort to line up new displays, develop inventive advertising and set up striking displays, we had no inclination to spread ourselves thin opening new branches," Lachman says. "Only when we were confident that the job had been done on the home front and that Bloomingdale's was well on the way to a leadership position did we give the green light for the Stamford store and a full branch network."

Bloomingdale's based its branch development on a secret strategy of avoiding competitive situations, so the earliest units were built away from shopping centers, malls and established department stores. Lachman feared that proximity to competitors would detract from Bloomie's emerging identity and jeopardize its still fragile image. This insistence on isolated locations changed only after Lachman felt confident that the Bloomie's name was well established and could hold its own against the field. The Short Hills, New Jersey, branch, opened in 1967, was the first Bloomingdale's store to be built in a modern shopping center.

The branch expansion has been distinguished by a high level of professionalism. Management picked its sites carefully, studying the pros and cons of all prospective locations to be sure that they met three key criteria:

- A base of at least 500,000 potential customers within a ten-mile radius.
- A market area family income level of at least double the national average.

- A community with a proved preference for tasteful and fashionable merchandise, evidenced by the prior success of other quality merchants in the area.

In a nutshell, Bloomingdale's focused on its most valuable market: white, upper-middle-class, well-educated executive and professional families. Prime targets were such high-income bedroom communities as Great Neck, Scarsdale, Short Hills, Manhasset, Garden City, Harrison, Greenwich, Georgetown—all of which are now serviced by Bloomingdale's branches.

"We never put a Bloomingdale's in any place where we didn't think we could bring with us the flavor of Fifty-ninth Street," Traub says. This prerequisite is crucial to the success of Bloomingdale's branch network. Real growth in modern department store retailing comes from merchandising expertise, and this is Bloomingdale's great strength. Bringing trendy fashions and innovative promotions to markets previously lacking this type of retail excitement is what it does best.

"People are tired of being mass merchandised to," says Philip Hawley, president of Carter Hawley Hale Stores, a national retail conglomerate. Hawley's statement refers to the attempt by many retailers to sell large quantities of commodity goods in sterile and predictable surroundings. The emphasis in stores like this —including Ward, Sears, Caldor, Penney and K-Mart— is on the mechanics of efficient selling rather than the selection of interesting fashion merchandise. Here financially oriented *operations* executives call the shots; at Bloomingdale's, the top brass, with the exception of Lachman, are imaginative merchants up from the buyer ranks.

For more than two decades now, the suburbs have been inundated with operations-oriented stores—mass merchandisers who have built thousands of units to sell tires, lawn mowers, double-knit suits and other uninspired goods to the local home owners. Many suburbanites, especially those in the more sophisticated communities, yearned for an alternative—for the trendy type of goods Bloomie's is famous for.

"Bloomingdale's emphasis on breaking fashion has been a key factor in their successful branch network," says Joseph Ellis, retail-industry analyst for Goldman Sachs. "They recognized that fashion would be a growth force in discretionary consumer spending and that many customers consider fashion to be essential in all merchandise categories, from clothing to linens. Bloomingdale's recognized early on what others failed to perceive: that department stores are ideally suited to merchandise fashion to *local* tastes and that fashion itself is a growth vehicle that has swept over wider and wider categories in apparel and nonapparel merchandise. A particularly well merchandised department store organization can provide the excitement of a hundred different small specialty stores in each of its branches and can develop fashion capabilities that far exceed that of its merchandising competition."

"Bloomingdale's caught the other big retailers sleeping on the job," adds Fran Blechman. "When Bloomie's started its branch network, even Saks, Bergdorf's, Lord & Taylor and the like were not in tune with the spreading fashion awareness in this country. These old-line retailers were not changing their stores to cater to the growing ranks of customers seeking something new and different; Bloomingdale's had the field to itself."

Also important to the success of the branches is the fact that Bloomingdale's sinks its teeth into each of the store's surrounding communities. By conceiving of the branches as more than depositories for merchandise—by establishing them as cultural, educational and amusement centers—Bloomingdale's keeps the spark of public interest extraordinarily high. Each branch is staffed with a local public/community relations director, responsible for supervising the unique Bloomingdale's mix of special events, charity affairs, adult education courses, parenthood classes and fashion shows. By investing in these extracurricular activities, Bloomingdale's makes itself part of the fabric of a community—a responsible corporate citizen rather than a commercial parasite. It also positions itself as a center of action, suburban style.

A look at an activity list at Bloomingdale's White Plains and Scarsdale branches is revealing:

- Interior Design Course—a six-week lecture course on interior design, in cooperation with Pace University School of Continuing Education, taught by William Spink, director of Interior Design, Bloomingdale's Scarsdale store, and Kathleen King, professor of Interior Design, Pace University, Pleasantville/Briarcliff. Mr. Spink focused on "Bloomingdale's Approach to Interior Design," and Ms. King focused on the "History of Furniture from Ancient Times to the Present Day."
- Cuisinart Cuisine—complimentary demonstration of the use of the Cuisinart Food Processor machine.
- Benefit Party—Bloomingdale's Scarsdale celebrated the opening of its fall designer rooms, "Overture to the '80s," with a musical evening for the benefit of the Westchester Symphony Orchestra. The musical highlight of the evening was a performance by the New York Pro Arte string ensemble.
- The Blooming Life—Bloomingdale's bloomed indoors in a week-long festival of plant life interpreted by Westchester experts—Amodio's Garden Center, Heathcote Florists, Lord and Bumham Greenhouse Company, Nabel's Nurseries and Sprain Brook Nursery. Flowers and plants were displayed throughout the store.
- George Plimpton on Sports—spectators went behind the scenes with George Plimpton as he recounted his observations of athletes' states of mind before, during and after the "big event."
- "Avedon Photographs"—famed fashion photographer Richard Avedon showed through slides his history-making retrospective show at the Metropolitan Museum of Art.
- "Garden with C. Z. and Elvin"—C. Z. Guest, well-known gardening author, and Elvin McDonald, garden editor of *House Beautiful,* dem-

onstrated the art of making the most of holiday centerpieces and floral arrangements with seasonal flowers and plants.

- Sweets for Holiday Giving—Anita Pritchard, author of *Anita Pritchard's Candy Cookbook*, tempted her viewers with her mouth-watering candy delights, all made with fresh natural ingredients based on old-fashioned recipes modernized for today's kitchens.
- Design Lecture/Tour—Ric Lawler, director of Interior Design, conducted complimentary tours explaining the concepts and trends he used in the White Plains designer rooms for the fall.
- Beauty Center Seminars—hair care, skin care and make-up techniques were demonstrated.
- Prenatal Clinics—a series for expectant mothers and fathers was conducted by Mrs. Yvonne Shapiro. Lecture demonstrations included prenatal care, development of the baby from conception to birth, delivery and care of the newborn.

"You can spend your whole life in that store if you want to," says Judy Zolt of White Plains. "You find yourself gravitating to Bloomingdale's—and only Bloomie's—because that's the only store that's exciting."

After two seasons of Bloomingdale's instruction in Chinese painting, cooking, marriage counseling and drug-problem solving, one Garden City woman summed it all up in a letter to the store manager: "I feel like I've received my college degree from Bloomingdale's U."

Success comes on many levels. For Bloomingdale's, the success of its branch network is several notches below that of its New York flagship. From the most profitable store in Bergen County to the least profitable in Fresh Meadows, all the branches (except New Rochelle) have proved themselves to be good, solid performers—ahead of local competitors, but nowhere near the superstar class of the Fifty-ninth Street store. Although Bloomingdale's management has undeniably brought a sense of excitement and fashion to the suburbs, it has never been able to make the suburban stores look and feel as dynamic as the flagship.

One reason for this is internal: trying to get Bloomingdale's buyers, store designers and fashion coordinators to think beyond the Fifty-ninth Street store at which they are based is a constant battle for top management. "The branches are good, but there's definitely something missing," says Ralph Lauren. "You don't walk into a suburban Bloomingdale's and get the same pulse that throbs through the New York store. Their branch stores shine next to some of the local competition but not next to their own mother."

Traub disagrees. "I have no reason to make excuses for any of the Bloomingdale's stores. We think they are fine examples of exciting merchandising—all of them. Granted, it's hard to perfectly duplicate Fifty-ninth Street anywhere else, but we purposely put the stores in areas with similar demographics so that we can conduct typical Bloomingdale's operations in the branches."

But despite Traub's claims that all is well, management is acting to try to bring more of the flagship's excitement to the branches. "The need to better present or merchandise the branches is a problem we are aware of and are working to correct," admits Gordon Cooke. "Every store and department manager, every buyer and merchandise executive, has been issued marching orders from the top to do more to coordinate promotions throughout the branches."

For the India promotion, a special branch store design coordinator was hired. Based at Fifty-ninth Street (and reporting to D'Arcy), the coordinator traveled to the branches to help them set up departments and displays first introduced in New York. Traub wanted every branch to have at least three shops with Indian themes: ready-to-wear, home furnishings and accessories. The coordinator took plans and sketches for these departments to the branches and worked on their implementation with local display managers. This set the precedent for an ongoing program, and a similar routine is now being followed for standard seasonal promotions, fall, spring and Christmas. Management hopes that the appointment of the design coordinator will alleviate some of the problems inherent in branch merchandising, but observers wonder just how effective one individual can be in this area.

"Bloomingdale's only real threat is that its branches could get lackluster," says David Bell, Bloomingdale's former director of design. "If management ever takes it too easy—rests on its laurels and forgets to keep the edge in the branches—the store could face its first real trouble. To tell you the truth, I personally believe they've fallen behind already—and I think the demands of the branch network have had a lot to do with this. That's why I tell young decorators coming out of school to work for Macy's now—that's where the action is."

Talk such as this rankles Bloomingdale's branch managers, executive management at Fifty-ninth Street and, equally important, the chiefs at the parent corporation, Federated Department Stores. Federated's management counts on Bloomingdale's, as the brightest star in its organization, to set the pace for all units and to make the company highly attractive to the investment community. So it is safe to say that Bloomingdale's branch expansion, and the effect this is having on the store's overall merchandising style, is being closely monitored by two masters: one in New York and one in Cincinnati.

# 9

# Where the Real Power Lies: Cincinnati?

*I'll never forget my first day on the job at Blooming-dale's. I rode up that rickety old wooden escalator, saw the shoddy surroundings and said to myself, "Krensky, I think you made a mistake." The higher up in the floors I went, the more certain I was that coming to work at Bloomingdale's was a terrible blunder.*

Harold Krensky
Chairman of the Executive Committee
Federated Department Stores

It is only fitting that Bloomingdale's, itself an over-achiever, should be part of a talented family. And so it is. Bloomie's corporate parent, Federated Department Stores, is the nation's largest department store group and is widely considered the best of its kind anywhere. Many of the prestige names in American retailing belong to the organization, each with a distinct identity and merchandising strategy. The unifying element that runs through the Federated empire is strength—that is, virtually all the divisions dominate the markets they serve. Federated is at the top of the cutthroat retail jungle—and it stays number one—because it is managed to perfection.

First impressions of Federated can be misleading. On paper, the corporation appears to be a loosely knit federation of largely autonomous and quasi-independent retail entities. This is the way chairman Ralph Lazarus and chairman of the executive committee Harold Krensky like to portray their company. It harks back to Federated's founding fifty-one years ago as little more than a holding company for its four charter divisions. The concept of independent stores working together for the common good has proved immensely successful for Federated throughout most of its existence and top management does everything possible to make it seem that this is still the *modus operandi*. But the truth is that the tough competitive climate of recent years has shaken Federated right down to its boots and caused a dramatic change in operating style.

Federated is in one sense a highly visible company and at the same time one the average consumer knows little about. The vast majority of Americans shop at at least one Federated store, and many frequent two or more. Federated remains obscure, however, because it is known to the public by its divisions only, rather than by its corporate identity. And those who shop at more than one Federated unit rarely know that they are in fact sisters in the same business organization. This is one of Federated's great strengths: all its operating divisions have clear and distinct identities, and in terms of public awareness, each stands on its own.

One important point to be made from the start: Federated is not a chain store outfit. The very distinction between each of the divisions is, in fact, part of what separates Federated from the chains. Generally, chain organizations such as Sears, K-Mart and J. C. Penney are highly centralized operations controlling hundreds or thousands of almost identical stores. Management determines what it considers to be the ideal store and every unit in the chain is designed to imitate the model. The accent here is on sterile and functional surroundings, central buying and hair-splitting efficiency. All major decisions are made at the headquarters level, and local executives are mostly glorified office managers. All stores in the chain sell under the same name, have similar physical layouts and stock virtually identical merchandise. Herein lies a great weakness of the chains: when it comes to fashion merchandise, consumer tastes vary too greatly across regions and localities to be well serviced by headquarters purchasing. Only those retail organizations granting genuine authority for merchandise selection to local managers can compete effectively in fashion goods. Although Penney's, Sears and even Korvettes have launched major advertising campaigns designed to position their stores as fashion centers for the trendy junior clothes market, it is all too obvious to discriminating consumers that they cannot deliver on the promise. "Divisional autonomy has always been what separated department stores from chains," says Arnold D. Becker, retailing specialist and vice president of Cresap, McCormick & Paget, the prestigious national consulting firm. "By centralizing, you start to homogenize things. You lose some of the local identity that is crucial in department store retailing."

By remaining fairly loose in structure and controls, Federated has, through the years, retained the high degree of local identity that let it cash in big in the fashion markets. From coast to coast, in every major region of the country, Federated is represented by at least one powerful division. Most are elite, high-powered merchandisers selling goods above the midlevel of the price spectrum. All appear to their customers to be independent corporations.

Federated's divisions are a mixed bag of retail ventures ranging from prestige department stores to supermarkets. Some of the divisions are similar to Bloomingdale's; others have little in common with their famous sister. Most are known to be quite profitable, others are just barely in the black. In general (except for A & S), the older, more established divisions—most of which are comprised of standard department stores—are the best performers. The glamour divisions—those most closely related to Bloomingdale's—are Burdine's and I. Magnin. Both carry trendy, relatively high-priced merchandise which appeals to the fashionable upper middle class. The stores are smart-looking and classy, featuring a wide selection of designer goods.

Burdine's—launched in 1898 as little more than a frontier trading post—now has stores throughout southern Florida's affluent communities, including Miami,

Dadeland, Westland, Pompano and Hollywood. A favorite shopping stop for vacationers and winter residents, especially in the Miami area, Burdine's also enjoys the patronage of transplanted New Yorkers hungry for a high-fashion retail environment.

I. Magnin, another Federated jewel, operates twenty-three stores from Seattle, Washington, in the north to La Jolla, California, in the south and eastward to Washington, D.C. I. Magnin & Company began in San Francisco in 1876 as the idea of Mary Ann Magnin, the founder and, until her death in 1943, the guiding inspiration of the company. The principles she established —for style, quality and taste—still remain at Magnin. The store was also one of the earliest American fashion retailers to see potential in branch stores and it opened its first, in Los Angeles, before the turn of the century.

The second tier of Federated divisions includes A & S, Bullock's and Filene's. These stores are positioned as lower-priced versions of Bloomingdale's, featuring merchandise that leans toward middle-of-the-road. The outrageous fashions (like those of Zandra Rhodes) that are the hallmark of Bloomingdale's are rarely found here.

Filene's is one of the more interesting of these divisions. Long famous for its exceptional bargain basement, as well as the quality merchandise on its main sales floors, Filene's is a Boston institution that was founded in 1852 by an immigrant tailor. One of the earliest stores was located on Boston's Washington Street, the crossroads of the city's subway system. It stands today as a fashion center not only for Boston but for much of New England. Filene's led the way in New England in building suburban branch stores, and today there are thriving units in major malls and shopping centers in Greater Boston; in the Cape Cod Mall at Hyannis; in Warwick, Rhode Island, near Providence; and also in Worcester and Chestnut Hill, Massachusetts. The 1977 opening of a branch store in Manchester, New Hampshire, marked Filene's entry into still another state. One of the best-known features of the downtown Boston parent store is the Automatic Bargain Basement, where goods must sell within thirty days or be given to charity. Clearance goods from Bloomingdale's and other Federated divisions often wind up here.

One of the few divisions that clearly break out of the Federated mold—and one that has experienced major financial difficulties—is Gold Circle. In contrast to the elaborate structures and lush interiors of Bloomingdale's and Burdine's, Gold Circle is a bare-bones mass merchandiser. It is, in fact, a chain store operation within Federated, stressing price, wide assortments and convenience. The division was started in 1967, and the first store opened in Columbus, Ohio, in the spring of 1968 and quickly gained wide customer acceptance. By the end of 1976 Gold Circle had established twenty-five branches in Ohio and two in Kentucky. An aggressive expansion program was started in 1975 with the opening of three new stores in Rochester, New York. Gold Circle entered the California market in 1976 with three branches in Sacramento and then moved into San Jose in 1977. Three new stores were opened in the Pittsburg, Pennsylvania, area in November 1977. Promotionally aggressive and designed to appeal to young, budget-minded families, the stores are all located in suburban shopping areas, each has about 100,000 square feet of floor space, all on one level, and most have adjoining leased grocery stores. Gold Circle has not to date achieved the success Federated had projected for it. Expansion into new markets was held up for some time until profits were boosted at existing units. Management now claims that Gold Circle is finally on the road to sustained profitability.

The Federated division most dissimilar to Bloomingdale's is Ralphs. With the acquisition of this major regional supermarket chain, Federated became a truly diversified retail empire. The move jells with Federated's master plan of bringing merchandising know-how to every type of retail operation.

Los Angeles was a sleepy town of eight thousand when George A. Ralphs opened his first grocery store, but from the little store on the corner of Sixth and Spring streets, George and his brother and partner, Walter, built a major business. Ralphs opened a second store in 1911, and by 1936 had expanded to twenty-five markets. Long before consumerism became fashionable, Ralphs was working to streamline its services, gearing them to its customers' special needs. Before the turn of the century, Ralphs built overnight accommodations, including stables, to make it easier for farmer customers from outlying areas to do business. Later, in Greater Los Angeles, Ralphs learned to boost sales by stocking foodstuffs with special appeal to the various ethnic groups living in the area. In 1967 Ralphs became a part of Federated, and under this parentage grew even faster. By 1978 the company was operating 100 stores in southern California and in northern parts of the state. Ralphs has its own dairy-processing and ice cream plant, deli kitchen, bakery and meat-processing center. But in spite of its rapid expansion, Ralphs has been a dark spot in Federated's earnings picture since 1976. Tremendous price wars in Ralphs' markets have had a devastating impact on the bottom line, producing slight losses for the division. Federated has learned all too well that the supermarket business is a tough one even for the experts—and even more so for those trained in the far different world of department stores.

The other Federated divisions are Boston Store, Bullock's Northern California, Goldsmith's, Gold Triangle, Lazarus, Levy's, Rich's, Rike's, Sanger-Harris and Shillito's.

Federated prides itself on the ability to cater to local tastes in spite of the fact that its divisions cover such a wide geographic area. Fred Lazarus, Jr., Federated's founder, liked to illustrate "the intricacies of keeping up with the customer by pointing out the regional variances of taste. In Federated's Eastern stores, merchandise is more tailored, usually more simple. As it comes further west, it's more ornamental. I think you could sell women's red underdrawers much faster in Cincinnati and Columbus than you could in New York or Boston. I don't think the women in the Middle West are any wilder, but it's just a difference in the taste level or what they think is a stunt or cute. The important thing is being alert to it, and testing it sufficiently to find out what's in demand among your customers.

"If it strikes, then you hit hard with everything that you have. It's a gift that someone with a statistical, legalistic mind, frozen up on the dollars and cents side of the business, can't learn very easily. It takes a flexibility of outlook and openness to innovation, experimentation. It's much easier to teach what the figures represent to a person who has this flexibility, than it is to teach a statistical person how to become flexible. The really good top manager is the guy who's enough of a schizophrenic to start out in the beginning with this knowledge of flexibility and customer demand, and learn the other."*

Federated's public stand on autonomy is found in this statement from a stockholder publication:

> Because the company founders felt that Federated should not become a chain of identical stores with a common name and common merchandise trying to appeal to a mythical common customer, new merchandising concepts have been developed and tailored to the changing needs of the American consumer. Operating control has remained at the local level where management can closely relate to the needs of customers and community.
>
> Federated believes that a corporation, like an individual, has a duty to be an involved citizen in the community. This is even more important for department stores. By the very nature of their presenting total services, department stores are involved with most of the major elements of society.

Although some of this is corporate fluff—and no longer as true as it once may have been—the statement does give some insight into exactly how Federated's divisions became part of the fabric of their local markets. Many of Federated's most important divisions are old established ventures, many with a long history of family ownership. In the majority of cases, all were

---

* Memorial pamphlet compiled by the Lazarus family.

acquired by Federated only after they had established themselves as major factors in their home communities. This legacy of independence is something Federated has always acknowledged and has tried to retain as much as possible. To his credit, Fred Lazarus recognized that relying on local expertise is the best way to profitably manage a far-flung business organization. As powerful merchants joined Federated throughout the years, existing management was asked to stay on to run the business, taking only long-term advice and direction from the headquarters office in Cincinnati. Although this hands-off policy is no longer always the rule—the divisions are often subject to much closer scrutiny these days—it applied to Federated's operations for most of its life, and still does to a greater extent than for any other comparable department store group.

One peculiarity of Federated's organization reflects the traditional emphasis on independence: each division has its own chairman as well as president. In most cases, large, multidivisional public companies such as Federated reserve the title of chairman for the head of the parent body; division chiefs are usually called directors, vice presidents or presidents. But Federated's division chiefs are called chairmen even though they have no boards of directors to supervise. The distinction is important because it reveals the extent to which Federated goes to preserve the identity of local management and to give the impression of divisional independence.

Federated gets high marks for the caliber of executives running its divisions: most are savvy and experienced merchants thoroughly familiar with their local markets. Appointments to the top two posts at each of the divisions must be approved by Cincinnati (Bloomingdale's chairman Traub and president James Schoff, Jr., were appointed to their positions in 1978 by Harold Krensky); all other posts can be filled by divisional management without Federated's approval. Obviously, the parent sets standards for the kinds of managers it wants to see in the middle and upper ranks, and these are routinely followed. The goal is a balanced executive team of chairman and president to head each division, which means dividing the responsibilities between a financially oriented manager and a strong, experienced merchant.

The former Lachman and Traub team at Bloomingdale's is a perfect example: Lachman made his mark as a corporate controller and always focused on the financial end of the business; Traub, as a buyer and merchandise manager who came up through the ranks, retained responsibility for the purchasing and selling of goods. Expertise in both areas is essential for the well-run department store, especially one experiencing the kind of major branch expansion that Bloomingdale's underwent during the Lachman-Traub era. "Federated's tandem management decisions are usually good ones," says Bartley S. Durant, chairman of the Emporium group, a San Francisco-based operation that competes with Federated. The two kingpins of the Federated empire, Lazarus and Krensky, also balance each other out. Krensky says that the ideal retail executive would be half Einstein, half Picasso. Lazarus, for his part, says it will always take two individuals working together to achieve that mix of talents.

At age sixty-five, and a second-generation Federated scion, Ralph Lazarus is the company's master merchant. His father, Fred Lazarus, Jr., helped change Federated in 1945 from a holding company to an active operating company—one serving as a central driving force for the formerly independent divisions. Although this plan was not initially favored by the divisional chairmen, Fred Lazarus got his way by pulling a gutsy power play: unless the others agreed, he threatened to remove the F. & R. Lazarus and Shillito's stores from the Federated family. The senior Lazarus was convinced that Federated needed some semblance of operating unity to meet the competitive demands of the coming postwar period. His threat succeeded in getting the others to fall in line. Lazarus became Federated's chief executive, and he opened a small headquarters office in Cincinnati.

Ralph Lazarus assumed the chairmanship in 1967 and has held it unchallenged for more than a decade. An indefatigable worker, he operates in a rather per-

sonal and informal style. Before visiting one of the
Federated stores, he is known to review carefully the
names of people he will be meeting with, including those
in lower management; thus when he arrives, he is able
to converse with his subordinates on a first-name basis.
This kind of recognition can be very endearing to middle management employees. Feeling that the "great
man" knows of their presence helps motivate them to
put in the long workdays Federated expects. Lazarus is
one of those talented manipulators who know how to
hit and hug, how to charm and terrorize. His major
function at Federated is the development of long-term
planning: determining how and where the various divisions should expand, reviewing new acquisitions and
generally spearheading the corporation's future growth
pattern.

Krensky, on the other hand, gets deeply involved in
day-to-day operations. When red warning lights flash in
the divisions, Krensky is the first to know about them
and to take corrective action. A cordial, friendly and
down-to-earth executive, Krensky is highly regarded and
widely liked throughout the industry. His forte is the
maintenance of strict financial controls, which he believes distinguishes a solidly run operation from a sloppy
one. This means carefully analyzing divisional performance on a monthly basis. If Federated's 10 percent
annual growth criterion is not achieved by any of the
divisions, Krensky wants to know it. And if he thinks
he alone has the answers, he will relate them to divisional management loud and clear. He is especially
sensitive to excess inventories. If, for example, financial
projections call for an economic slowdown, Krensky
uses the full force of his office to get divisional managers to toe the line and reduce inventories. This is
indicative of the changing nature of Federated's par-
ent/division relationship. The absolute autonomy of the
past is gradually giving way to limited doses of central
control. This is not the image Federated wants to project, however, and so it is carefully downplayed.

Krensky dislikes the reputation he has gained as a
hard-nosed financial man, preferring to think of himself
as a well-rounded merchant. And observers in and out

of Federated give him high marks in this regard, calling him a gracious and talented man, with a trained eye for fashion as well as balance sheets. In an exclusive interview (only the second in his thirty-seven-year retail career) with the author, Krensky reminisced about his life, the development of Bloomingdale's and the present-day Federated: "I came to Bloomingdale's after stints as a newspaperman and as an executive with a Boston retail outfit. I always wanted to live in New York, so when the Bloomingdale's offer came, I jumped at it. I was so much of a New Yorker at heart that even when I lived in Boston I rooted for the Yankees, not the Red Sox."

A former chief of Bloomingdale's, Krensky came to the store in 1947 as a young merchandising executive. It was at this time that J. E. Davidson was first planning the store's transformation—a process in which Krensky would play a major role in the years to come. He recalls: "It was a very exciting place to work as a young man. Ever since I was a child I had wanted to work in New York. When I finally got there I couldn't believe it was really happening to me." Perhaps this explains the man's continuing love affair with the city and with Bloomingdale's. In a highly unusual setup for a top executive of a multibillion-dollar organization, Krensky does not work at the Cincinnati headquarters. Instead, his office and residence are in Manhattan, just a city mile from Bloomingdale's. "The crazy thing about this company is that the president can live wherever the hell he wants to," says a Federated staffer. "I wish I could do that." Krensky communicates daily with headquarters, attends board meetings in New York and Cincinnati, and logs 150,000 air miles annually visiting the Federated divisions.

Krensky lives in New York because he likes it best and considers it home. He is still known to occasionally ride the subway to Bloomingdale's, enter the store through the subway entrance and make his way up the floors, checking out the activities as he goes along. Krensky's jaunts to Bloomingdale's are the only divisional visits he makes without first calling the store principals to announce his coming. It is not the man's style to make surprise spy missions; his stops at Bloomie's go unannounced because they are usually for pleasure rather than business. "He likes to stop and chat with salespeople," says a former Bloomingdale's vice president. "Krensky is a genuine gossip—if there's any dirt to be known about someone, he's the man who can tell you about it. Not that he would say anything truly bad—he's really a delightful person."

It is obvious that Krensky's supervision of Bloomingdale's is a labor of love. This is important, as it gives Bloomingdale's a powerful ally at headquarters—a crucial factor in getting the money for branch expansion. All divisional requests for new branches—as well as all capital expenditures of $1 million or more—must first be approved by Krensky, Lazarus and president Harold Goldfeder and then by the board of directors. Having a friend at the top helps to move things along.

Federated is a massive retail organization. The dynasty boasts 323 stores; 46,372,000 square feet of space; $2.5 billion in assets; $242 million in long-term debt; 15,851 managers and professional employees; 54,179 sales workers; 16,813 office and clerical workers; 3,551 craftsmen; and 1,817 technicians. Women comprise 81 percent of the sales workers and 48 percent of the managers and professionals, while ethnic minorities account for 14.5 and 8.7 percent respectively. Federated's total annual sales* exceed $4.9 billion; pretax income $384 million; net income after taxes, $196.5 million; and common stock per-share earnings top $4. The company's sales break down regionally as follows: West, 28 percent; Southeast, 17 percent; Midwest, 21 percent; Southwest, 11 percent; and Northeast 23 percent. Of total department store sales, 41 percent are in cash and 59 percent by credit. Flagship stores account for an average of 27 percent of total sales; branch stores the remaining 73 percent. (Here, again, we can see the comparative strength of Bloomingdale's flagship store, which accounts for about 40 percent of that division's total sales.)

---

* Figures as of January 1978.

## NET INCOME

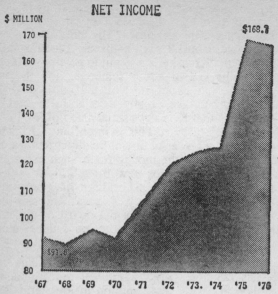

$ MILLION

$168.7

## NET SALES

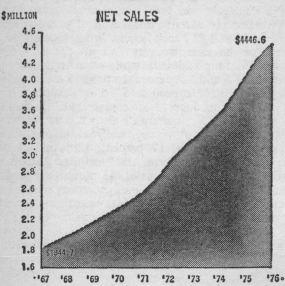

$MILLION

$4446.6

## COMMON STOCK DATA

| | Dividend per share |
|---|---|
| 1959 | .50 |
| 1960 | .52½ |
| 1961 | .55 |
| 1962 | .58¾ |
| 1963 | .63¾ |
| 1964 | .72½ |
| 1965 | .77½ |
| 1966 | .83¾ |
| 1967 | .85 |
| 1968 | .92½ |
| 1969 | .97½ |
| 1970 | 1.00 |
| 1971 | 1.00 |
| 1972 | 1.04 |
| 1973 | 1.08 |
| 1974 | 1.16 |
| 1975 | 1.22 |
| 1976 | 1.38½ |
| 1977 | 1.49½ |

The graphs and table above clearly illustrate Federated's continuous sales growth, long-term earnings growth and excellent common stock dividend record.

With more than 48 million shares of stock outstanding—much of it owned by institutional investors, including pension funds and bank trust departments—Federated is a closely watched company on Wall Street. Its stock is one of the most widely followed on the New York Stock Exchange, and is often touted by professional analysts at most of the big brokerage concerns. Federated's popularity with investors stems from its image as an aggressive fashion merchandiser; the company is seen as leading the retail field—calling the shots and setting the trends—and that's the kind of image that gives an otherwise bland retailing stock a bit of "sex appeal" in the market. Some of the best-managed and most consistently profitable corporations in the U.S. have luckluster stocks. The reason is clear: in spite of Wall Street's sophistication, even the big money managers want a stock they can get excited about. Federated manages to keep "the street's" attention largely because of the magical appeal of its prestige stores, notably Bloomingdale's. When it comes to department store stocks, Wall Street favors those with an excellent track record for selling fashion.

According to the Goldman Sachs report on retailing and retail stocks:

> Long-term investments in department store companies should be restricted to those companies characterized by a management philosophy that encourages fashion "risk-taking" in a wide variety of classifications. This is done with the recognition that, *properly executed,* risk-taking on a *cumulative* basis results in accelerated sales volume and gross profit dollars that more than offset higher dollar markdowns. We seek managements whose growth programs are well defined in *merchandising,* as well as in expansion and financial terms, whose quest for market penetration derives from an understanding of the inherent growth potential realizable in more intensive merchandising of existing units as well as through new store openings. Such managements tend to build an atmosphere of excitement and motivation within their organizations that is conducive to growth.

The smell of trouble in any one of Federated's divisions can cause hand wringing on Wall Street. This is especially true if the bad news concerns one of the glamour units, Bloomingdale's or I. Magnin. For this reason, and because of competitive pressures, Federated keeps a tight lid on divisional statistics. The company's sales, profits and other key operating highlights are not broken down by division; a single, aggregate total is all that is given. Generally speaking, Federated releases the minimum information the Securities and Exchange Commission requires a public company to report. Questions concerning divisional finances are routinely labeled proprietary and are not answered, so that Wall Street, individual investors and the press are forced to guess or estimate. Federated prefers it this way because management is then able to keep its secrets and to manipulate the news about its overall corporate performance. Quite often, management goes overboard in its penchant for secrecy; for instance, Federated will not even reveal the number of employees at its Cincinnatti headquarters. Although Krensky claims this is due to competitive pressures, the real reason appears to be a severe case of corporate paranoia.

Federated tries to conceal the fact that some of its divisions have been forced to relinquish a good measure of their former autonomy—partly because it is widely known that Cincinnati plays a strong role in managing divisional affairs only when there is real trouble in the field. Wall Street knows that any sign that headquarters is calling the plays at Foley's, Burdine's or Ralphs is a signal of trouble brewing. That can cause Federated's stock to fall.

Bloomingdale's is exceptional in that it gets a rather long leash from Cincinnati. The reason is that the division has never experienced a serious business decline. Not so, however, at its nearby sister division, Abraham and Straus. Founded in 1865 by Abraham Abraham and his friend Joseph Wechsler, A & S has grown from meager beginnings to become the biggest Federated division. The founders had only $5,000 of starting capital; today A & S is one of the largest stores in the world and a Brooklyn institution that has expanded to serve most of Long Island as well. Abraham was one of the few Brooklyn businessmen to back the controversial Brooklyn Bridge. After it was completed he moved his store to a new Fulton Street location with 145,000 square feet, five times as large as his store on lower Fulton. It was one of twenty-eight expansions in the store's first hundred years. In 1893 Wechsler retired; Isadore and Nathan Straus entered the business for a brief period of years and the company name was changed to Abraham and Straus. In the same year Simon F. Rothschild, Abraham's son-in-law, became a partner in the firm. In 1929 he and his son, Walter N. Rothschild, Sr., were among those instrumental in forming Federated Department Stores, Inc., of which Simon was the first president. The A & S expansion to Long Island began in 1950 with a store in Garden City. In 1952 the spacious Hempstead store (528,000 square feet) was built. Five other Long Island branches followed. A & S took its first "regionalization" step when it opened a major branch store in New Jersey in 1971.

In recent years A & S has become a real problem child for Cincinnati. Once the biggest profitmaker in the Federated family, A & S prospered until the early 1970s.

In 1973, a pivotal year, the division's long string of record earnings came to an abrupt end. Performance flattened, falling well below the parent company's objectives for that year. The new chairman, Sanford J. Zimmerman, the first nonfamily member to run A & S, said at the time: "Our performance last year was not good and we have been asked by Cincinnati to change gears." Krensky's public reaction was far more severe: "It is necessary for A & S to totally rethink its business."

This "rethinking" originated not so much from A & S's Brooklyn headquarters as from Cincinnati. A & S is so big, with annual revenues estimated at more than $500 million, that problems at the division have an immediate impact on Federated's aggregate earnings. Neither Lazarus nor Krensky was inclined to take this matter lightly; nor were they willing to let the new chairman tackle the problem on his own. The signs were too ominous and there was simply too much at stake to play a polite game of corporate "wait and see." An immediate inquiry into the reasons behind A & S's disappointing performance revealed deep-seated problems. Most notably, the solid middle-class community that once surrounded and supported the mammoth Brooklyn store had fled to the suburbs in the 1960s and early '70s. Less affluent consumers, many members of minority groups, moved into the area, gradually supplanting the traditional A & S customers. Local management did not, however, at the same time reposition A & S to reflect this change in the market. The store simply continued to market itself in the traditional way: as a middle-of-the-road, price-promotional store, featuring widely distributed brand-name apparel, housewares and furniture. The now dominantly black and Hispanic community in the surrounding areas simply did not respond to this kind of store. To make matters worse, A & S, which was for years a responsible and highly regarded pillar of the Brooklyn community, soon became a symbol of hated "white authority." Black militants viewed the store as a parasite taking money from the people and giving little in return. After a widely publicized shooting of a young black man in 1976, for example, pickets marched around A & S for more than a month, demanding that the store use its alleged power with New York's mayor to assure swift punishment of the assailant.

To counter these nagging problems, Krensky and Lazarus worked more closely with divisional management than any Federated principals had ever done throughout the corporation's history. Their strategy called for a four-pronged attack: First, upgrade the merchandise lines and reposition the store as a trendier fashion retailer. The new A & S would be similar in concept to Bloomingdale's, but with somewhat lower-priced and less sophisticated merchandise. Second, invest $6 million in a complete refurbishing and remodeling of the deteriorating Brooklyn store. Third, use modern marketing techniques to reach potential A & S customers located in parts of Brooklyn never before serviced by the store. (To attract these pockets of affluent, white brownstone dwellers in Park Slope and Brooklyn Heights, and to appeal to middle-income working blacks, A & S embarked on a sophisticated marketing program featuring a direct mail campaign sorted by zip code to identify the highest-income neighborhoods.) And finally, the store's community relations staff was to work on improving its image with the local community by supporting black history events, African art shows, and crafts displays. A similar program was instituted at A & S's big Hempstead, Long Island, branch, which had turned into a money loser.

After a good deal of conceptual work, major capital expenditures and direct action by the parent company, Federated claims that the big A & S division did get back on track. There is some reason to doubt this, however, what with the early retirement in January, 1980 of A & S's Chairman Alan B. Gilman. Industry sources believe that Gilman was pressured to resign due to the continuing problems at A & S.

There is, however, a lingering fallout from the A & S episode—it has made divisional autonomy much less of the sacred cow it once was. At Federated, autonomy was an unwritten law which depended on precedence, as much as anything else, for its continuation. Once the precedent of corporate noninvolvement was broken —regardless of the reason—the entire concept became easier to challenge in the future. This has had major implications. Edward Goodman, the former A & S president, who parted company with Federated in 1975, has placed some of the blame for his division's troubles on interference from Cincinnati. "What we had were fundamental differences with Federated on how the business should be run. We were always pushing to grow and expand and we were always being turned down by Cincinnati."

This is not to say that Federated no longer respects the *principle* of autonomy. In most cases, Krensky and Lazarus still believe that the best way to run a business like Federated is to have local management call most of the shots. "The most important function the top officers of Federated have is to appoint capable people to run the divisions," Krensky says. Still, Lazarus and Krensky are now less hesitant about butting into divisional affairs when they consider it necessary. To make their influence felt on a regular basis, they have also instituted new controls throughout the organization. The Cincinnati headquarters staff has more than doubled in the past four years, and a central computer operation has now been installed. As a direct result of this, every division gets monthly reports on projected economic conditions in its market area, as well as comprehensive computerized projections for each spring and fall, designed to keep divisional managers current on merchandise trends, changing income levels and industrial activities. The purpose of the reports is to provide reliable input for buying, inventory and promotional decisions and to give Krensky and Lazarus some guidelines for reviewing divisional budgets. For example, if the seasonal projection prepared for Bloomingdale's warned of an imminent downturn in the New York economy and Bloomingdale's ignored this projection and planned continued ambitious buying, Krensky would set up a meeting with Traub to discuss the situation. Typically, Krensky will argue for leaner inventories in response to a pessimistic projection; Traub, on the other hand, may insist that the gloomy figures will not affect his customers. In most cases, arguments on both sides result in a compromise solution. Although Krensky insists that the final decision here rests with the divisional chairman, this is misleading. Sitting face to face with the president of Federated and being warned by him that divisional buying plans were excessive and potentially disastrous, few store chiefs would want to put their jobs on the line by obstinately refusing to cooperate. Krensky's warnings, whether they take the form of dictates or not, have a tremendous impact on divisional policies. Careers, after all, are at stake.

This internal jawboning is, in fact, the way headquarters generally chooses to direct the divisions. Krensky and Lazarus recognize that they can go just so far before the concept of autonomy is completely destroyed. "We rolled up our sleeves and did some hard work at A & S," Krensky says, "but that was mostly in sitting down with the principals and working with them to redirect the store. I was tempted, believe me, to just go to A & S, give that division two years of my time, and turn it around myself. My specialty as a manager is turnaround situations, so the challenge was very tempting. But you just have to control yourself."

Self-control is important because the Federated organization functions on at least the appearance of divisional independence. Any arbitrary removal of autonomy (without the obvious crisis conditions of an A & S) would seriously damage the relationship between the parent and all its divisions and cause a great deal of ill will with top divisional executives. Local Federated managers pride themselves on the feeling of running their own business. If this were taken away, many would probably leave the company. "All we have to do is say that from here on in we call the shots, and a lot of our top people would say that the whole Federated concept is a crock," Krensky admits. "Taking away their autonomy would be like sending our best people to our competitors."

So Federated wants to continue to preserve the impression of "healthy" divisional autonomy, despite the fact that this autonomy has been diminished somewhat over the past five years. The truth is that retailing is becoming a tougher and tougher business, with increasingly aggressive competitors in all major markets; to Federated that mandates the need for more divisional supervision than ever before in the corporation's history. The bottom line is this: Yes, the divisions are relatively independent; no, they are not in business for themselves.

"In managing a far-flung organization like this" Krensky remarks, "one thing is of prime importance: credibility. Remember, you have about forty top executives out there [chairmen and presidents], all of whom are capable, aggressive and dynamic. The only way they'll respect your decisions is if they know that you, too, have been at the front lines—that you've got a Purple Heart on your chest to prove that you've come through the battles of running a division. They all know I did my duty at Bloomingdale's and Filene's—that I'm thoroughly familiar with the pressures they are under. Without this experience, I'd be considered an ivory tower egghead."

This is more than a matter of personal vanity. The fact that there are strong, experienced managers at the helm in Cincinnati builds greater respect for Bloomingdale's and the other Federated divisions throughout the retail trade.

## 10

# The Trade

---

*"Just what Marvin Traub is up to always gets a lot of attention in this business. He's a hard man to keep up with and he sets the pace for the most influential store in the world. People in the trade like to refer to him—behind his back, of course—as Marvin Bloomingdale. The man is completely devoted to the store and has been all of his working life. Those of us who have worked with him know that he never really wanted anything except to be the chairman of Bloomingdale's. Legend has it that his mother dropped him off there as a young child and never came back to claim him.*

*A former Bloomingdale's vice president*

The long, deeply rooted grapevine that runs throughout the retail industry is a marvel of informal communications. No other business has anything to compare with it. Just as soon as a major store develops "secret" plans for new branches, merchandising themes or executive appointments, news of the action usually spreads throughout the industry. This is part of the game, the way of life. For retailing is a gossipy business, rife with rumors, scandals, press leaks and endless shop talk between colleagues and competitors. The fact is retail people can talk about their business virtually nonstop. The intensity of retailing—the constant pressure to produce ever greater profits, the long hours and the grueling schedules—thoroughly absorbs those involved in the business. Add to this the egocentric notion that retailers are a special breed, harder-working and more pressured than the nine-to-fivers who toil at most of the nation's offices.

"We're the only ones who get report cards on our performance every single week," says Harold Krensky. "Computer printouts on the current week's sales versus sales for the same period a year earlier always let us know exactly how we are doing. This applies to the officers of the store, the vice presidents, merchandise managers, buyers, store managers and department managers. We are all accountable. If you don't think that jangles the nerves, try it sometime."

This feeling, a cross between martyrdom and self-pity, prompts many retailers to limit their social contacts to associates in the business—other merchants, manufacturers and designers. "It's a feeling that only other retailers will understand them—only others in the business can sympathize with what they go through," says Cathy Spellman. "They like to talk about the business a lot and so they naturally enjoy the company of others who share the same interests. There's nothing snobby or arrogant about it. In fact, it's all very natural."

Much of the shop talk extends beyond the confines of individual stores or store groups. Executives at one store commonly talk about their jobs and their employers with colleagues at a competing store. This happens not as part of some sinister spy system but because retailing, from a career standpoint, is a dynamic business. People who go to work for major retailers rarely stay with the same employers until retirement. More often, the individual makes three to seven changes during his career, moving from store to store and frequently from city to city. Unlike the more staid industries, such as petroleum or computers, the Texacos and the IBMs, retailing does not frown on this intercompany movement. Although it is not applauded, it is nevertheless regarded as part of the natural career cycle. Management recognizes that in retailing, such mobility is often the only way rising executives can get to the top.

This revolving door of talent in and out of the major stores has produced a far-flung association of retail executives that transcends company lines. Friends who worked together buying housewares at Bloomingdale's often remain friends when one leaves to take a new post at Macy's. The merchandise manager who leaves Filene's to assume a vice presidency at a key resource is unlikely to drop his old ties at Federated. It is a loyalty that stems as much from business as from social reasons: maintaining friends and associates throughout the industry helps executives perform better on the job. Retailing is so competitive and fast-moving that top managers must stay abreast of breaking developments in and out of their own limited field or company. By sharing news, tips, projections, insights and hunches, merchants keep each other well informed. They also feed the grapevine, and by doing so, ensure that secrets, if they ever exist, are short-lived. "There is often a camaraderie among people who have worked for the same store," Spellman says, "that tends to get stronger as one or both of them leave. They stay in touch, perhaps lunch together every other week, and share stories about their new jobs. They don't mean to reveal secrets, but in the very process of conversation, they mention things that are enlightening to the other party."

As a result, merchants are remarkably well versed in their competitor's affairs. Who will be appointed to what position? Who is opening a big new branch in Dallas? Who will be named a "launch store" for Saint Laurent's Opium? Who is losing money? Who is making lots of it? Who is being forced to mark down Calvin Klein's men wear line only four weeks into the season? This is the kind of talk that is bandied about every day at lunch, every evening at cocktails. Retailers simply want to know—and the best make it their business to know—as much as possible about everyone else in the trade. Given this nosy, inquisitive atmosphere, virtually everyone in the business is subject to scrutiny. But none more than Bloomingdale's. In the retail industry—and those trades associated with it—Bloomingdale's is the center of attention, the subject of the most conversation. As the recognized leader of trendy, high-fashion retailing, the store takes center stage and lives with a spotlight trained on its face. For those who work in the retail trade, Bloomie's-watching is one of the favorite pastimes. Even giant Sears, by far the nation's largest retail organization, for years kept a memo in its New York office directing fashion buyers to visit Bloomingdale's no less than once a month to soak up new merchandising ideas. This, even though Sears does not consider itself in competition with Bloomingdale's; the visits were prescribed for inspiration.

As a perceived kingpin of its industry, Bloomingdale's garners the wide range of emotions and attitudes reserved for leaders. It is loved and hated, envied and imitated, denigrated and praised, despised and adored. In most cases, however, the feelings expressed about Bloomingdale's are based on petty personal biases: those who need Bloomingdale's, and who live by selling to it, praise it up front while all the time cursing under their breath. Those who compete with Bloomie's frequently scoff at it in public, only to work like hell just to keep up. The truth is, of course, that Bloomingdale's is a major force in the retail industry, widely credited with having an extraordinary impact on suppliers, competitors and customers.

The "trade," as it is called, is actually a diverse group of entities involved in planning, producing, promoting and selling consumer merchandise. One highly important segment of the trade, the design community, gives Bloomingdale's much of the credit for making the designer influence a major factor in American fashion.

For the most part, the famous apparel designers are a strange breed. Catapulted to national attention in less than a decade, they enjoy more fame and have amassed greater wealth than the most optimistic among them ever imagined. Who could have predicted that the men and women who make clothing for the rich and powerful would become almost as rich and powerful as their clients? This rapid rise to prominence has left many designers infatuated with their own celebrity status. Hobnobbing with actors, politicians and socialites, they are wrapped up in a social whirl of sixteen-hour days that combine both business and pleasure. Few can resist the call to the latest party, much less the invitation to meet mayors, governors, the President or the First Lady.

Add to this the power, money and prestige of having one's name on millions of shirts, suits, sheets, shoes and sunglasses. Understandably, most designers have developed egos of enormous proportions, clearly evidenced by their attitude toward Bloomingdale's. Many of their careers were launched by Bloomie's; others have come to rely on the store as a major sales outlet. For these reasons they praise the store in public, mouthing all the appropriate things one is expected to say about a rich and powerful benefactor. Privately, however, the talk takes a different tone. Most reveal a deepseated belief that they are better and more powerful than any one store—that Bloomingdale's did not make them but was simply fortunate enough to discover their talents. Although they want badly to retain Bloomingdale's business, they find it hard to conceal the attitude that they are indestructibly talented—the princes of the business. Generally speaking, they respect Bloomingdale's for its role in cultivating the designer craze, but they are too arrogant to give the store more than passing credit for their success.

For some, this arrogance has infected the whole of their personalities and carried over into their operating style. Calvin Klein, who wanted to be a fashion designer "ever since I was old enough to push a pencil," was making only $75 a week as late as the 1960s. Designing coats for Dan Millstein, Klein believed he could do better by going into business on his own. His friend, and now business partner, Barry Schwartz, who was then running a supermarket in Manhattan, borrowed $2,000 from the store to bankroll Klein's sample dress and coat collection. The prototype line proved to be a winner and provided the first spark for a company that now sells men's and women's clothing and fragrances to fashionable stores throughout the world. Today Klein is a multimillionaire who owns two country homes and a fabulous New York apartment, and drives a Rolls-Royce.

The trappings of wealth and power have apparently gone to his head. The author's experience was that Klein's offices are staffed by secretaries and receptionists who treat callers in a rude and hostile manner. Unless there is a visible business connection at stake, telephone messages go unanswered, letters unopened. Klein refuses to deal with the public or the press unless he himself can call all the shots. Told by a friend at Saint Laurent's Opium party that his new men's wear collection was selling out at Saks, Klein said, "Nothing I make stays on the racks long—you know that. How could you think anything else?"

Although this kind of blatant arrogance is not representative of all the designers (Ralph Lauren and Bill Blass are notable exceptions), in the privacy of their own offices most are more than slightly irreverent toward Bloomingdale's. They view it as an institution that has peaked—a store that has lost some of its dazzle. Many are annoyed by Bloomingdale's constant pressure on them to participate in theme promotions, which they view as a time-consuming waste and, even worse, as involvement in "tacky" events (like the India blitz). Almost unanimously, the top designers reveal a greater affinity for the carriage-trade specialty shops like Bendel's, Saks and Bergdorf's. The wild enthusiasm many of Bloomie's customers have for their store is not shared by the very designers whose names dot its walls, boutique signs and labels. If they respect the store at all, it is mostly because of what Bloomie's was in the past and because it can still move great quantities of their merchandise. Certainly, they feel no great loyalty. Told that a world-famous designer credits him privately for his first big break, Harold Krensky says, "That's incredible; he hasn't communicated with me more than once in the last ten years."

To many of her major resources, Bloomingdale's is a tough, demanding, customer. Manufacturers who sell to Bloomingdale's on a regular basis say that the pressure from Fifty-ninth Street is intense. The perfectionism of the store's buyers often causes them to insist on being involved in the production process from the very start, which can be an aggravating intrusion to the smaller vendors and those most dependent on Bloomie's. With a discriminating customer looking over your shoulder, it is virtually impossible to take shortcuts or to opt for economies of production that might otherwise be hard to detect. The problem is especially severe for those resources Bloomingdale's contracts with to produce its unique or private-brand merchandise. Here buyers come armed with specific designs, fabric selections and production schedules. Purchase commitments are based on the assurance that the manufacturers will produce their lines precisely according to Bloomingdale's exacting specifications. What's more, buyers often demand exclusive rights to sell the merchandise in all of Bloomingdale's market areas. In a typical example, a Seventh Avenue junior clothes house is asked to produce a 25,000 run of trendy cowl-neck sweaters in light pastel colors. Bloomingdale's agrees in advance to purchase the 25,000 units, providing the garments meet the agreed-upon specifications. Bloomingdale's own label is sewn in the sweater, which cannot be sold to any other retailer in the Mid-Atlantic states. This is called "selected distribution." What happens to the rest of the manufacturer's production run is not Bloomingdale's concern.

"They are ball-busters supreme," says a former Bloomingdale's executive now with a major financial services outfit. "Cocky and uncaring is probably the best way to describe it. When Bloomingdale's knows it has a manufacturer over a barrel, it just makes its demands and expects compliance. If there is a lack of cooperation, then the hell with them: Bloomie's will find someone else to take the order. Manufacturers throughout the apparel and furniture industries hate Bloomingdale's for this arrogance. The store's vendors are perpetually bitching and complaining about how miserable Bloomingdale's makes their lives. What really bothers the vendors is when they are asked to do

something special for Bloomingdale's, like produce a
way-out sofa. Bloomingdale's buyer tells the manufacturer that this will be the big new look. Maybe it will
be in Bloomingdale's, but when the supplier tries to sell
it outside New York, he finds he's stuck with a warehouse full of duds. The items that sell well at Bloomie's
don't always sell well elsewhere."

Edwin Bobrow, consultant to mass merchandise suppliers, agrees. "It's hard to be a department store
vendor today. You have to be flexible enough to satisfy
a great variety of stores. Macy's, Gimbels, Bloomingdale's, Saks—all want different things from you, and
Bloomingdale's ranks among the toughest."

The problem extends beyond design and performance
specifications. In recent years, the question of inventory levels has emerged as a major cause of friction
between Bloomingdale's and its suppliers—a development not limited to Bloomingdale's alone, but sympto-
matic of department stores in general. After decades of
cyclical earnings—with the bottom line often deflated
by sudden recessions—retailers have moved to reduce
the impact of adverse economic conditions. This is done
primarily by keeping tight reins on inventory levels
and by ordering less rather than more of projected merchandise requirements. Merchants have come to recognize that by carefully balancing inventories they can
weather the effects of economic slowdown without
incurring heavy losses. It is the combination of swollen
inventories with simultaneous reductions in consumer
spending that causes real havoc; excess merchandise
must be drastically reduced and in many cases cannot
be sold at all. Although merchants can do little to
manipulate consumer confidence, they can manage one
part of the equation by limiting inventories. With merchandise levels carefully tuned to current sales, a
downturn may cut revenues but will not produce the
seas of red ink that flow when excess goods are moved
at clearance prices. Federated, as we have noted, is
especially sensitive to inventory levels: it demands that
divisional chairmen be highly cautious and conservative
in this regard. The corporate headquarters staff in
Cincinnati projects economic conditions up to five

years in advance, and store chiefs are expected to keep abreast of the figures.

"There's no doubt that Bloomingdale's especially has been cutting their inventory levels over recent years," says Jill Curry, an editor at *Chain Store Age* magazine. "They have adopted a more hesitant approach than ever before. Since their trendy merchandise is particularly vulnerable to heavy markdowns, they must make sure to keep inventory levels lean. Although I think they've always recognized this, they have become even more gun shy since the mid seventies."

This hard-nosed stance on inventories poses yet another dilemma for manufacturers: they must produce enough to satisfy Bloomingdale's and other customers' requirements, while being increasingly wary of excess production. What is most disturbing to them is that powerful stores like Bloomingdale's are now forcing vendors to assume more and more of the inventory function by demanding that orders be shipped on a delayed basis. The idea is to accept additional deliveries only after the market proves that it can and will absorb current inventories. "A number of the traditional store functions are switching over to the manufacturers," Bobrow says. "Some stores are demanding, for example, that inventories be counted and price-tagged by the manufacturers."

Vendors are disturbed by these developments. Most of the fashion resources are small firms that find it extremely difficult to make gradual deliveries, to warehouse goods at their own cost and to wait for drawn-out payments on completed merchandise. This extended cycle has a devastating effect on cash flow—always a precarious factor in the apparel trade. The feeling that the giant stores are making their small suppliers assume greater levels of risk and service is bitterly resented.

All the bitching and moaning aside, however, Bloomingdale's is still, in some ways, a plum of a customer for most of the resources that serve her. As one supplier of men's accessories noted: "Nothing good is easy—and doing business with Bloomingdale's is good—

very good. You get tsuris, sure, but a lot of gelt in the pocket too."

The truth is that the vast majority of the vendors selling to Bloomingdale's are sharp and savvy entrepreneurs who know their way around the retail trade, and are pushovers for no one. They are willing to accept Bloomingdale's tough standards, and to work with the store in a cooperative "partnership selling" effort, because above all else, they respect Bloomie's awesome selling power, its merchandising expertise and its ability to launch new products into the mainstream. The trade is well aware of the fact that Bloomingdale's Fifty-ninth Street is the greatest store in the world and that no other retailer of its size can touch its sales volume per-square-foot. "Although Bloomie's doesn't like this description because it doesn't sound chic enough, the store is, for some lines, a mass merchandiser," Bobrow comments. "Everyone knows that they can move a hell of a lot of high-fashion goods there. This has earned the store a great deal of respect in the industry."

"In spite of all the problems and complaints about dealing with them, the trade is still in awe of Bloomingdale's," Curry says. "Most of the people in the business still believe Bloomingdale's does what it does better than anyone else."

The intense personal relationship between Bloomingdale's and its suppliers—whether good or bad—does not apply across the board. There are those large, well-established vendors whose relationship with the store is routine and matter-of-fact. Most are companies with successful brand-name products, to whom Bloomingdale's is just another store. There are no consultations on merchandise design or production and no squabbling about Bloomingdale's dictatorial tactics. No single store has much power with these leading resources, and Bloomie's buyers, like their counterparts from other stores, just go to the manufacturer's showrooms, survey the samples and place their orders. In some cases, Bloomingdale's actually needs the vendor more than the vendor needs Bloomingdale's, and any sign of the store's notorious arrogance simply would not be tolerated. A good example is Bloomingdale's relationship with Izod. Customers come to Bloomingdale's with the express intention of purchasing Izod shirts, slacks, sweaters, tennis shorts and the like. It is a classic line—a perennial favorite that people expect the store to carry. For its part, Bloomingdale's would not be caught without the full Izod collection. It is profitable, builds traffic, pleases customers and most important, keeps Bloomie's shoppers from going elsewhere for their beloved "alligator clothes." "We appreciate having Bloomingdale's as a customer," says Izod president Vin Draddi, "but our business wouldn't be materially affected if Bloomingdale's disappeared from the face of the earth. They are only one of our top twenty customers, and we have thousands of customers all over the world."

Draddi's attitude is typical of those in the trade who have amassed staggering wealth without the aid of the merchants. When Draddi (who, as noted previously, already owned the prestigious and successful house of David Crystal) started selling the Izod shirts in the early 1950s, he found stiff resistance wherever he turned. The garments sold for eight dollars then, which was considered too expensive for casual wear, and they were also called "strange and funny looking" by the store buyers. Finding no ready market for his "alligators," Draddi decided to give the shirts away to friends and golf buddies, including John Wayne, Bing Crosby, Bob Hope and the Duke of Windsor. Little did he know it at the time, but this gesture sowed the seeds for a phenomenal business. The real spark came when President Eisenhower showed up at a golf tournament wearing an Izod shirt. Fashion reporters made note of it, word spread through the media and soon a mystique began to surround the alligator emblem. By the mid 1950s, Izod became the chic label of the country club crowd. To many, the alligator was a sign of affluence— of membership in an exclusive club. "The people got this fashion started, not the stores," Draddi comments. "The merchants started calling us for orders only after their customers demanded it."

\*    \*    \*

Bloomingdale's reputation in the trade is also colored by the large corps of its alumni now holding down top positions at other organizations. Members of this so-called Bloomingdale's Legion are among the most prominent names at major retailers, leading apparel and furniture makers, fashion and decorating magazines and international advertising agencies. Many left Bloomingdale's for grander personal rewards; others were fired. Although their attitudes are biased, and in some cases bitter, it is interesting to note that most of them hold rather similar views of their former employer. To a man (and woman), they all refused to be quoted by name, obviously mindful that they may want to return to Bloomingdale's in the future. This in spite of the fact that most complain bitterly about Bloomingdale's sweatshop environment—the grueling work days, the Saturday hours and the pressure to devote at least some Sundays to paper work and other catch-up duties. Traub is portrayed as an indefatigable executive—a workaholic who gets in earlier than anyone else and stays later. This pace, they say, is imitated by the top-level seventh-floor executive staff, who in turn take the whip to their subordinates. As a result, the exhausting work schedules are mandatory for $18,000-a-year assistant buyers as well as for $80,000-a-year vice presidents. Trade gossip is clear about this: behind the scenes, Bloomingdale's is no picnic.

"Bloomie's is terribly understaffed," says a former Fifty-ninth Street store department manager now working at Macy's Herald Square. "Everyone in a professional capacity there does the job of two or three people. Bloomingdale's is preoccupied with its image to the public, but cares little about how it treats its own staff. You are supposed to toe the line, do the work, know your place and shut up. It's the old 'if you can't stand the heat, get out of the kitchen' attitude.

"The environment at virtually all other stores is different. This need to prove that the staff can take any punishment—can be worked to near exhaustion—is purely a Bloomingdale's phenomenon. Everyone in the trade knows this and weighs this factor before accepting a job at Bloomie's. At stores like Macy's, you don't have to work ninety-seven hours a day to prove yourself. They have more respect for you than that."

Many of the Bloomingdale's alumni insist that the store has lost some of its best people in recent years—that standards have declined and the work load has intensified to the point where some of the most talented people have abandoned ship. The feeling is—and this is shared by objective observers as well—that for one reason or another, the superstars of Bloomingdale's recent past are no longer generating the magic the store built its reputation on. Critics point to the fact that Barbara D'Arcy, so influential in the development of the furniture department, has been kicked upstairs to supervise store design. Kate Murphy, the great fashion innovator, and Joe Schnee, the brilliant merchandise manager, are both dead. Bob Myers, once president of George Jensen and later a Bloomingdale's furniture vice president (called by one knowledgeable observer "the finest hardgoods merchant in the nation") has departed. Arthur Cohen, the marketing whiz who sparked Bloomingdale's catalogue ventures, is now with J. Walter Thompson. David Bell, the long-reigning chief of the interior design staff, took his leave to form Design Multiples. Cathy Spellman, who introduced Bloomingdale's to television advertising and who brought a new sense of excitement to its promotions, also entered the ranks of self-employed.

The consensus is clear: Although Bloomingdale's still gets the cream of the crop of retail job candidates—and although it still boasts an extraordinary amount of talented people on the payroll—some of the magic has left the store. Former employees who visit Bloomie's now or who maintain contacts on the staff agree with this view. Many blame it on the current crop of managers, whom they consider too numbers-oriented. The feeling is that no one has the time or the inclination to work with young people to develop new talent. This emphasis on human relations—the great strength of Jim Schoff, Sr. (father of the current president), Katie Murphy and Joe Schnee—seems to be missing. "They turn out buyers so quickly now that they can't be nearly as good as Bloomie's buyers of the 1960s and early

'70s," says the Bloomingdale's alumnus now with Macy's. "Everyone in the trade knows that the training programs have been diluted, the standards lowered and the emphasis switched from quality of work to quantity. The store is growing so rapidly—building so many branches—that speed and work load have become the all-important factors. You just walk through the store and see it before your eyes—so much of the excitement is gone."

"The store has lost some of its luster precisely because it has lost some of its real stars," Jill Curry adds. "It's known in the trade that the buying staff is not what it used to be." Mary Merris of *Women's Wear Daily* puts it this way: "Bloomie's is still very good, but it never gained back some of the magic Katie Murphy took with her when she died."

Still, it must be said that hostility on the part of former employees—now in some cases competitors—is to be expected. What's more, many of those who chide and downgrade Bloomingdale's have been quick to apply Bloomie's merchandising concepts to their new places of employment. Theme promotions, designer shopping bags, in-store boutiques, active community relations, customer cooking courses, fashion coordinators —all were developed by Bloomingdale's and are now being duplicated by her alumni in stores across the country.

Perhaps the most accurate barometer of Bloomingdale's image in the trade comes from those merchants in other cities who do not compete with the store head-on. And there Bloomingdale's is viewed as the master of high-fashion, conceptual merchandising—as the retailer with the most pizazz, the most loyal customers and the most revenue per square foot. It is also seen as a great source of ideas—as the model for how a profitable store can be run.

Not that local or regional department stores in the nation's heartland want to be mini or quasi Bloomingdale's. Most know that Bloomingdale's caters to the kind of special, unusually sophisticated market that does not exist on any large scale in the heartland. What these merchants do know, however, is that certain aspects of Bloomingdale's operations can be duplicated anywhere. Imaginative techniques for merchandise presentation, in-store promotions, conceptual advertising and community relations can be transplanted to the Deep South or to the Midwest or to the Plains states. To remain fresh and appealing, merchants throughout the nation must introduce new ideas and concepts regularly. For many, Bloomingdale's is their inspiration.

The best evidence of this—and of Bloomingdale's exalted position in the trade—is the fact that store executives from coast to coast make it a point to spend time at Bloomingdale's when they are in New York. "Bloomingdale's is considered the must place to visit by all out-of-town buyers," says Murjani's Warren Hirsh. It is common for large store groups, like Nordstrom's on the West Coast, to send staffers on regular pilgrimages to Manhattan for the express purpose of keeping up with the latest happenings at Fifty-ninth Street. Even in the most parochial towns, where the man on the street has never heard of Bloomingdale's, the merchant community knows of the store and holds it in great esteem. "Bloomingdale's is my favorite store in the world; it's absolutely the best in the business," says Margaret Dadian, chief buyer for Kay Campbell stores, a chain of twenty-odd moderate-priced junior clothes shops in the Midwest. "Although most people here don't know of Bloomingdale's, the more affluent, better-educated classes do and they all want to visit the store when they go to New York.

"I visit New York every six weeks to do the buying for our stores, and I certainly never miss a chance to stop at Bloomingdale's when I'm in town. On Monday nights, in fact, Bloomingdale's is a gathering spot for out-of-town merchants. The routine is to have dinner and then head to Fifty-ninth Street to see what's new and exciting—and you can bet that there's always something to learn.

"Believe it or not, my love affair with Bloomingdale's contributed to my losing a daughter-in-law. I once said that the most important thing I did in New York was to visit Bloomingdale's, then my grandchildren. I was being facetious, to be sure, but the statement got in print and my former daughter-in-law used it against my husband to show that I cared more for Bloomingdale's than for her children."

In parts of the trade, the very name Bloomingdale's is synonymous with avant-garde merchandise. The store is seen as a gambler, an innovator, a daring tester of the new and unproved. "The feeling here is that they just act from the top of their heads," Dadian adds. "An idea comes up and they try it. That's why if someone shows merchants in the Midwest a piece of furniture or an item of clothing that's considered hip or outré, we say, 'Oh, that's very Bloomingdale's.' It's become a generic term."

Even radically different stores, like the mighty Sears, respect Bloomingdale's abilities. "Sears' customers and Bloomingdale's customers are two different groups," says Wiley Brooks, Sears's assistant director of national news. "We don't compete with them, but we do recognize that they are very competent merchants. There is something to be learned from them as well as from any good store." Brooks's reserve is to be expected from a close-to-the-vest publicity man for Sears. The giant Chicago-based merchant is the biggest in the nation and it considers itself the king of retailing.

But the truth is that Sears sales and profits have stalled in recent years and top management has been trying one device after another to light fires under its massive organization. To bring greater balance to its merchandising thrust, and to boost net profits, Sears has therefore been trying harder than ever to position itself as a source of fashion apparel. "Fashion is where the money is and we have been making a greater effort in this area," Brooks admits.

It is for this approach that Sears has used Bloomingdale's as a source of ideas and inspiration. Young buyers, interior designers and merchandise managers view Bloomingdale's as *the* place to learn how to buy, sell and present fashion. This is so deeply ingrained in the trade that salesmen traveling the country try to use Bloomingdale's as a selling point. "They come to us and say Bloomingdale's just bought fifty thousand of their blouses. That alone is supposed to convince others to buy—and sometimes it does," Dadian explains. "This appeal is effective, however, only if the merchandise involved is not considered extreme."

Even within the Federated family, Bloomingdale's occupies a position of prominence. Bloomie's sits at the head of the corporate table. It is the acknowledged mover and shaker for the entire organization, setting the trends and laying the foundation for developments that, in many cases, surface months or years later at Filene's, Burdine's and I. Magnin's.

Although a major effort is made to disguise this, there is no denying Bloomingdale's leadership image inside the Federated organization. Lazarus and Krensky prefer to play this down, fearing that public adulation of Bloomingdale's will lead to a favorite-child syndrome. Other divisional chiefs are obviously aware of Bloomie's status, and some are resentful of it. After all, Federated's organizational structure pits the store groups against one another for expansion funds and capital improvements, and perhaps most important, it forces the divisional heads to compete for spots in the Federated high command. So although Krensky admits that "Bloomingdale's has a major impact on the Federated divisions," he prefers to limit his remarks to that.

It is known that within the Federated family, Bloomingdale's is admired, copied and closely observed; but its image is also deflated by the divisional chiefs. The rationale is that Bloomingdale's is so successful—and can afford to take risks the others cannot—simply because it has an extraordinary customer base. To these detractors within the organization, Bloomingdale's success must be attributed to its location rather than to its management prowess.

As we have seen, Bloomingdale's image in the trade varies greatly. Just how one views Bloomingdale's depends almost entirely on the observer's relationship to the store.

High-fashion retailing is an extremely tough, aggressive and, in many ways, dirty business. There is outright theft of ideas, duplication, imitation and heavy reliance on whatever power play one can muster to force events in a particular direction. Arm twisting, back biting, jealousy, cutthroat tactics, sabotage, spying, blackmail and bribery all characterize this multibillion-dollar, hyperactive industry in which great sums of money and international reputations are earned and lost with dizzying speed. One thing most consumers never perceive is that in spite of its overall size, retailing is predominantly an industry of small businesses. Seventh Avenue apparel resources are mostly family-owned outfits that live and die by the seasons; two bad years and the shop closes. The corporations of name designers like Von Furstenberg and Blass are also comparatively tiny outfits, light-years away from the Fortune 500 industrials. Even the stores themselves operate as small outfits: each department is run as an independent business headed by a buyer.

The significance here is that retailing is an industry dominated by personalities—a fish-bowl world of people working together and battling one another for power and wealth. In this environment, statements and feelings about rivals, competitors, colleagues and partners are colored by heavy doses of envy, fear and paranoia. Those who say they hate Bloomingdale's are often those who have been beaten by the store, those who claim to love Bloomie's usually depend on it. Still, through all this lying, bickering and bitterness, Bloomingdale's emerges as that very special retail institution just about everyone in the trade knows, watches, thinks about and in one way or another is personally involved with. Above all, Bloomingdale's arouses emotions.

Perhaps the most knowledgeable observer of Bloomingdale's—a man who grew up in the retail trade and is considered by many to be its senior statesman—is Stanley Marcus, chairman emeritus of world-famous Neiman-Marcus. As Marcus sees it, Bloomingdale's is regarded in the trade as the one store that learned how to combine department store and specialty store features into a single operation. "Traditionally, department stores simply put out great assortments of merchandise and let the buyers choose what they liked best," Marcus explains. "When it came to blenders, for example, the department store might stock fifteen different models. Specialty stores, on the other hand, were expected to do some of the product selection for their customers. They would therefore test all available blenders and carry only the two or three management thought to be best. In specialty store selling, management is not objective: it introduces its personal tastes into the buying process."

Bloomingdale's, Marcus claims, brought this aspect of specialty store operations to department stores and has thus freed the big merchants to put their personal stamp on merchandise selections. "Bloomingdale's is recognized as the innovator in this regard and as the one that still does it very, very well. The most important thing I can say about Bloomie's is that ever since they got moving as an extraordinary store, they taught many others how to do things right. Thanks to Bloomingdale's, the industry has never been the same."

# 11

# Clouds over Fifty-ninth Street

*No one could spot me for a hard-core Blooming-
dale's freak—the kind who, twenty minutes late for her
own wedding, would be halfway down the aisle of
the Young East Sider shop, rummaging frantically for
something new, something blue.*

Lois Gould, "Confessions of a Bloomingdale's Addict"
New York Magazine

Bloomingdale's has built its power base, in part, on its
ability to make "freaks" of otherwise intelligent and discriminating consumers. To maintain its extraordinary
growth throughout the 1980's, Bloomingdale's must
continue this remarkable hold on the public. The question is can it do so?

Although crystal-balling is always difficult in business, indications are that Bloomingdale's is moving off
the fast track it has blazed along on for more than thirty
years now. There are signs, in fact, that the store is
becoming a victim of its own hype—that the very laws
of the business in which it has prospered—the high-
fashion retail trade—rule against its continued dominance of it. No single institution, it seems, can plant its
flag at the precipice of this volatile business for more
than a fleeting period. Bloomingdale's has commanded
the top spot longer than any of its predecessors—and
longer than anyone predicted. But alas, its grip may be
slipping.

Actually, this should come as no surprise. Postwar Bloomingdale's has always been in a precarious position. As "beautiful Bloomie's," the darling of New York's social set, the store has made its bed with an extremely fickle group. Hard-core Bloomingdale's customers are firm believers in "newness for newness' sake." To appeal to them, fashion must be white hot—new and fresh and seemingly ahead of the times. Bloomie's "freaks" have been conditioned by their store itself to discard current styles at the first sign of a new trend or fad. Practical considerations such as durability, classic appeal and value are frowned upon as bourgeois, blue-collar, Archie Bunker hangups.

Bloomie's "freaks" are also, for the most part, fashion groupies—people determined to do what is considered cool, chic and in vogue. As such, they are highly susceptible to bandwagon psychology. No sooner do the beautiful people of show business, society and business fame—the real fashion leaders—claim their latest discovery than the groupies fall in behind. For example, the beautiful crowd—Halston, Minnelli, Capote, Nureyev, and company—switched their social allegiance in recent years to four different discos: Regine's, New York/New York, Studio 54, and Xenon. With each change, the new place became the glitter capital of the world, the *Time* magazine story of the week. Equally important, the previous hot spots were relegated almost instantly to second-class citizenry, suitable "for tourists only." As Jackie O., Leonard Bernstein, Margaux Hemingway and Calvin Klein moved on, so did the faceless groupies from the upper East Side. Bloomie's "freaks" will not get caught dead at the wrong place.

Over the years, Bloomingdale's has encouraged this mentality. The store's classic advertising campaigns have portrayed the very image of the Bloomie's ideal—young, chic and sophisticated people moving through life with great style and poise. At work, Bloomingdale's people are pictured as smartly dressed, always climbing toward ever greater success. Socially, Bloomingdale's people hustle, sip Dom Perignon and party till dawn. They know the "right" places to cut their hair, dance and dine. They are thoroughly convinced of their own superiority and, most important of all, conspicuously fashionable. The postwar Bloomingdale's has always identified closely with current social trends. Its photos for newspaper ads have used as backdrops the "in" restaurants and discos; models have been posed playing tennis, jogging and roller skating; in-store themes have moved from Chinese to Indian to country and western; and promotional events have capitalized on fads like backgammon and marathon running. Bloomie's feeds its hard-core "freaks" a steady diet of change—change for change's sake—and they gobble it up, spit it out and move on to the next diversion.

Certainly, this hyper-fashionable corps of Bloomie's "freaks" represent only a small segment of the store's customers. They are just one group, mostly upper East Siders, responsible for a tiny fraction of Bloomingdale's sales. Still, they constitute a powerful and highly visible minority that gives the store much of its cachet. Bloomie's "freaks" tend to be the innovators, the fashion leaders, willing to try a new fashion long before it is accepted or comfortable to do so. They make it possible for Bloomingdale's to venture far afield with its trendy merchandise—to gamble on the likes of Zandra Rhodes and Kenzo—and to sell enough of these avant-garde goods to retain its fashion edge without going broke in the process. They are similar to the kind of people owner Steve Rubell allowed in, free-of-charge, to Studio 54 when that disco was immensely popular and mobbed by hopefuls waiting on line for a chance to gain entry. "I let some Broadway chorus people, young actors and the like in here without waiting in line and without paying. They bring excitement to the place because they are free, uninhibited and great dancers." Many Bloomie's addicts are outrageous, sexy and irresistibly attractive. They are important to Bloomingdale's because they are the kind of people others watch and imitate. Keeping them loyal to Bloomingdale's has proved to be a pivotal factor in the store's success.

Until now. But suddenly, without warning or reason, there are rumblings of discontent among Bloomie's "freaks." To some, it is no longer *de rigueur* to shop at Bloomingdale's. Worse yet, there are signs that among the superstars of New York's social set, Bloomie's is becoming a dirty word. "To put it straight out, it is now becoming chic to put down Bloomingdale's—to say nasty things about the store and to avoid shopping there," says Nancy Benson, fashion editor of *Cosmopolitan* magazine. "A lot of the superfashionable people in New York are now walking around telling everyone that they can't stand Bloomingdale's. There's a drastic change of attitude taking shape here—you can't help but notice that." *Chain Store Age* editor Jill Curry, a longtime Bloomie's shopper, agrees: "Bloomingdale's is definitely losing some of its magic. There are a number of problems at the store that are making it less of the glamour baby it once was."

Just why an institution like Bloomingdale's loses some of its appeal can never be traced to a set of rational and logical factors. Rarely is life so simple. Bloomie's success defied clear-cut, classic explanations; so, too, will its decline, if that should come about.

Still, some specific complaints about the store are being made by a broad spectrum of customers. They are legitimate, practical criticisms which, if unheeded by Bloomingdale's, may cause serious problems in the future. And they are particularly ominous because they emanate not only from the hard-core "freaks" but from the great masses of occasional customers.

Gripe number one is that Bloomingdale's is difficult to shop in. Both the Fifty-ninth Street store and the branches are accused of being poorly organized from the shopper's point of view. Customers complain that there is no "flow" to the store layouts—no orderly progression of departments or merchandise categories. The dizzying effect of b'way—although an undeniably dramatic touch—adds to the confusion. The clutter of boutiques, displays and theme environments has grown out of hand. Trying to make sense of it all—to locate and select specific merchandise—can be frustrating, time-consuming and just plain irritating. This is especially true for apparel purchasers. Clothing is widely dispersed throughout the stores, and even related lines are often floors apart. In the New York City store, for example, women's sportswear can be found below the main levels and all the way to the third floor. "It's so annoying to buy clothes in Bloomingdale's now because you have to run all over the place looking for what you want," Benson says. "That's very hard when it comes to apparel since you have to try the stuff on. It means going from one dressing room to another, often floors apart. You take your clothes off. You put your clothes on. You take an escalator to another floor. Again, take your clothes off—put your clothes on. With everything so scattered all over the place, it's terribly exhausting. It seems as if you have to pick up and move eighteen times just to make a selection."

Bloomingdale's penchant for moving things around —for constantly changing the look of the store with new boutiques, new merchandise and entirely new departments—also rubs many customers the wrong way. Hardly a month goes by without major changes in store layout. For several promotions, especially Christmas, the look of the store changes drastically. "I do most of my Bloomingdale's shopping at lunchtime," says Steven Forrest, a senior writer at a New York advertising agency. Typical of many successful, beautifully dressed Manhattanites living and working on the East Side, Forrest is a discriminating shopper who's losing his appetite for Bloomie's. "Since I am pressured for time, I like to know just where in the store to get what I need. With Bloomingdale's, you never know. One day there's a Kenzo boutique in one place; the next day Calvin Klein has the spot. One day there are business shirts in one corner; the next day it's Indian madras ties. I don't have the time or the inclination to figure out these puzzles. Sure, Bloomingdale's has an information booth, but who wants to keep running back and forth to that every few minutes? You don't know what's out of place or what's been changed until you start walking through the store anyway."

Bloomingdale's service—or lack of it—is also a sore point. Critics claim that the store's recent emphasis on branch expansion has taken its toll on an already dismal service record. Sales clerks are few and far between, they are hastily trained and are poorly supervised. Management is stretched thin; what time they do have is devoted to the flash and flair of inventive retailing rather than to the nuts and bolts of attentive service. Many believe that poor service will cause the most trouble in the new branch stores, where customers getting their first taste of Bloomingdale's may be less willing than the New York crowd to tolerate the inconvenience.

Another potentially serious problem is related to Bloomingdale's merchandise selection. Many Bloomingdale's defectors believe that the store is becoming more cautious and conservative, leaning toward those fashions that are acceptable to a wider range of consumers. Gone, they say, is the adventurous spirit of the past decade, the willingness to regularly support and promote obscure designers. Again, the blame for this is placed on the branch expansion—the logic being that the bigger the Bloomingdale's empire becomes, the bigger its merchandise orders have to be, the more people it must attract, and the less risk it can accept. In short, the closer Bloomingdale's comes to resembling a mass merchandiser, the more it loses the appeal on which its fame and riches are based. "What's starting to happen to Bloomie's now is that they are blending into the scenery with other stores," Benson comments. "You're starting to find, without exception, the same merchandise there that you see everywhere else. It's becoming harder and harder to find something truly unusual at Bloomie's. That's disappointing to me and to many of my friends because that's been the main reason why we used to shop there so often—to pick up that little treasure no one else had." Adds Jay Bloom, third year law student at New York's Columbia University, "When you want to find the best of the new in men's wear, you have to go down to Barney's, not Bloomingdale's. Barney's outclasses Bloomie's by a wide margin plus it has the unusual items Bloomie's no longer carries."

Taken together, the gripes against Bloomingdale's must be seen as warning clouds on the company's horizon. As a business grows, it must sharpen its skills and capitalize on its strengths to attract new customers and to build market share. Reputation and good will are powerful tools for accomplishing this: by jeopardizing its invaluable reputation, Bloomingdale's may be damaging itself at this crucial juncture in its history. The most troubling aspect of this is that management may be helpless to defend itself against the most dangerous development: the slowly emerging impression, now limited to a small group of fashion leaders, that Bloomie's is a "has been."

No less an authority on retailing than Stanley Marcus, himself a Bloomingdale's admirer, agrees that trouble may be brewing. "I'm hearing a lot of reports that there is disillusionment setting in about Bloomingdale's. Friends and associates in New York tell me that Bloomie's stores are disorganized, confusing and hard to shop at. Others say the stores change too quickly and that service is poor. The salespeople are trained to get people in and out as quickly as possible, rather than attentively waiting on their needs. I would say that Bloomingdale's—in terms of its greatness and its popularity—has peaked."

This feeling that Bloomingdale's has "peaked" is shared by such knowledgeable observers as Bill Blass, Halston and some top trade editors and key manufacturers. Most agree that the problems besetting Bloomingdale's are not new—that poor service, dizzying layouts and rapid merchandise changes have characterized the store since its postwar transformation. In fact, it is even acknowledged that some of what are now viewed as problems proved to be strengths in the past; people liked the chaos, the change, the zany confusion of it all. The important distinction is that these facets of Bloomingdale's operating style are starting to annoy increasing numbers of customers—and the first signs of revolt are coming from those who were most loyal to the store. How long the problems have existed is not the issue; what's important is that they are now being aired by an influential group.

How Bloomingdale's will deal with these problems is difficult to say. Publicly, at least, Traub has chosen to ignore them. "Bloomingdale's gives its customers the exciting environment they expect from us. We don't confuse them, we excite them. I make no apology for our service or our stores, both of which are excellent."

One can only guess that management's attitude will change if the anti-Bloomingdale's sentiments develop to the point where they have a significant impact on sales.

One aspect of Bloomingdale's future is easy to predict: the competition will be much tougher. For decades, Bloomingdale's has had what amounts to a free ride in capturing the affluent, fashionable consumers in its market areas. From the first years of its upgrading, the store found that it had little competition in luring the choice East Side consumers whom management had set its sights on. The same proved true in suburbia: wherever Bloomingdale's went, it found a vacuum in the retail marketplace. The truth is the other great names in New York retailing were not on their toes. The same period that saw the emergence of an enlightened Bloomingdale's was, for other store groups, a time of turmoil, poor management and lack of direction. While the others returned from the war years seemingly intent on doing things the old ways, Bloomingdale's implemented its master strategy to win over a new generation of consumers. Without knowing it, the competition was building its own gallows; for in business, companies must consciously move ahead or they will invariably fall back. It is impossible to simply hold one's ground. By trying to defy this business law—by attempting to stay just as they were—the competition was playing right into Bloomingdale's hands. As the only new act in town, Bloomie's could easily command the spotlight and steal the show.

Worse yet, Bloomingdale's competitors fell into a state of neglect. Without clear plans for their future growth, and without the continuity of management that characterized Bloomingdale's, the others simply foundered, allowing their businesses to decline. The great Fifth Avenue stores—including Lord & Taylor and Saks—became dull, stuffy and out of sync with the times. Catering almost exclusively to older consumers, they alienated the young, affluent groups that are so crucial to healthy department stores. Worse yet, Macy's and Gimbels, two of the legendary giants of the business, deteriorated badly. Reflecting the gradual decline of the Herald Square area, both stores became sloppy and dirty, and lowered their merchandise standards to appeal to the blue-collar groups that frequented the area. Macy's Thirty-fourth Street, the largest store in the world and once a shining example of American retailing, was rapidly becoming a white elephant: sales and earnings were on the skids, and management seemed incapable of turning the lumbering giant around. While uptown Bloomingdale's was showing off its exciting new look, Macy's resembled a huge warehouse, with mountains of merchandise simply piled up in ugly and mundane surroundings. Even the main floor—the focal point of every department store—resembled a bargain-basement area, featuring bins of cheap silverware and sale apparel.

Bloomie's competitors also failed to perceive the opportunities in ready-to-wear designer apparel, in-store boutiques, trendy furniture and the revolution in men's fashion. "Bloomingdale's came to power at a time when the retail community was taking a long nap," says Ralph Lauren. "No one else was interested in fresh, inventive approaches to selling. Bloomie's knew where it was going—it dared to be different—and it captured the public's imagination in the process."

Bloomingdale's proved, through its extraordinary success, that it was the king of the high-fashion retail business—that it knew how to sell and grow and make money better than anyone else. By the time a new generation of management took the reins at Saks, Macy's and Lord & Taylor, Bloomingdale's had a twenty-five-year head start on the pack. It was not until the mid 1970s that the rest of New York's big merchant community turned on the juice, got their acts together and consciously went after the very market Bloomie's had been monopolizing for years.

Traub is the first to admit that the competitive situation has changed drastically. "It's a whole new ball game in retailing now. Saks, Bergdorf, Lord & Taylor and Macy's have vastly improved managements and they are more capable and more aggressive than they have been for years. We have much better and tougher competition now in New York and in suburbia. Everyone is on their feet. Don't get me wrong, however. I welcome this change. It makes us more alert and alive, and it behooves us to stay the best in the business. We can beat all these competitors at what is essentially our game."

Traub's optimistic statements obviously reflect his sense of good public relations. No business manager wishes to give the impression of running scared, and Traub wants to leave no doubts about his confidence in Bloomingdale's. And the man does seem to believe that Bloomingdale's can survive any threat and stay on top.

Others are less certain of Bloomingdale's competitive advantage. The reason for most of these doubts can be summed up in one word: Macy's. The grand old lady of retailing is alive and kicking again—and is as strong a force in retailing as she's ever been. Some big names in the industry, including Stanley Marcus, believe that Macy's now is, or is becoming, the number one store in the country. "For years, Bloomingdale's had the lead—it was head and shoulders above all other department stores. But now Macy's has caught up to the point where I believe it to be the best department store in the country. Macy's president, Ed Finkelstein, is a genius; and I think he'll take an even wider lead over Bloomingdale's. This is not to say that Bloomie's will go to the devil, but just that its days of dominance are over."

Arnold Becker, retail consultant for Cresap, McCormick and Paget, has a similar view. "Ed Finkelstein is a very exciting fellow. The best proof of that is what he did with Macy's Cellar: he shook up Bloomingdale's, and the rest of the retail business with that. He used The Cellar as a hook to get people to come back to Macy's Herald Square, and it has worked marvelously. I think Macy's is the most exciting store in the country now."

There's no doubt that Macy's has become one of the new stars in retailing. Designers, resources, trade editors and merchants throughout the industry rave about Macy's the way they used to rave about Bloomingdale's.

Macy's is proving itself in the marketplace too. In 1976, sales at the Herald Square store were roughly

$165 million per year; they are now more than $200 million and are expected to reach $300 million by the early 1980s. Clearly Bloomingdale's toughest challenger now and in the immediate future, Macy's has built its new-found success on the very same three ingredients used by postwar Bloomingdale's: renovation, innovation and upgrading. Just as Davidson had done three decades earlier when taking over the helm at Bloomingdale's, Finkelstein looked at Macy's and recognized immediately that affluent, upscale consumers could be drawn to his stores. First, however, he had to give them good reason to return. Finkelstein's strategy was to invest heavily in the Herald Square store—to pour substantial time, dollars and talent into restoring the behemoth on Thirty-fourth Street to its former glory. In doing so, he spent $15 million dressing up the physical structure, peeling away old paint and plaster to reveal the original charm of the ornate walls and ceilings, reorganizing merchandise displays into theme and designer boutiques and, as his crowning achievement, replacing the bargain basement with The Cellar. In addition, apparel and furnishing lines were upgraded, and the emphasis changed from traditional to trendy fashions.

Macy's branch network has also been vastly improved. In White Plains, New York, for example, where Macy's and Bloomingdale's compete head on, Macy's has renovated the entire store and is now considered by many local residents to be the most exciting merchant in the city. In junior clothes especially—a key market for trendy stores—Macy's offers a wider and more daring merchandise selection. In terms of outright aggressiveness, Macy's is showing that it is willing to work harder to build market share: it keeps late hours every week night and is open Sundays from ten to five. Bloomingdale's keeps only two late nights and closes Sundays (except during the Christmas season).

"The best way I can describe the new Macy's is to recount an experience when I was in Mexico on a buying trip," says Stanley Marcus. "I was dealing with a small producer of craft items. He told me Macy's buyers had just been in the week before and had placed some orders. This was very unusual because the man can produce only small quantities of goods. Big department stores generally want very large orders; they will not deal with minor vendors. The Macy's people weren't concerned with this traditional outlook. They told the Mexican they'd put the crafts in only one of their stores if they had to. That's a sign of both good buying and good merchandising—it shows originality."

Macy's is not Bloomingdale's only problem. It faces tough competition on its upper flank as well. A reawakened Saks has moved full swing into trendy designer clothes, all the while maintaining its position as a higher-priced store. Saks is featuring the collections of Oscar de la Renta, Halston, Louis Vuitton and Cacharel, and adds to these an important element lacking at Bloomingdale's—attentive service. Saks sales personnel are widely regarded as the best in the business. They make it a point to know regular customers by name, to never leave a customer in the middle of a sale, and to be thoroughly familiar with their merchandise lines.

As a specialty store, Saks is far more flexible than Bloomingdale's. Since Saks does not carry furniture, it can expand faster and to a wider geographical area than its department store competitors. Furniture requires much more elaborate warehousing and distribution facilities; and it therefore complicates the expansion process. Saks plans to take full advantage of its flexibility by opening fifty new stores across the U.S. in the 1980s.

One of the last merchants to catch the modernization fever, Gimbels is also coming on strong as a tougher competitor in the midprice bracket. Elliot Stone, Gimbels chairman, ordered the company's first major remodeling efforts in years. Gimbels, as well as Macy's, has recognized that renovations of existing stores, even at the current rate of about $2 million per 100,000 square feet of selling space, is more economical than building new branches from scratch. In addition to polishing up its stores, Gimbels is taking the now standard moves that will bring it into even closer competition with Bloomingdale's—emphasizing fashion apparel, eliminating major appliances, and replacing staid merchandise displays with such floor theatrics as in-store disco sets—music and all.

The upgrading is obviously working. Prestige resources, including Estée Lauder cosmetics and Yves Saint Laurent men's wear, which for years refused to sell to Gimbels because of its unfashionable image, have now agreed to do so. Changes like this have already had a major impact: only months after it was renovated, sales at Gimbels' branch in Paramus, New Jersey, increased by 20 percent. And this kind of improvement has taken place at other Gimbels branches as well.

Certainly, tougher competition will not obliterate Bloomingdale's. Stores like Gimbels, especially, have a long way to go before graduating to the Bloomie's league. The important point is that Bloomie's is facing much sharper competition across a broad front. In Manhattan, all signs point to some erosion of its popularity with the movers and shakers of the fashion scene. In the suburbs, the newly awakened Macy's, Saks, Lord & Taylor, A & S, Filene's and Garfinckel's will make it harder for Bloomie's to sustain its dynamic growth.

Still, Bloomingdale's is a great institution—the originator and master architect of the modern department store. It is a formidable competitor in its own right, still capable of feats of one-upmanship that would make the store's founders glow. A good example is Bloomingdale's Main Course, a counteroffensive to Macy's Cellar. Caught off guard by Finkelstein's great success, Traub started planning The Main Course just as soon as The Cellar was unveiled. "We were all conscious of what a great job Macy's had done with its Cellar, and I knew Bloomingdale's was planning some sort of answer to it, but I had no idea what it would be," says Federated's Krensky. "I was having lunch with Marvin and he asked me to come on up and see what was being done on the sixth floor. I loved what I saw at first sight, and so has the public. The Main Course has drawn a tremendous amount of traffic.

"I think this is a good example of how well our organization works, and it indicates how Bloomingdale's will be able to meet the challenges of the future. Sure, the competition is much, much tougher, but Bloomingdale's is up to the test. When you have talented local chairmen on the scene making the key decisions, they know how to respond to anything."

Observers in the financial and consulting communities agree that Bloomingdale's is still strong. "Bloomingdale's recent history is that of a dominant store," says Arnold Becker. "It has dominated some of its markets for years. It is always hard to knock off a dominant store because its roots run deep and because it tends to have tremendous resources. Bloomingdale's has a tough challenge ahead to regain its fashion leadership. That takes great smarts and agility; but I think they'll do it. I think they could be number one again."

It seems likely that for the future Bloomingdale's will be relying more and more on its branches. The slower growth rate it will experience in Manhattan should be partially offset by the opening of new branch stores. Both Federated and Bloomingdale's say that there are plenty of opportunities for expansion and that new units will be opened throughout the coming decade. As to how many new stores there will be and exactly where they will be located, no one is saying.

Traub does insist, however, that Bloomingdale's expansion will come within its existing market region (Washington, D.C., to Boston, Massachusetts). "It's far more important that we continue to grow in our current markets than open new territories. I look for expansion in the Philadelphia, Boston and Washington areas. We have no shortage of growth opportunities. People lose track of the fact that Bloomingdale's has already expanded greatly. We have opened ten new stores in ten years and we have proved that we can succeed outside New York."

Traub's comments reflect his annoyance at the constant speculation concerning Bloomingdale's ability to transplant its sophisticated brand of retailing to Southern, Midwestern or West Coast markets. As *Time* magazine noted in its Bloomingdale's cover story: "Ice cream made from Himalayan mangoes may not sell as well in the suburbs of Spokane as it does on Manhattan's East Side."

This kind of statement bothers Traub, and rightly so. He manages a business that is geared for New York, not for Spokane or Peoria. It is unlikely that Bloomingdale's will ever move far from its home in the Eastern corridor. This assumption is based not only on Bloomingdale's merchandising style, but also on the nuts-and-bolts considerations of capital expenditures, distribution and logistics. First, it is impractical for full-size department stores to open single branches in distant cities. If Traub wanted to take a flier at an experimental store in Chicago, he would be limited by what is known as the "cluster concept": this holds that for stores to commit to major geographical expansion, they should open three or more units at the new location simultaneously. Typically, a cluster of stores is built around a major metropolitan area, with the branches scattered through the nearby suburbs. All the units are serviced by a single warehouse and distribution center, which is built simultaneously with the stores. The cluster concept is particularly important for hard-goods merchants. Stores selling major appliances, electronic equipment and/or furniture require costly facilities to effectively bring the merchandise to market and to service customers. Current thinking holds that this investment in facilities is sound only if several stores are built in the new market. K-Mart—a discount operation that is one of the nation's most successful chains—brought the cluster concept to widespread attention during the past decade. The company's dramatic expansion has followed a set pattern: four or five stores ring a metropolitan area and are serviced by a single warehouse. Its success has been closely observed throughout the industry. Lord & Taylor, which has announced plans to expand in Chicago, will open several new stores simultaneously.

All Bloomingdale's existing branches are close enough to New York to be serviced by New York warehouses, but any more-distant moves would require new distribution facilities—and the price tag for that would be steep. "If Bloomingdale's wanted to go into the Chicago market—which it does not—it might want to build four stores there," says Lawrence Lachman. "That would cost more than $100 million—an amount you can't justify considering the fact that there is plenty of growth in our existing markets."

The feeling in the investment community is that Bloomingdale's will, indeed, stay away from distant and untested waters. "Federated definitely believes in the cluster concept," says Joseph Lez, a retail analyst for Cresap, McCormick and Paget. "Just look at Bullock's North: that Federated division came to be a separate entity simply because of the need to open a lot of stores in one area and to have them serviced by local distribution facilities. If Federated took Bloomingdale's to Chicago or Pittsburgh or Dallas, they'd have to launch several stores, and that $100 million–plus investment is more than they'll want to gamble with in parts of the country that may not be suitable for a Bloomingdale's type of operation. I look, instead, for Bloomingdale's to open more stores in the Boston, Washington and Connecticut areas. First, they are doing well in these areas; second, they are proved factors there; and third, there is still room for growth. That's a combination of factors too good to resist."

Putting together all the bits and pieces of available wisdom—of expert projections and financial analyses—the scenario for Bloomingdale's goes something like this: Bloomie's loses its unchallenged leadership of the Manhattan fashion scene. But the flagship store still continues to generate healthy sales, though at a markedly slower growth rate. The focus turns more and more to the branch network, which by 1990 will grow to twenty stores, accounting for more than 90 percent of Bloomingdale's gross sales. Bloomie's will remain a robust and vital business, still loved by many, but with less of the mystique that earned it a place in the stars for thirty years.

Says one observer: "Bloomie's is like a great rock star who's starting to slip from the charts. While her albums used to rocket to number one and she used to sell out Madison Square Garden months in advance, she's now getting edged out by two hot new groups from down-town. She won't die and fade away—no, she's been too popular for that. She'll simply get married, move to the suburbs and make the kind of albums the mellow stations play. She'll stay rich and important, but she'll always be the kind of woman about whom parents say to their children: 'You should have known her when.' "

# Index

Abraham, Abraham, 189-190
Abraham and Straus, 37, 159, 176, 177, 189-194, 212, 227
activities and events, 45-46, 52, 71, 90-91
  branch stores, 169-171
advertising agencies, 115-116, 118
advertising and advertising department, 8, 27, 33-34, 51, 86, 90, 96, 114ff.
  attitudes toward, corporate, 114-116, 121-126
  and branch stores, 139, 172
  competition and, 117, 128-129
  co-op ads, 125-128, 139
  costs, 115-116, 123, 125-127, 137, 138
  in-house department, 114ff.
  image ads, 130
  institutional ads, 127-128
  marketing technology and, 128-133
  media selection, 120
  and national promotions, 133-136
  pace of, 117
  positioning strategy, 131-133
  recall rating, 117

salaries and working conditions, 118
staff (see also names), 118ff.
television and radio, 115, 117, 118-119, 128, 136-140
turnover, staff, 118, 120
Unique Selling Point strategy, 129
see also Promotions; Publicity and public relations
advertising, by suppliers, 105, 125-128, 133-136, 139
Air-India, 90, 92
Allen, Woody, 1
Altman's, 13, 156
American Express, 90
apparel, see Fashions; Men's wear; Women's wear
Arden, Elizabeth, 59, 60
Assatley, Richard, 127
Associated Dry Goods, 84n
At Your Service department, 16-17
Avedon, Richard, 119

banking department, 36
bargain basement, 60
Becker, Arnold D., 176, 192, 224, 228
Bell, David, 40, 109-110, 113, 173, 208

Bendel's, 12, 17, 201
Benson, Nancy, 153, 218, 220
Bergdorf's, 12, 169, 201, 223
Bergen County (N.J.) branch, 160, 171
Bergerac, Michel, 60
Blass, Bill, 13, 45, 63, 74-75, 82, 83, 144, 201, 213
  on decline of store, 221
  on influence of Bloomingdale's, 153
  sheets, 146
Blechman, Frances, 165, 169
Bloom, Roslyn, 155-156
Bloomingdale, Irving, 38
Bloomingdale, Joseph B., 25-32, 38, 136
Bloomingdale, Lyman (grandson), 46
Bloomingdale, Lyman G., 25-32, 38, 136
Bloomingdale, Samuel, 38
Bloomingdale's Great East Side Bazaar, 26
Bloomingdale's Perrier Marathon Run, 52
Bobrow, Edwin, 203, 204, 205
Bon Marché, 152
Bonwit Teller, 70, 99
*Boston Globe*, 90
boutiques, 3, 9, 54ff., 69ff.
  men's, 58
  "swing," 13, 62, 102
  women's wear, 99ff.
Bourdin, Guy, 11
branches, 48-49, 69, 155ff.
  activities and events, 169-171
  advertising and promotions, 139, 172-173
  apparel store, 161
  competition between, 161-163
  and competitors, 167
  costs of opening, 157
  customer service, 219-220
  design, interior, 157-159, 218
  expansion, future, 228-229

  failure, New Rochelle, 163-164
  furniture, 160-162
  home furnishings specialty, 160-162
  and image, 7-8, 44
  influence on merchandise policies, 113
  locations, 5, 43-44, 160, 167-168
  merchandise selection and, 220
  merchandising style, 171-173
  planning for, 44, 167-169
  profitability, 8, 44, 156-157, 160, 165-166, 171
breads, 41
Brooks, Wiley, 211
Bullock's, 177
Burdine's, 177, 178, 189, 212
*Business Week*, 47, 53-54, 143-144
buyers, 74-76, 101-102
  costs of department absorbed by, 86
  media, 120
  salaries, 72
  training, 43, 106-107, 208-209
  and vendor relationships, 72, 89, 90, 106-107

Cacharel, 62, 226
Caldor, 168
Canton Trade Fair, 75, 76
Capezio, 13
Carson, Johnny, 19
Carter Hawley Hale, 84n
catalogues, 11, 34-36, 115
celebrities, as customers, 1-2, 16, 18-20, 115
Cellar, The (Macy's), 61, 64, 224, 225, 227
Chapdelaine, George, 141, 152-153
charge cards, 20
Charles of the Ritz, 133-135

Chestnut Hill (Mass.) branch, 160-161
China Passage, 9, 69-75 *passim*, 77, 88
clothing industry, 93-95, 100, 102-107
*see also* Fashions
Cohen, Arthur, 11, 19, 139, 208
Colgate-Palmolive, 144
competitors, 60-62, 128-129, 159, 166, 222-227
communication among, 196-199
countering, 61-62, 227-228
evaluation of Bloomingdale image, 209-214
Federated divisions as, 159, 161-162
inter-branch, 161-163
*see also* names
Cooke, Gordon, 8, 18, 120-121, 172
advertising, 131-132, 136
branch stores, 172
displays and promotions, 8, 10, 90, 172
on exclusivity, 15, 16
on trendiness, 23, 81
cosmetics department, 58-60
*Cosmopolitan*, 148
credit cards, 20, 156-157
Cresap, McCormick & Paget, 176, 224, 230
Curry, Jill, 204, 205, 209, 218, 224
customer service, 19-23, 109-110, 219-220
customers, 1-4, 7-8, 11-12, 16-21, 42, 48-53, 133
dissatisfaction of and potential for decline, 216-222
*see also* Image and mystique, Bloomie's

Dadian, Margaret, 210-211
D'Arcy, Barbara, 78-79, 88, 90, 106, 111, 112

store design, interior, 157-159, 172, 208
David Crystal, 126
Davidson, J. E., 38-45 *passim*, 49, 62, 76, 79, 97, 113, 184
image of store, 95
DBA Ltd., 127
decline, potential for, 153, 173, 202, 209, 215-231
decorating services, 109-110
de la Renta, Oscar, 10, 226
delicacies, *see* Foods and delicacies
Deneuve, Catherine, 19
departments, 53, 58-65
early, 31, 36
financial management, 86-87
location, 58-65, 218-219
upgrading, 39-46
*see also* names
designers, 9, 12, 45, 54ff., 63, 74-75, 95-98, 102, 199-201
*see also* names
Dior, Christian, 100
displays, *see* Promotions
Draddi, Vincent de Paul, 126, 138, 206
Durant, Bartley S., 182

earnings, *see* Profitability
Elias, Lois, 47
Elizabeth, Queen, 18, 115
Ellis, Joseph, 14n, 169
Ellis, Perry, 62
employees and staff, 66-68
and customer service, 19-23, 219-220
offices, 65-66
salaries and working conditions, 21, 66-67, 72, 118, 207-208
training, 21, 22, 43, 106, 208-209
turnover, 118, 120-121, 207-208
unions, 21, 66-67, 163-164
escalator, 32

*Esquire,* 148
Evans, Bob, 154
*Evening Mail,* 33-34
exclusivity
   atmosphere of, 15-20
   of merchandise, 79-81, 99-
      100, 201-203

fads, 7-8, 62
Farkas, George, 71
fashions
   advertising (*see also* Adver-
      tising and advertising de-
      partment), 116ff.
   buyers, 106-107
   coordination, 73-75, 90,
      98ff.
   high fashions, stress on,
      14-16
   influence on, 3-7, 142ff., 200
   men's, 3-4, 60, 95, 96-98
   promotions (*see also* Pro-
      motions), 8ff.
   sales, 93
   supplier relationships, 82,
      94-95, 99, 102-107, 201-
      206, 213-214
   upgrading of lines, 93ff.
   women's, 10-14, 51, 55-57,
      62-63, 81-83, 85-86, 93ff.
   *see also* Designers
Fass, Steve, 61
Fathers Day television campaign, 137
Faure, Michel and Chantal,
   100
Federated Department Stores,
   45, 152, 174-195, 203
   Bloomingdale leadership,
      212
   and branch operations, 157,
      160, 163-164, 173, 228-
      230
   competition, interstore, 160,
      161-162
   divisions (*see also* names),
      175-179
   executives, 181-185, 194
   as investment, 185-187

merger of Bloomingdale's
   with, 37
operating policies, 37, 73,
   175-176, 179ff., 188ff.
organization, 174-175, 180-
   181, 185
profitability, 84-85, 113,
   185-189
Filene's, 37, 162, 177, 198,
   212, 227
financial management, 39, 62,
   84-87, 113, 157
   *see also* Prices and pricing;
      Profitability
Finkelstein, Ed, 60-61, 224,
   225, 227
Foley's, 189
Food and Drug Administra-
   tion, U.S., 40-41
foods and delicacies department, 14, 40-42, 60-61,
   64-65
Ford, Charlotte, 62
Forrest, Steven, 219
Forshner, Cheryl, 51
40 Carrots restaurants, 19,
   115, 151
founding and early history,
   26-38
franchises, 115
Fresh Meadows (N.Y.)
   branch, 43, 160, 167, 171
Frogurt, 150-153
furniture department, 42-43,
   78-81, 88, 95, 107-113
   buyers, 107, 111
   customer services, 109-110
   model rooms, 64, 78-79,
      110-112, 149
   pricing, 108-109, 111, 112-
      113
   profitability, 108
   trendiness, 107-108

Garbo, Greta, 1
Garden City (N.Y.) branch,
   159, 160, 162
Garfinckel's, 166, 227

gay market, 52-53
Gerald, John, 79
Gimbels, 21, 42, 43, 48, 203, 222, 226-227
Givenchy, 10
glassware department, 63
Glynn, Mary Joan, 120
Gold Card system, 20
Gold Circle, 178
Goldman Sachs, 14, 77, 169, 188
Gonzales, Betsy, 127
Goodman, Edward, 192
Gould, Lois, 215
Green Room, 62-63
Grey Advertising, 119
Gumport, Bob, 40-41
Gutner, Elizabeth, 147-148

Haire, Bill, 127
Halston, 9, 75, 100, 103, 216, 226
    evaluation of store, 22-23, 51, 221
    fashions, women's, 12, 22-23, 45, 54-56
    fragrances, 58, 59
    India promotion, 92
    on influence of Bloomingdale's, 7, 154
Halston Boutique, 55-56
Harris, Ellen, 14n
Hatfield, Julie, 161
Hawley, Philip, 13, 168
Hemingway, Margaux, 1
Hill, Sandy, 115
Hirsh, Warren, 104-106, 145, 147, 210
Hoffman, Dustin, 19
home furnishings, 9, 42-43, 64, 72, 77-81
    branches, 160-162
    buyers, 106
    decorator services, 109-110
    leadership, 145-147, 149-150
    model rooms, 64, 78-79, 91, 110-112, 149

sheets, 146
supplier relationships, 103-106, 202-203
    see also Furniture department
Hood Dairies, 141, 150-153
House & Garden, 148
House Beautiful, 148, 149

image advertising, 130
image and mystique,
    Bloomie's, 1ff., 24-25, 38ff., 47-48, 82-83, 114, 155-156
    and branches, 7-8, 43, 218, 220
    decline, potential for, 153-154, 173, 201, 209, 215-231
    trade evaluation of, 209-214
    see also Influence
imports, 3-4, 43, 69, 73, 75ff., 87ff., 95
    standards, 40-41, 88
India Fantasy promotion, 9, 87-92, 172
influence, 7, 72, 141ff.
    and branches, 155ff.
    decline, 153-154, 201
    on fashion, 3-7, 142ff., 199-200
    on food habits, 150-153
    on home furnishings, 145-147, 148-150
    on merchandising, 13, 53-54, 209-214
    media and, 148-149
innovativeness, 2ff., 112-113
Izod, 13, 60, 126-127, 138, 206

Jacobs, Melvin, 55
Jenkintown (Pa.) branch, 160
Jody Donohue Associates, 57
Jordan Marsh, 152

Kenzo, 147-148, 217
Klein, Anne, 45, 62

Klein, Calvin, 9, 45-46, 106,
  200-201, 216
  apparel lines, 60, 62, 102,
    103
  fragrances, 58, 59-60
K-Mart, 6, 168, 175, 229
Knapple, Richard, 91, 112
Knight, Jerry, 166
Koch, Edward, 49
Kohlenberg, Stanley, 59-60
Korvettes, 156, 176
Krensky, Harold, 49, 97, 183,
  201
  fashions, men's, 96
  fashions, women's, 45, 55
  and Federated Department
    Stores, 175, 181, 183-185,
    189-194 passim, 197, 203,
    212, 227-228
  image of Bloomingdale's, 95
  merchandising, 128

Lachman, Laurence, 24, 38-
  39, 49, 66, 102, 168, 182
  boutiques, 103
  branches, 5, 160, 163, 164,
    167, 230
  departments and, 87
  image of store, 5, 38, 42,
    94-95
  supplier relationships, 44,
    45, 94
Lauder, Estée, 58, 59, 227
Lauren, Ralph, 4, 9, 12, 46,
  57, 93, 98, 103, 201, 223
  branch stores, 172
  buyer relationships, 74, 106,
    107
  fragrances, 59, 95, 98
  on influence of Blooming-
    dale's, 153-154
  men's fashions, 4, 62, 95-98
  women's fashions, 10, 62,
    98
Lazarus (F.) & Company, 37
Lazarus, Fred, Jr., 179-180,
  182
Lazarus, Ralph, 175, 182-183,
  190-194 passim, 212

Lehman Brothers, 37
Levine, Carl, 76, 106
Lez, Joseph, 230
Lincoln Center, 91
Lindsay, John, 45, 49
lingerie promotions, 10-11
Lord & Taylor, 70, 107, 152,
  157, 166, 169, 222, 223,
  227, 229
L'Zinger, 127

M., Mrs., 22, 68
MacGraw, Ali, 154
Macy's, 21, 37, 58, 60-61, 128,
  203
  as competitor, 8, 64, 128,
    173, 222-227
  profitability, 48, 84n, 157
Magnin, I., 128, 176-177, 188,
  212
Maharishi Mahesh Yogi, 87
Main Course, The, 64-65, 139,
  227
Manhasset (N.Y.), 160, 162
Manhattan store, 1ff.
  and branches (see also
    Branches), 48-49
  building at Fifty-ninth
    Street, 29-33, 58
  centennial, 45-46
  customers, characteristic,
    see Customers; Image and
    mystique
  customers, dissatisfactions
    of, 217-222
  departments (see also De-
    partments; names), 40-
    46, 58-65
  departments, early, 31, 36
  design, interior, 53-54, 58-
    65, 218-219
  founding and early history,
    25-38
  location, 26-30, 36, 49-50
  neighborhood, 38, 39, 48-
    52
  success, modern, 1ff., 47ff.

transformation and upgrading, 2ff., 38ff., 94ff.
*see also* subjects
marathon, Bloomingdale's/ Perrier, 52
Marcus, Stanley, 15, 17, 213-214, 221, 224, 225-226
Mastroianni, Marcello, 19
Matthau, Walter, 19
Mazur, Paul, 37
McDonald, Tim, 139
media relations, 17-18, 53-54, 70, 90-91, 92, 120-121, 148-149
men's wear, 3-4, 44, 60, 95, 96-98
merchandise
  conservatism, trend to, 220-221
  decisions, and Federated Department Stores, 193
  exclusive, 80-81, 100, 202
  innovativeness on decline, 112-113
  inventories, 193, 204
  mix, 11-17, 53-54, 105
  mix, early, 27-28, 34-35, 39
  stock-turn rate, 5-6
  and theme promotions, 69-70, 73ff.
  trend-setting, 13-14, 70ff., 96, 103-104, 107, 168, 210-211
merger, 37
Merrill Lynch, Pierce, Fenner & Smith, 165
Merris, Mary, 94, 102, 209
Mic Mac, 100
Missonis, 9, 16, 62
Monroe, Earl ("The Pearl"), 19
*Morning Break* (TV show), 139
Morning Lady, 127
Murjani, U.S.A., 56, 104-106, 125-126, 145
Murphy, Katie, 85, 98-102, 208
Myers, Bob, 208

Neiman-Marcus, 17, 152
Nevins, Bruce, 52
New Rochelle (N.Y.), branch, 43, 156, 160, 163-165, 167
*Newsweek*, 148
*New York Post*, 70, 120
*New Yorker*, 92
*New York Times*, 37, 52, 70, 72, 81, 90, 91, 120, 127, 130, 131, 136
  *Magazine*, 116

offices, managers, 66
Onassis, Jackie Kennedy, 16, 19, 92, 216
Opium promotion, 133-136

partnership buying, 82
Penney, J. C., 168, 176
Perfumer's Workshop, 62
Perrier, 52, 137
Pet Rocks, 7
*Philadelphia Inquirer*, 90
Plaza, 62
Polo, 58, 95, 96, 97-98, 102, 103
  (*see also* Ralph Lauren)
positioning strategy, in advertising, 130-133
prices and pricing, 12, 15, 28, 39, 80, 83-84, 107-108
  furniture, 108-109, 111, 112-113
Procter & Gamble, 144
profitability, 5-6, 14, 39, 44, 48, 77, 80-81, 84-86, 108
  and branches, 7-8, 44, 112, 156-157, 159, 165-166, 171
  and decline of innovativeness, 112-113
  Federated Department Stores, 84-85, 113, 185-189
promotions, 7ff., 53, 57, 69ff., 97
  and branches, 173
  designers and, 75, 201

promotions (*cont.*)
  personnel and organization,
    114ff.
  *see also* Advertising and
    advertising department;
    Publicity and public rela-
    tions; specific promotions
publicity and public relations,
    17-20, 53-54, 57
  attitudes toward, corporate,
    114-115, 122-124
  in-house department, 114ff.
  media and, 17-18, 53-54, 70,
    90-91, 92, 120
  and national promotions,
    133-136
  staff (*see also* names), 118
  *see also* Advertising and
    advertising department;
    Promotions
Pure Jeanius, 62

quality control, 40-41, 87-88

Radziwill, Lee, 19
Ralphs, 178-179, 189
Redford, Robert, 1
Reeves, Rosser, 129
resources, relationships with,
    87-88
  and advertising, 125-128,
    134-136, 139-140
  fashions department, 82,
    93-95, 99, 102-107, 201-
    206, 212-213
  foods and delicacies depart-
    ment, 41-43
restaurants, in-store, 19, 65,
    115, 151
Revlon, 58, 59, 60, 122
Rhodes, Zandra, 10, 11, 52,
    177, 217
Rich's, 128
Rive Gauche, 101, 102, 133
Robsjohn-Gibbings, 110
Roselon Industries, 127
Rothschild, Simon F., 190
Rothschild, Walter N., Sr.,
    190

"Round-About New York"
    guidebook, 33
Rubell, Steve, 217
Rubinstein, Helena, 58, 60
rugs, 9, 80
Rykiel, Sonia, 16

Saint Laurent, Yves, 9, 45, 59,
    62, 100, 227
  fragrance promotion, 133-
    136
Saks, 13, 17, 21, 151, 157,
    201, 203
  as competitor, 128, 135,
    169, 223, 226, 227
sales, *see* Profitability
Sant'Angelo, Giorgio, 62
Sarabhai, Mrinalini, 91
Sasson, 62, 123
Saturday's Generation, 60
Scarsdale (N.Y.) branch, 160,
    162, 170-171
Schnee, Joseph, 5, 137, 138,
    208
Schoff, James, Sr., 38, 49, 208
Schoff, James, Jr., 181
Schwartz, Barry, 200
Schwartzman and Buchman,
    architects, 30
Sears, 156, 168, 176
  avoidance of comparison
    with, 42, 43
  recognition by of Blooming-
    dale's merchandising
    methods, 199, 211
*Seventeen*, 147
Shaw, Doris, 21, 72, 84, 108,
    110, 120, 121, 138, 149
sheets, designer, 146
Shillito's, 179, 182
shopping bags, 115, 119
shopping services, 16-17
Short Hills (N.J.) branch,
    160, 167
Sidel, Helene, 127
"Sighs and Whispers" cata-
    logue, 11
Simon, Frank, 4, 96, 97

*60 Minutes* (TV show), 53, 115, 120

slogan, 15, 57, 131

Spa, The (Cambridge, Mass.), 150

Spellman, Cathy Cash, 121-125, 135-138, 197, 198, 208

Spock, Benjamin, 19

Springs Mills, 63, 146

staff, *see* Employees and staff; names

Stamford (Conn.) branch, 44, 160, 167

Stern, Nancy, 152

stock-turn rate, 5-6

Stone, Edward Durell, 162

Stone, Elliot, 226

Stone, Lee, 19

Straus, Isadore and Nathan, 189

Streisand, Barbra, 19

Supermania, 62

suppliers, *see* Resources, relationships with; names

television and radio
   advertising, 117, 118, 128, 136-140
   and publicity, 53, 115, 120
   tie-ins, 115

Terporten, Jack, 151

test marketing, 144-147

*Time,* 2, 53, 120, 148, 216, 228

Torres, Ida, 67, 164

Traub, Marvin, 9-10, 17, 32, 41, 49, 52, 66, 71-73, 106, 182, 193, 196
   advertising and public relations, 70-73, 121, 124, 136, 137
   and branches, 158, 159, 160-161, 162, 165, 168, 172, 228-229
   competition, countering, 62, 223-224, 227
   customer dissatisfaction and, 221

employee relations, 207

fashions, women's, 45, 81, 105

furniture department, 111, 113

image of store, 5, 49, 51, 83, 105

India promotion, 88, 90, 91

merchandising, 9-10, 111

quality control, 88, 103

store design, 158

trend setting, 13-14, 70ff., 96, 104, 107-108, 146ff., 168, 210-211

Tribune Builders, 30

Tysons Corner (Va.) branch, 139, 156-157, 160, 165-166

Ultimate Fantasy promotion, 87-92, 172

"umbrella" scheme of merchandising, 2-3

Unique Selling Point, 70, 129

United Store Workers, 163-164

Vanderbilt, Gloria, 19, 56-57, 62, 105, 106, 125, 145, 149

*Vogue,* 91

Von Furstenberg, Diane, 45, 85-86, 213

Von Furstenberg, Egon, 45, 85-86

Vuitton, Louis, 226

*Wall Street Journal,* 53, 120, 143-144

Ward, 168

*Washington Post,* 90, 117, 120, 166

*Washington Star,* 120

"We Believe" advertising campaign, 81, 127, 131, 142

WFAS (Westchester, N.Y.), 139

Wechsler, Joseph, 189

White Flint (Md.) branch,
    139, 160, 166
White Plains (N.Y.) branch,
    139, 156, 160, 164-165,
    170-171
window treatments, 96-97
women's wear, 10-14, 44, 54-
    58, 62-63, 85-86
  boutiques, 99ff.
  couture lines, 82-83
  failures and near misses,
    86, 92
  Paris knock-offs, 81-83

parity goods, 104
supplier relationships, 82,
    93-95, 99, 102-107
  *see also* Designers; Fashions
*Women's Wear Daily*, 12
WTOP (Washington, D.C.),
    139

Yasmin Ali Khan, Princess, 18
Yogurt, frozen, 150-153

Zimmerman, Sanford J., 190
Zolt, Richard, 80, 149-150

No one who buys it,
survives it.

# THE HOUSE NEXT DOOR

A terrifying novel
by
## Anne Rivers Siddons

28172  $2.75

 BALLANTINE BOOKS

G-1c

# Beauty is as beauty does...